Why Iowa?

Why Iowa?

How Caucuses and Sequential Elections Improve the Presidential Nominating Process

DAVID P. REDLAWSK,
CAROLINE J. TOLBERT,
AND TODD DONOVAN

THE UNIVERSITY OF CHICAGO PRESS   CHICAGO AND LONDON

DAVID P. REDLAWSK is professor of political science and director of the Eagleton Center for Public Interest Polling at Rutgers University. His recent books include *How Voters Decide: Information Processing during an Election Campaign* (2006) and *Civic Service: Service Learning with State and Local Government Partners* (2009), and he is coeditor of the journal *Political Psychology*.

CAROLINE J. TOLBERT is professor of political science at the University of Iowa, Iowa City. She is coauthor of, most recently, *Digital Citizenship: The Internet Society and Participation*, with Karen Mossberger and Ramona S. McNeal (2008), and, with Daniel A. Smith, *Educated by Initiative: The Effects of Direct Democracy on Citizens and Political Organizations in the American States* (2004). She is coeditor, with Bruce E. Cain and Todd Donovan, of *Democracy in the States: Experiments in Election Reform* (2008).

TODD DONOVAN is professor of political science at Western Washington University, Bellingham. In addition to being the author of *State and Local Politics: Institutions and Reform* (2010), he has coauthored or coedited several books, including *Demanding Choice: Opinion and Voting in Direct Democracy* (1998), and *Reforming the Republic: Political Institutions for the New America* (2004), both with Shaun Bowler.

The University of Chicago Press, Chicago 60637
The University of Chicago Press, Ltd., London
© 2011 by The University of Chicago
All rights reserved. Published 2011
Printed in the United States of America
20 19 18 17 16 15 14 13 12 11   1 2 3 4 5

ISBN-13: 978-0-226-70695-5 (cloth)
ISBN-13: 978-0-226-70696-2 (paper)
ISBN-10: 0-226-70695-8 (cloth)
ISBN-10: 0-226-70696-6 (paper)

Library of Congress Cataloging-in-Publication Data
Redlawsk, David P.
    Why Iowa? : how caucuses and sequential elections improve the presidential nominating process / David P. Redlawsk, Caroline J. Tolbert, and Todd Donovan.
        p.   cm.
    Includes bibliographical references and index.
    ISBN-13: 978-0-226-70695-5 (hardcover : alk. paper)
    ISBN-13: 978-0-226-70696-2 (pbk. : alk. paper)
    ISBN-10: 0-226-70695-8 (hardcover : alk. paper)
    ISBN-10: 0-226-70696-6 (pbk. : alk. paper)   1. Primaries—Iowa.   2. Presidents—United States—Nomination.   3. Presidents—United States—Election—2008.
I. Tolbert, Caroline J.   II. Donovan, Todd.   III. Title.
    JK2075.I82R43   2011
    324.2777'0152—dc22

                                                                    2010013981

To the many men (and a growing number of women) who have spent long, cold winters, hot summers, and beautiful springs and falls in Iowa, pursuing their dream of the presidency. These public servants, propelled by a desire to serve their country and to make America better, have often failed and sometimes succeeded, but in all cases contributed to a robust debate about the nation's future. The Iowa caucuses would not be what they are without them.

Tonight what we have seen is a new day in American politics. A new day is needed in American politics like a new day is needed in American government. And tonight it starts here, in Iowa. But it doesn't end here. It goes all the way through the other states and ends at 1600 Pennsylvania Avenue, one year from now.

MIKE HUCKABEE, upon winning the 2008 Iowa Republican caucus

This is obviously a bit like a baseball game, first inning. Well, it's a fifty-inning ballgame. I'm going to keep on battling all the way and anticipate I get the nomination when it's all said and done.

MITT ROMNEY, upon coming in second in Iowa

Contents

Preface

The Iowa caucuses have been a source of fascination, disdain, excitement, and frustration since the fateful decision of the Iowa Democratic Party to move its 1972 caucuses to January 24, leapfrogging over the venerable New Hampshire primary to become the first candidate test of the presidential nomination campaign. Jimmy Carter's 1976 campaign consequently used the caucuses as a springboard to national recognition, through the brilliant strategy of telling the media that the results in Iowa would matter. Even though Carter came in second—he lost to "uncommitted"—the media focus that he achieved with his "victory" in Iowa gave his campaign the momentum that he used to reach the presidency. Since Carter, every competitive presidential nomination campaign has run through Iowa, and the Iowa caucuses have become an institution.

As an institution, however, the Iowa caucuses have not been subjected to the level of scrutiny by political scientists that most of our other political institutions have endured. Perhaps this is because they come around only once every four years. Or perhaps it is because they—like campaigns in general—are rather ephemeral. The run-up to the caucuses elicits great attention from us, but the moment they are over our focus shifts elsewhere. In any case, there have been only two book-length monographs and another edited volume that focus directly on the Iowa caucuses.

This is not to say that political scientists have ignored the caucuses entirely. The extensive literature on the presidential nominating process includes specific papers and chapters on Iowa, generally oriented toward explaining Iowa's role in winnowing the candidate field and influencing

(or, for most of the research, *not directly* influencing) the eventual outcome of the campaign. In 1988 Peverill Squire hosted a conference at the
University of Iowa, resulting in his edited volume, *The Iowa Caucuses
and the Presidential Nominating Process,* as well as some on-the-ground
reports from the caucuses published in the journal *PS: Political Science
and Politics.* Throughout this book, we build on the work that came before us. But it also seems well past time for this work to be updated.

Twenty years later, during the week of the 2008 Iowa caucuses, the
Iowa Political Science Department once again hosted an Iowa Caucus
Conference sponsored by the Benjamin F. Shambaugh Fund. The conference was held with the full recognition that 2008 would be a unique
presidential election year, because both the Republican and the Democratic parties had strongly competitive nomination campaigns. Participants at the conference, ourselves included, attended candidate rallies
and observed the Iowa caucuses in action on the evening of January 3.
Dave Redlawsk even chaired his precinct caucus! We have fond memo-
ries of attending the caucuses that snowy evening with a large group of
political science observers. All eyes were on Iowa before the caucuses,
and the meeting provided a unique opportunity to connect political science research to real-world politics through interaction with media, political candidates, and voters by observing the caucuses. Selected papers from the conference were published in January 2009 in "Reforming
the Presidential Nomination Process," a *PS: Political Science & Politics*
symposium edited by Caroline Tolbert and Peverill *Squire.*

Our goal in revisiting the role of the Iowa caucuses is to both update and extend our understanding of the role played by this small, homogenous, midwestern state in defining the parameters of the nomination campaign for the forty-nine states that come after. After laying the
groundwork of the process in part 1, we spend the second part of this
book developing a more complete and complex understanding of the
Iowa caucuses themselves, including a chapter that we bill as an insider's guide to how the caucuses really work. We then turn in part 3 to
consider how the outcome in Iowa reverberates throughout the country as the remaining candidates move on to the next stages in the nominating process. Finally, we close the book by looking at reform—at how
Americans view the current process and what changes they might support, and then proposing a reform of our own. In doing so we recognize
both the value of Iowa—and of other small states where grassroots pol-

itics can be meaningful in a modern media-driven age—and the need for change.

While writing this book we did not always agree. Some of us are greater fans of election reform than others. But in the end we all believe that the Iowa caucuses, as currently constituted and as likely to remain for 2012, are worth better understanding for both their good points and their bad.

Acknowledgments

This book began as a simple class project to give our undergraduate students some hands-on data collection experience by conducting polls ahead of the 2008 Iowa caucuses. As our students became more engaged in the project, so did we. Fortunately, we were embedded in what became the most exciting and intense Iowa caucus and presidential nomination season any of us had seen. As the project grew, we were fortunate to gain significant financial and personal support through then University of Iowa provost Mike Hogan and the College of Liberal Arts and Sciences. With this funding the Hawkeye Poll carried out numerous telephone surveys of voters from Iowa and across the country, allowing us to build the unique data sets reported in this book.

We are also indebted to a number of our students who worked on various phases of this project over the last three years. Iowa graduate students William (Bill) Franko and Daniel Bowen, and Western Washington undergraduate student Rob Hunsaker carried out some of the key data collection and analyses in this book, with Bill also handling most of the meticulous detail work on the figures. We appreciate their hard work and good humor. Allison Hamilton spent many hours overseeing the Hawkeye Poll call center, helping to ensure high-quality data. Amanda Keller also worked in the call center, overseeing callers and helping things run smoothly, and James Rydberg deserves recognition for his early data analysis and two years of assistance with the Hawkeye Poll. We also thank Sang Ki Kim for his work tracking down many citations, and Howard Sanborn for his call-center supervision.

We especially want to thank Iowa undergraduate Brigid Freymuller, who became our right-hand, go-to (and any other cliché we can think of) person, managing all aspects of the Hawkeye Poll as well as our statewide in-caucus survey. It is not too much to say that without Brigid the Hawkeye Poll simply would never have gotten off the ground. Ben Earnhart, who served as our technology guru, and Kevin Leicht, director of the Iowa Social Science Research Center, deserve thanks as well for their support of the Hawkeye Poll and its use of the SSRC.

We would be remiss if we did not recognize the staff in the Political Science Department at Iowa as well. They had to process dozens of student employees working for the Hawkeye Poll, which is never easy. Thank you, Wendy Durant, Carole Eldeen, and Karen Stewart. And, of course, thanks to those dozens of students who came through our classes and found themselves learning more than they expected about survey research as they carried out Hawkeye Polls.

We also acknowledge the Benjamin F. Shambaugh Fund at the University of Iowa for supporting a conference in early 2008 at which all three of us had the chance to present many of our ideas to a group of very accomplished scholars. We wish to thank those in attendance for their valuable feedback and for educating us on the presidential nominating process research more generally: John Aldrich, Lonna Atekson, Daniel Bowen, Marty Cohen, Linda Fowler, Michael Hagen, Audrey Haynes, Thomas Holbrook, Richard Johnston, David Karol, Michael Lewis-Beck, Cherie Maestas, William Mayer, Barbara Norrander, Tracy Osborn, Ronald Rapaport, Tom Rice, Peverill Squire, Walter Stone, Michael Tofias, and Lynn Vavreck. They helped us make this book better, but are certainly not responsible for any of the places we might have gone wrong.

We would like to give special recognition to Tracy Mayfield, then an undergraduate student at Tufts University. Tracy called Dave Redlawsk out of the blue one spring day, saying she would be in Iowa City for the summer and asking if there was work she could do. The answer, of course, was yes, and Tracy spent the summer researching many details about the history of the Iowa caucuses, working diligently and beyond our expectations. She also spent part of that time in a shelter during the historic Iowa flood of 2008, since she had to evacuate her residence. Even so, she kept her sense of humor and worked through it all.

To Connecticut senator Christopher Dodd, who met with us at the Village Inn in Iowa City, we offer our thanks for providing insights into the experience of running for president. David Bonior, former Democratic whip in the U.S. House of Representatives and a visiting political science professor at Iowa, spoke at one of our graduate seminars and provided helpful feedback on our reform proposal: a caucus window and a national primary. David was kind enough to tell us he liked the idea, which we consider high praise, coming as it does from someone who has firsthand experience in Iowa as a campaign manager. We also thank the Republican Party of Iowa and the Iowa Democratic Party for their assistance in getting our in-caucus survey into their respective precincts. Both parties allowed us to include the pencil-and-paper survey form in their official caucus materials, which helped ensure a great response rate from those asked to complete the survey.

Each of us has some personal acknowledgments to make as well. Todd Donovan would like to thank Western Washington undergraduate students in his Parties, Campaigns and Elections courses whom he has too often forced to agonize over the question, why Iowa? Why not us?

Caroline Tolbert acknowledges her coauthors, not only the two who share authorship on this volume, but the many she has had the honor of working with over the years. Collaborators make the study of politics rewarding and interesting. She also acknowledges her husband, Dave, for his support, encouragement, and creative ideas.

Finally, Dave Redlawsk would like to acknowledge the influence of his late grandmother, Gertrude Brindley Parnell, who nurtured his early love of politics, even though she lived in England and he in the United States. While he may have known much more about the British House of Commons than Iowa back then, she introduced him to the excitement and the drama of campaigns and elections on both sides of the ocean.

PART I

Framing the Argument

CHAPTER ONE

Why Iowa?

Because the Rules Matter

On the day of the Iowa caucus, my faith in the American people was vindicated. What you started here in Iowa has swept across the nation. So, the people of Iowa, I will always be grateful to all of you! — Barack Obama, campaign speech, Des Moines, Iowa, October 31, 2008

Imagine 2008 without the Iowa Caucuses

January 20, 2009. The new president is taking the oath of office, capping a campaign that was both improbable and yet inevitable. As she raises her right hand, President-elect Hillary Clinton considers the road that got her to where she is. It began in New Hampshire, with her easy win in the nation's first primary nomination contest over first-term Illinois senator and political upstart Barack Obama and second-time candidate and former North Carolina senator John Edwards, among others. No doubt her regional strength—after all, she was the junior senator from New York—played a significant role in her victory in New Hampshire, followed quickly by good outcomes in Nevada, where labor carried her to victory, and South Carolina, where her husband's strong standing with the African-American community helped her run even with Obama. By the end of the February 5 Super Tuesday primaries (so called because close to half the states held their primaries that day), Clinton was the Democratic Party's nominee.

Her general election opponent, former Massachusetts governor Mitt Romney, had a tougher time against his main opponents, former New York City mayor Rudy Giuliani and Arizona senator John McCain. With New Hampshire as the starting point, Romney capitalized on his regional connections and battled to a draw with McCain, who had won the state in 2004. Giuliani, who had been the national front-runner mainly on name recognition, could not raise enough money to offset the millions Romney could put into the campaign. Once Romney showed his strength, conservatives who saw both Giuliani and McCain as RINOs, or Republicans in Name Only, flocked to his campaign, despite the efforts of former Arkansas governor Mike Huckabee, who had no money, no name recognition, and no prospects. Unfortunately for Romney, 2008 was simply a Democratic year. Despite his strong campaign, voters worried about a declining economy and the collapse of financial markets elected Clinton the first female president of the United States.

*   *   *

Of course, none of this actually happened. New Hampshire was not the first nomination contest in 2008. Iowa was, with its January 3 caucuses. But it is interesting to consider the question: what if 2008 didn't begin in Iowa? Hillary Clinton may have won the Democratic nomination, as she narrowly won New Hampshire's primary despite being upset earlier in Iowa. The momentum from New Hampshire could have propelled her to victory. Moreover, since 1980 all but two candidates who raised the most campaign money the year before the nomination contests began ended up winning their party's nomination (Aldrich 2009; Cohen et al. 2008). In 2008 the candidates with the most money going into Iowa were Clinton for the Democrats and Romney for the Republicans. Whether Romney would have won without Iowa is more speculative, but certainly his campaign was derailed there by Huckabee, who was relatively unknown on the national stage but who overcame a lack of both money and organization to win Iowa. Romney placed second despite outspending everyone else in Iowa. As it turned out, after losing Iowa, Romney also lost New Hampshire to John McCain, who then rolled up enough winner-take-all primary victories to claim the Republican nomination on Super Tuesday.

For Hillary Clinton, her seemingly inevitable path to the nomination stalled in Iowa, where Obama, a lesser-known if not underdog candidate, won on the strength of superior organization and intensive efforts to mobilize young voters. Obama's surprising win in Iowa not only began to let the air out of the Clinton invincibility bubble, but also showed voters nationally that white voters in Iowa would in fact support a black man for president. By exceeding initial expectations, the momentum from winning Iowa may have contributed to Obama's success as the Democratic nominee, much in the same way that President Jimmy Carter gained momentum from his surprising victory in Iowa back in 1976.

Iowa's Role in Electing America's First Black President

Was Iowa critical in the election of America's first black president? The national survey analysis we present in this book shows that winning Iowa did in fact generate the momentum propelling Obama to victory in the 2008 Democratic Party nomination. Yet Iowa did not propel Huckabee to the Republican nomination, though it seems likely it fatally wounded Mitt Romney's campaign. This book demonstrates that more than thirty years after Carter discovered the magic of Iowa, early contests such as Iowa and New Hampshire proved critical in shaping how voters beyond those states evaluated the candidates in 2008. The path that Carter followed from Iowa to gain the elusive "momentum" that candidates seek may have changed somewhat, but we suggest it is still clearly marked. That early contests can be crucial in determining who wins the nomination raises several normative questions that we address in detail in subsequent chapters.

Obama's path in 2008 may have been similar to Jimmy Carter's in 1976. But Obama isn't like Carter. Carter is white and Obama is black. That alone is difference enough. The United States fought a Civil War over equal rights for African Americans. Andrew Delbanco in the *New York Review of Books* (Pinckney et al. 2008) reminds us that "it's been sixty years since the Dixiecrats walked out of the 1948 Democratic convention, more than forty since George Wallace stood in the schoolhouse door, and twenty since the elder George Bush ran his Willie Horton ads." But even though the race card may still be played in some campaigns and in some parts of America, as we write an African-American man sits in the Oval Office. By any account it is not trite to focus on the historical nature of the 2008 presidential election, given our nation's experience with slavery and race relations.

Our national survey data show that winning (mostly white) Iowa was critical to perceptions that Obama could win the nomination (what is called "viability"), and that viability was in turn the most important factor predicting a vote for Obama in subsequent primaries and caucuses.

His overall success in the presidential nomination contest may be rooted in his come-from-behind victory in the Iowa caucuses and the momentum it generated that propelled him forward. Although many would agree that the Iowa caucuses were important, at least in this campaign, early nominating events, including the New Hampshire primary, may be more important in a systematic way than has often been recognized by pundits and scholars (Hull 2007). This is particularly so if you believe the rules of the game help determine who wins and who loses in politics. In 2008 without Iowa, Hillary Clinton may have been the Democratic Party's nominee, as the opening vignette suggests. Without Iowa, America may not have a black president. Just as the rules of the Electoral College gave Texas governor George W. Bush a victory in the 2000 elections, despite Vice President Al Gore's having won more votes, the Iowa caucuses may have been instrumental in electing Barack Obama in 2008.

The Rules Matter

Rules matter. A truism, perhaps, but research on presidential nomination campaigns rarely goes beyond this truism to understand how in fact they do matter. This book focuses on understanding how election rules, and institutions in general, and Iowa in particular, influenced the 2008 presidential election and nominating process. And although 2008 may have been sui generis at least for the Democrats, we argue that the rules governing the presidential nominating process matter generally, consistent with published research (Norrander 1996, 2000). Our twist is to focus on *Iowa* rules.

In this book we examine in depth two critical rules of modern presidential nomination campaigns, both connected to the unique role of Iowa. The first is that Iowa holds caucuses rather than a primary. The nature of the caucus process conditions how candidates campaign and how the media interpret the results. The second is that Iowa votes first, and nomination campaigns develop sequentially, moving from one state to another. This sequential election process has important implications for who wins and who loses in the end. Taken together, these two rules—and many additional, smaller rules that are embedded in them—define the modern nomination campaign: the strategies candidates use, the information voters learn, the way voters make decisions, and the final outcomes.

Building on and extending Christopher Hull's (2007) work on Iowa's role in the nominating process in the late 1990s and early 2000s, we argue that the Iowa caucuses have become more important in recent presidential elections, and play a greater role than they have in the past. This is in part a function of the mass media's growing attention to the Iowa caucuses. The evolutionary metaphor to describe this change is punctuated equilibrium, in that the old system has experienced an abrupt and consequential change. At the same time, the increasing importance of Iowa has given rise to a growing sense among political scientists and the general public that there is no rational reason to grant Iowa (and New Hampshire) special status. The conventional wisdom is decidedly hostile toward Iowa (and at times New Hampshire) and the impact its privileged position has on the selection process. This hostility is rooted in the notion that this small midwestern state carries such outsized influence (Winebrenner 1998).

To be blunter, Iowa has been trashed by many who see caucuses in general and Iowa in particular as unrepresentative and biased. This perspective has always been long on speculation and short on empirics. There are positive aspects to Iowa's procedures that have been ignored. What we saw in 2008 was that electoral rules can be greatly influenced by exigent circumstances. Thus, Iowa's role in the 2008 election, on close inspection, looks to have been quite edifying. This book sheds new light on the benefits of Iowa, while at the same time calling for reform of the presidential nominating process.

The two important rules governing presidential nominations structure the second and third parts of the book: caucuses versus primary elections (part 2) and the sequential nature of subsequent primaries (part 3). Part 4 then examines how voters perceive the fairness of the existing process and how the presidential nominating process can be reformed. Here we learn that national opinion polls show that most Americans favor reform, but they may not recognize the benefits derived from the current system. In each of these three parts, we show how the rules matter, and how they shape aggregate outcomes (candidate vote share), individual political behavior, participation, public opinion, campaign strategy, and more. We propose a reform that merges both sequential and simultaneous election rules, along with caucus and primary rules. We conclude with our policy proposal: a caucus window followed by a national primary.

Caucuses are different from primaries, and their rules call for different campaigns. [They favor grassroots campaigning, and require voters to be more attentive. As a result, fewer voters attend caucuses, but those who do are generally more aware and involved than voters elsewhere. The unique nature of a caucus means that candidates must structure their campaigns to find proverbial needles in the haystack: the voters who will come out for hours on a cold winter night in Iowa. We argue that this process makes candidates better. They must build effective organizations, spend time in living rooms and VFW halls, and engage in retail politics, meeting voters face to face. Whereas most primaries result in large-scale media campaigns and short airport tarmac appearances, caucuses—especially in Iowa—require a kind of campaigning that seems part of a bygone era, but which ultimately strengthens successful candidates and provides more information about all candidates, not only to Iowans but to all voters.]

Our argument carries with it a story about the role of the mass media in making Iowa what it is today, and how the media themselves become part of the story. Iowa's election rules (caucuses, sequential voting) are the wheels that start the process and propel a candidate toward the nomination, while media attention to the Iowa caucuses is like the grease that lubricates the state-by-state sequential election process. The news media give disproportionate attention to front-running candidates they expect to do well in Iowa. If results in Iowa depart from initial expectations, media attention shifts to those candidates who beat expectations, whether they actually win or not. This shift in national media attention helps determine who is packing their bags for New Hampshire and Super Tuesday and who is packing to go home. Using data from nomination contests over a thirty-year period (1976–2008), we provide evidence of a macro process in which changes in the amount of news coverage candidates receive from the days preceding the Iowa caucuses to the days after—changes associated with unexpected election results— significantly affect how well candidates do in later primaries and in ultimately securing their party's nomination. We then unpack the micro foundations of these behavioral dynamics by drawing on a national survey of public opinion we conducted during the 2008 primaries and caucuses. We find a similar dynamic at play, in which voters rely on information about the results in Iowa and New Hampshire. Voters' knowledge of the winners of Iowa and New Hampshire shapes their perceptions of whether they think a candidate can win the nomination. This, in turn, shapes voter choice in states that cast ballots after Iowa. Widespread public awareness of the winners of early nominating events, such as the Iowa caucuses, results from intensive news media attention given to the earliest contests. Our national survey data show that knowledge of Barack Obama winning (mostly white) Iowa was critical to perceptions that Obama could win the nomination. In turn, perceptions of Obama's viability were the most important factor predicting a vote for him in subsequent primaries and caucuses.

One additional point frames our argument. The presidential nomination literature—especially with regard to Iowa's role—needs to be updated. Nelson Polsby (1983), John Aldrich (1980), and Larry Bartels (1988) each wrote definitive political science books on nomination politics. These were published twenty to thirty years ago, and much has changed since then, including new campaign strategies incorporating information technology, online campaigning, and aggressive state frontloading (scheduling primaries and caucuses near the beginning of the delegate selection season to have a greater impact on the process). Although there has certainly been more published since then, much of it builds on the conventional wisdom that came out of this early work.

Caucus Rules

One important rule structuring the nominating process is some states' use of caucuses instead of primary elections to select presidential candidates. Iowa not only votes first in the current nomination schedule, but it is a caucus state that goes first in that process, which specifically structures modern presidential nomination contests. Instead of making the more simplistic and obvious claim that the rules matter, we develop the argument that the structure and rules of the Iowa caucuses differentiate them from both primaries and other caucuses when (1) all the major candidates campaign extensively in Iowa, (2) candidates emphasize retail, face-to-face contact, and (3) candidates reach out to groups that are less likely to be targeted in traditional elections. Although the literature argues that the rules matter, we draw attention to Iowa's relatively unique process for selecting presidential candidates.

The fact that the caucuses are multicandidate elections and, on the Democratic side, use proportional representation with a modest threshold to allocate delegates means that underdog candidates have a chance of winning some delegates to their party's national convention, staying in the race longer, and maybe even winning it all. The Democratic

Iowa caucus includes a second round of voting, where if a voter's first-choice candidate is deemed unviable, she can vote for her second-most-preferred candidate. We find evidence of more sincere voting and less strategic voting in Iowa under this rule than among voters in later states. Republicans, on the other hand, take a single straw-poll vote in their caucuses, and the candidate with the most votes wins. These rules have implications for who wins in the Iowa caucuses.

One major effect of the caucus process is that it is harder for voters to participate in what are effectively party meetings. The result is significantly lower turnout compared with primaries. We explore the demographic composition of 2008 Iowa caucus participants and find that, perhaps because turnout was much higher than usual, those who came out to vote were quite representative of Iowa voters generally. One potential advantage that party caucuses have over most primaries for turnout is that people do not have to register to vote beforehand to participate on caucus night. In highly competitive nominations, this means a high proportion of caucusgoers may be first timers, as occurred in 2008.

Because of their lower turnout, caucuses test candidate campaigns in complex ways requiring extensive organization. It is harder for candidates to reach caucus participants because there are fewer of them in the population, so grassroots mobilization—retail politics—is critical, as opposed to the mass media campaigns found in most competitive primary states. Thus, a key difference between a primary and a caucus is the type of campaigning required. Caucuses lend themselves well to strong organization and retail methods of campaigning. Such grassroots mobilization is harder to quantify than mass media campaigns. One of the contributions of this book is a unique set of survey data measuring grassroots politics in 2008.

The Iowa precinct caucuses reward candidates who excel at organization (Trish 1999). We find Hillary Clinton had relatively weak organization in Iowa compared to Barack Obama. In 2008 Obama outspent his competitors in Iowa by almost double, yet the money was spent largely on grassroots mobilization efforts. Had the New Hampshire primary been the first nominating event (even though it is a small population state), the 50-plus-percent turnout at its primary would mean much more campaign funds spent on television and radio advertising in order to reach a mass audience. Mitt Romney—echoing the example of publisher Steve Forbes in 1996—may have lost Iowa in 2008 despite leading the Republicans in campaign spending, in part because so much of his money was spent on mass media campaigns rather than grassroots mobilization. So caucus rules interact with candidate campaign strategies as well.

The rules governing the nominating process also affect delegate allocation—the winner-take-all system generally used by the Republicans, versus proportional allocation of delegates used by the Democrats—which affects how quickly the parties can coalesce around one candidate in a highly competitive environment (Kamarck 2009).Thus, we center much of this book on Iowa's role as the first state to weigh in on the nomination contest. We look at its role as a caucus state, not just as the first state. At the same time, we do not ignore what comes later.

Sequential Voting Rules

The second important rule of American presidential nominations is their unique sequential election process, which can have direct consequences for the outcome of a campaign. Competitive presidential nominations are decided in a series of state caucuses and primaries held during the early months of a presidential election year. Any process has to start somewhere. Since 1972, the small state of Iowa has been first, with candidate visits there and media attention increasing dramatically over time. As has often been assumed but rarely shown, Iowa may be critical for the underdog candidate who does better than expected, like Carter, Colorado senator Gary Hart, and Obama. But having Iowa go first and New Hampshire second has consequences not just for Iowa and New Hampshire but for voters in the rest of the country. Most often those consequences have been to narrow the field and to limit choice, but as 2008 showed, sometimes if the competitive stars align just right, voters participating later in the process can be influential as well.

Most scholars of voting and elections study simultaneous elections, such as midterm and presidential elections, where vote totals are all reported at roughly the same time. Sequential elections are based on temporal dependence, meaning that future events are not independent of past events; later nominating events are conditioned on earlier ones. People at the end of the process see very different campaigns than people at the start of the process. Unlike general election voting, candidate choice in nomination campaigns is complex: the campaigns are constantly changing, candidates drop in and out of the race, and the cue of party identification is missing, since contests are among candidates of the same political party. The sequential nature of the nominating events introduces different dynamics at different points in the process due to a continually changing information environment and the potential for strategic voting in what is an iterative learning process across the states (Morton and Williams 2001; Cain 1978). One benefit of sequential voting is that voters making decisions later in the process have more information about candidates, including horse race information provided by polls and past election outcomes, delegate totals, candidate traits, and ideology and policy information, because of the earlier electoral events (Battaglini, Morton, and Palfrey 2007; see also Lau and Redlawsk [2006]). This may give later voters the opportunity to make more informed and perhaps better decisions than they would have otherwise, while earlier voters may be relatively disadvantaged. At the same time, voters in states that go early in the process may have an undue influence on the outcome of the nomination battle. This leads some to express concerns about representation and fairness in the current nomination system.

Iowa votes first, and yet the issue is really not Iowa per se. The more general argument is that early nominating events shape perceptions of whether candidates can win the nomination (viability) and the presidency (electability), which in turn shape candidate choice in later primaries and caucuses. In 2008 Iowa may have mattered for Obama, but in other years New Hampshire matters or Super Tuesday matters, for different candidates and in different elections. At the same time, how these early nominating events shape voting nationally is part of one general process. A strong finish in early nominating events builds "momentum" by generating increased media coverage, monetary contributions, and campaign volunteers. Agenda-setting theories show us that public visibility through media coverage invokes candidate salience, and salience is a necessary condition for candidate viability. In turn, perceptions of viability lead to subsequent primary election successes, as well as more media exposure, more campaign donations, and perhaps more support in later races (Bartels 1987, 1988; Mayer 1987). Candidates thought to be underdogs who beat the odds and do better than expected in early nominating events gain momentum, and the increased media attention that ensues earns them a closer look by voters in subsequent primaries (Aldrich 1980).

Electoral sequence structures how, and where, knowledge about the winners of early nominating events will be distributed and thus will shape voting in later states. Indeed, the national survey data we present here demonstrate that perceptions of the candidates shift even in a very short time period. Candidates doing better than "expected" as defined by the news media are rewarded by voters. We provide evidence over a thirty-year period of a macro process in which the change in media coverage of candidates before and after the Iowa caucuses significantly affects candidate vote share in the New Hampshire primary. In turn, changes in media coverage post Iowa and post New Hampshire affect candidate vote share in primaries nationwide. We also find that the state-by-state sequential election process affects levels of political participation (both traditional and online politics) and even attitudes toward reforming presidential nominations. The sequential rules governing the nominating process are important in complex ways, in that sequence interacts with media exposure of early nominating events to shape voter decision making. The media's effect on the nominating process works within the sequential election rules highlighted in this book.

Reforming Election Rules

We know from the literature on election reform that the rules matter by structuring outcomes in politics. We also know the rules governing elections can and do change. Iowa has faced a great deal of criticism, because the state and its caucuses are both seen as unrepresentative. Other rules that could be used to select presidential candidates include a system of rotating state primaries or a national primary held on a single day. One rationale for a national primary is that it represents only a modest change from Super Tuesday, which with twenty-four states voting on one day in 2008 approximated a national primary. In the following chapters, we not only empirically measure public opinion in terms of support for a national primary (chapter 10) but also examine, in chapters 8 and 9, how voting on Super Tuesday affects interest in the nomination campaigns and media attention. We find that voting on Super Tuesday is linked to increased knowledge of which political candidate won the early nominating events compared with those voting after Super Tuesday. This suggests that we can look at Super Tuesday voters as a proxy for how voters would respond to a national primary. National opinion polls show most Americans favoring reform of the presidential nominating process. A system run under different rules could likely result in different campaign strategies, different candidates, and different outcomes.

We conclude the book with our own unique proposal for reform of presidential nominations.

Our Argument: In Three Parts

Following chapter 2, which summarizes what happened in 2008 and reviews the existing literature on presidential nominations, this book is organized into three additional parts. Since Iowa votes first in this sequential process, it is the beginning point for us as well. Part 2 focuses on Iowa, exploring the rules governing the Iowa caucuses, differences between the two parties, participation in the caucuses, candidate campaigns, and how caucuses differ from primaries. In chapter 3 we provide an insider's guide to how the Iowa caucuses *really* work, with details about the different rules Republicans and Democrats follow on caucus night and the implications those rules have for candidate campaigns. We also examine challenges to the caucus system and responses by its defenders. Chapter 4 examines the nature of the campaigns in Iowa in 2008, using data from our Iowa caucus surveys, which asked caucusgoers about candidate contacts, as well as aggregate data on candidate activities in Iowa. We look at where the candidates focused their efforts and the resulting substantial increase in voter turnout over prior caucus years.

From chapter 4's focus on the campaigns, in chapter 5 we move to the voters, examining participation by Iowans in the process, particularly in light of the intensity of the candidate campaigns. We look at who caucused in 2008, and consider the conventional wisdom that caucuses are dominated by party activists who do not represent mainstream voters. For whatever reason—probably the degree to which the campaigns mobilized voters—we find that caucus attendees in 2008 looked a lot like Iowa voters more generally. We take up this question of the nature of Iowa caucusgoers in more detail in chapter 6, comparing findings of earlier studies with the reality on the ground in 2008. It is certainly true that the caucus process itself makes participation more difficult than in a primary, suggesting that those who turn out must be more motivated than the typical primary voter. But using our Iowa caucusgoers survey data to examine the demographic and attitudinal characteristics of these voters in 2008, we find that on a number of bases these voters were not the unrepresentative party activists that conventional wisdom seems to assume they always are.

Following our in-depth examination of the Iowa caucuses, part 3 broadens the analysis to other states, examining the role of early states in the nominating process in general. This section explores the impact of sequential voting rules on candidate performance over time, the role of the news media in amplifying results from early states, the dynamics of individual-level vote choice, and political participation in primaries and caucuses. Do the Iowa caucuses and the New Hampshire primary have the ability to alter preseason rankings of candidates' odds of winning their party's nomination? Chapter 7 demonstrates how election outcomes in Iowa and New Hampshire condition voter decisions in other states. We draw on data from 1976 through 2008 to examine how news media attention to candidate performance in Iowa affects outcomes in later states. Editors and reporters set early expectations about how candidates might do in Iowa, and then shift attention to candidates who exceed these expectations. Momentum associated with a highly visible early contest is thus not so much about winning; instead it is about doing "better than expected." This chapter shows that changes in media attention to candidates associated with the Iowa result significantly influence the candidates' overall performance in subsequent primaries.

Chapter 8 turns back to 2008 to further examine how momentum worked in the presidential nomination season. Voting decisions are made by individuals, so we need to use data at the individual level to understand how early events condition voter perceptions in later ones. Our national survey data suggest that knowledge of winners of the Iowa Democratic caucuses increased perceptions that Obama would win the nomination, which in turn increased the probability that a person would vote for Obama. But knowledge of which candidates won Iowa did not predict perceptions of candidate momentum for other Democratic or Republican candidates running in 2008. Thus, the general findings over time presented in chapter 7 appear to apply again in 2008, at least in the context of the highly competitive Democratic campaign.

We end this section by again considering citizen participation in chapter 9, but here we compare that participation and interest in later nominating events—Super Tuesday and the Pennsylvania Democratic primary—with Iowa, and we look at both traditional and newer online modes. In 2008, turnout in primaries (at least for the Democrats) was high throughout the process, and actually increased slightly over time. We find that the intense Iowa caucus campaign meant Iowans were more likely to participate both online and in traditional (offline) activities

than registered voters nationally. But sequence mattered, and later voters may have benefited from information from early events; registered
voters at Super Tuesday and the later Democratic primary in Pennsylvania were more interested in the nomination and were actually more
likely to follow campaign news than were Iowans. Competitive nominating events and online politics also appear to reduce the bias of primary
electorates. As the case of Pennsylvania shows, we suspect that if another state were exposed to the candidate campaigns and media attention that Iowa receives, we would find similarly high levels of online and
traditional political participation.

No book on presidential nominations would be complete without a
careful consideration of calls for reform of the process. Iowa's unique position has generated a great deal of pushback from other states and from
those who argue that the current system is too drawn out, too focused
on one or two small unrepresentative states, and too frontloaded. Part 4
focuses on historical attempts to reform how we nominate presidential
candidates in the United States, and outlines goals for reforming the
process. In addition, it presents public opinion data on different election
rules that could be used to structure presidential nominations, including rotating state primary order and holding a national primary. Drawing on national survey data, chapter 10 finds high support for reform of
the nominating process when people are asked their general preferences.
More important, support for reform is conditioned by self-interest defined by an individual's state of residence, especially its population size
and voting sequence (early or late). That is, voters seem to know whether
the current system is "good" for them or not. We end this book with
chapter 11, where we ask whether the rules governing presidential nominations should be changed. The final recommendation is a compromise
among us three authors, which we are brought to by the data and analyses that run throughout the book. We conclude with our policy proposal:
a "caucus window" followed by a national primary.

This book illuminates how the Iowa caucuses work, how the presidential nominating process works, and, finally, how we might update
or reform the process. No one has put together all the pieces of the
process—caucus rules, candidate campaigns in the caucuses, participation in the caucuses, voter turnout in the caucuses, analysis of candidate
performance over time across states, the dynamics of vote choice nationally, participation online and offline in primaries and caucuses, and, finally, public opinion on reforming the process—like we do here, updat-

ing our understanding of U.S. presidential nominations. With the notable exception of Hull's (2007) work and some papers by Adkins and Dowdle (2001; Dowdle, Adkins, and Steger 2009), little recent scholarship has focused on either Iowa or the implications of the sequential nominating process. As Kamarck (2009) notes in her recent book on presidential primaries, the sequential nature of the system structures how delegates are won, and delegates are what candidates need in order to win the nomination. While she focuses on how sequencing and delegate selection rules affect candidate strategy and how candidates try to game the system itself, we are interested in how the first state—Iowa—creates the initial conditions to which both candidates and voters must respond. As we update the literature from the perspective of 2008, we recognize both the unique aspects of this recent nomination battle and election, and the lessons that we may draw going forward, given the likely continuation of a sequential nominating process in future years.

The path Carter followed from Iowa to the White House has changed since 1976, so we have recommendations for how the nominating process can be modified and improved. Still, by book's end, we hope that we will have persuaded the reader of the clear benefits to the nation as a whole of beginning the presidential nominating process in small-population states (Iowa or others) where healthy grassroots politics is possible, and where voters can become informed and aware of the campaigns. Yet we underscore both the need for significant reform of U.S. presidential nominating process and the benefits of continuity. In so doing, we answer the ever-elusive question: why Iowa?

CHAPTER TWO

What We Know and What We Don't about Presidential Nomination Campaigns

One definition of crazy is to keep doing something that's never worked, while expecting it will be different this time. That's a bull's-eye description of the loony system used to nominate candidates for the U.S. Presidency. Every four years, we try again hoping against hope that this time it will work. — Professor Terry Madonna (2004), referring to the 2004 presidential campaign

Crazy or not, the current presidential nomination system has been more or less in place for nearly forty years. Although there has been some tinkering around the margins, and states have fallen over one another trying to get to the head of the line for the benefits of being early participants in the nominating process, for the most part the system has been relatively stable despite the constant criticism it receives. This stability is more a result of the political parties' and the states' inability to agree on anything better than satisfaction with the system. But while the guiding rules have remained relatively constant, much has changed in the years since Iowa took the lead in the sequential nominating process. We have seen the rise of information technology and online campaigning, greater attention to the so-called invisible primary, and skyrocketing presidential campaign costs. All this has happened while one-third of the population seems uninterested in the existing parties, claiming to be nonpartisans or independents, which generally excludes them from participating in the nominating process in many states.

In this chapter we set the stage with a very brief summary of what actually happened in 2008—the most competitive nomination campaign in recent history—followed by a review of the extant literature on presidential nominations. We examine the conventional wisdom that has developed from this research, much of which is based on data that is at least twenty years old. We set the stage for the rest of the book, where we examine how the rules of the game and its sequential nature operate to define the modern nomination system, and offer a brief introduction to proposals for changing the nominating process. We close this chapter with a discussion of our methods and data, describing a series of surveys we conducted in Iowa and nationally to develop our understanding of the 2008 nomination campaign.

A Brief Summary of the 2008 Presidential Nomination Campaign

The presidential nomination calendar of 2008 was marked by the most aggressive frontloading in recent history, which ironically may have only increased the importance of early nominating events, such as Iowa and New Hampshire. Frontloading is the trend in which states schedule their primaries and caucuses near the beginning of the delegate selection season to have a greater impact on the process. In 1976, 10% of national convention delegates were chosen by March 2, and the number only grew over the next thirty years. As part of their ongoing efforts to address frontloading and other problems, both the Democratic National Committee (DNC) and Republican National Committee (RNC) revised the schedules and rules in anticipation of the 2008 presidential primary elections and caucuses. Even so, 70% of the 2008 delegates were chosen by that same date.

Ugly battles over the nomination calendar pitted some state parties, notably those in Florida and Michigan, against others, primarily those in Iowa and New Hampshire. This conflict led to the dates and sequence of nominating events remaining uncertain until late 2007. Moreover, because Florida and Michigan moved their primaries to earlier dates than they were supposed to under party rules, the entire primary calendar was pushed to very early in 2008; the Iowa caucuses were held just three days into the new year. Florida and Michigan were threatened with what seemed at the time to be severe punishment. The RNC threatened them with the loss of half their delegates to the GOP national convention, and the DNC initially ruled that the states would lose all their delegates to the Democratic convention. Although the parties largely relented after their nomination contests were settled, concern over what to do about Florida and Michigan dogged the candidates, campaigns, and parties for months. The Florida and Michigan delegates were among New York Senator Hillary Clinton's best hopes for the winning the nomination, and their fate was still uncertain before the last round of primaries in June. Concerns about frontloading make reform of the nominating process particularly salient (see Tolbert and Squire [2009]). Indeed, just before the national conventions, each party announced that it would undertake significant reviews of its nomination system in preparation for 2012 (Balz 2008; Shear 2008).

Once things got under way on caucus night January 3, the Republican campaign unfolded much as it has in past contests—that is, relatively quickly. After losing the Iowa caucuses to upstart Mike Huckabee, John McCain managed a comeback in New Hampshire. Aided by the GOP's reliance on winner-take-all (or most) delegate selection rules, McCain eliminated all serious competition (except for Huckabee) by the end of Super Tuesday on February 5, and by March 5 he had won an outright majority of delegates. The Democrats, however, battled much longer, with Obama's victory certain only after the very last primaries on June 3, when he had won enough pledged delegates to ensure that Clinton could not overtake him. Although some complained that the Republican nominating process was too short, eliminating choice for states coming after Super Tuesday, many of the same people complained that the Democrats' campaign went on too long as Clinton and Obama traded states, with Clinton winning or holding her own in many primaries, while Obama's organizational advantages overwhelmed her in caucus states. In the end, of course, Obama trounced McCain in the general election, completing his Iowa-assisted rise from first-term U.S. senator to president.

Revisiting Presidential Nomination Politics

Like the treasures in grandma's attic, the literature on presidential nominations is valuable but badly in need of updating, as much of the research we rely on for conventional wisdom was conducted in the 1970s and 1980s. Our understanding of the nominating process in place since 1972 has been eroded by a changing world. The race in 2008 unfolded in a number of ways that contradicted prevailing expectations. It had long been assumed, for example, that there were "only three tickets out of Iowa," meaning that a candidate's finishing below the top three in either party ended his or her chances. Senator McCain, however, managed to become the nominee even though he finished fourth in Iowa, albeit missing the third position by only a 424-vote margin (Tolbert and Squire 2009).

Other departures from the conventional wisdom were more meaningful. Again, it was long held that the dynamics of the current nominating process made it likely that the nominee from each party would be determined relatively quickly. The winnowing function performed by the early contests would inevitably take a large field of candidates and rapidly reduce it to a smaller and smaller group (Winebrenner 1998). Once two or three candidates were left, voters would quickly shift in favor of the eventual nominee. Although the rules on the Republican side produced this expected quick verdict, those on the Democratic side did not allow easy resolution of a seemingly never-ending contest.

Conventional wisdom also maintains that winning the Iowa caucuses does not matter very much; winning New Hampshire or doing better than expected is the ticket to success (Adkins and Dowdle, 2001; Mayer 2004). And while Hull (2007) argues that Iowa is more important than it gets credited, many pundits rehash the idea that the Iowa caucuses are more a sideshow than anything else. Yet in 2008 Obama's win there clearly gave him the momentum that created the competitive campaign through which he secured the Democratic Party nomination; Huckabee's win, in contrast, did not really lead him anywhere, though it did fatally wound Romney.

Another unexpected outcome in 2008 was a surge in political participation, in part because the Obama campaign was remarkably successful in getting young supporters out to the polls. Turnout in presidential primaries normally declines over time as the field of candidates is winnowed and a clear winner emerges (as happened with the Republicans in 2008). Yet the 2008 Democratic contests were the most competitive in modern history, with the long battle generating record turnout in primaries and caucuses across the nation. Turnout in the 2008 New Hampshire primary set a record for Democrats, while Iowa turnout broke records for both parties. Turnout in state primaries from January through May was about one-third of the voting eligible population across the nation—the highest since 1972, driven by the competition between Obama and Clinton. Such competition may reduce bias in the compo-

sition of the electorate and foster party-building activities (Stone, Atkeson, and Rapoport 1992).

Other changes in presidential nominations in election years before
2008 deviate substantially from our understanding of the process, which
is derived from the 1970s and 1980s. Candidates begin fund-raising years
before the first nominating event, drawing on elite patrons (Cohen et al.
2008) in what has been called the invisible primary (Aldrich 2009). Financing elections has changed, as candidates increasingly opt out of
public funds. Combined with the frontloaded calendar, early money
may matter more now than it had in the past.[1] We should note, however,
that in 2008 neither party's 2007 money leader actually won the nomination, challenging claims that the invisible primary is what determines the
nominee.

Notions of the importance of the invisible primary may have to
change, especially with the advent of online campaigning. Although the
broadcast media continues to play a powerful role in informing the public about the candidates, online media and online fund-raising have become increasingly significant since 2000 (Hull 2007; Mossberger, Tolbert, and McNeal 2008; Bimber 2003). The Internet did not exist when
much of the key literature on presidential nominations was written. New
media and new information technologies may alter the role that initial
financial advantages have provided front-running candidates by giving
upstarts a means to translate early success into campaign funds over-
night. Newer technologies may also level the playing field somewhat by
allowing underfunded, lesser-known candidates to reach voters directly
via e-mail, listservs, candidate Web sites, YouTube videos, blogs, and social networking resources such as Facebook and Twitter. The diversity
of online media—which includes mass, small-group, and interpersonal
communication—can make candidate campaigns more cost-effective
and able to reach wider audiences because of the relatively low cost and
twenty-four-hour availability of the Internet (Mossberger, Tolbert, and
McNeal 2008). Online fund-raising has become increasingly important,
as demonstrated by McCain when he first sought the nomination in 2000,
and by former Vermont governor Howard Dean's pioneering Internet
campaign of 2004. Although trailing Hillary Clinton in funds heading
into Iowa, Obama's victory in November 2008 was made possible in part
by the huge amounts of money raised: $730 million accrued from 3 mil-
lion donors, much of it raised online. It is clearly time to revisit our understanding of presidential nomination politics.

At the same time, readers might rightfully ask whether 2008 was unique and not to be repeated. One election out of the eight since former Georgia governor Jimmy Carter won in 1976 does not make a trend. That the early front-runners and leading fund-raisers of 2008 did not win their nominations and that competition was as intense as it was for the Democrats may be a relatively rare event, but it is significant nonetheless, because many structural features of the 2008 contest will likely remain in place. We do know that 2012 is likely to be different, even if nothing changes structurally and the rules remain the same. For one thing, the Democrats most likely have their 2012 nominee, since a sitting president running for reelection rarely faces a serious challenge (one exception was Jimmy Carter in 1980, who had to fight off a strong challenge from Massachusetts senator Edward Kennedy). Moreover, unless the Republicans change their winner-take-all rules, their nomination is likely to follow the typical path, ending relatively early when one candidate wins enough pluralities to gain a large percentage of delegates to the national convention.

However, without substantial, unforeseen rules changes there will likely be future contests in one or both parties similar to what occurred in 2008. We side with Hull (2007) in arguing that understanding the increasing role of Iowa as the first state to vote in the current nomination schedule, and the rise in nontraditional (online) campaign strategies, makes investigating what happened in Iowa and across the country in 2008 important, if only to document for the next presidential election cycle both the continuity and the change inherent in nomination politics of the early twenty-first century. No matter the future importance of Iowa itself, or whether it will remain first—the issue of the sequential nature of the primary season is not going away soon. One thing that has remained constant in the modern nomination system is its sequential nature. Examining this in the context of Iowa, as we do here, gives those interested in reform an opportunity to learn from the current system as they continue their attempts to design a better nominating process.

Part I. Caucus Rules: Updating Conventional Wisdom

If Iowa is important in structuring the options for primary and caucus voters nationwide, how representative is the state compared with the rest of the nation? How representative are the Iowa caucuses of Iowans themselves? How do Iowans respond to the onslaught of candidate campaigns and mass media attention, and how effective are the campaigns in reaching Iowa caucus participants? Do Iowans make rational and informed decisions? How do caucuses and primaries vary in selecting presidential candidates? If Iowa does indeed matter, understanding the nature of caucus participation is critical.

A key difference between Iowa and New Hampshire (and most other states) lies in Iowa's use of a caucus versus a primary system. Caucuses are lengthy local party meetings used to conduct party business and select delegates to future county, district, and state conventions, which ultimately cast votes for delegates to the national conventions. In primaries voters simply show up and vote as they would in a normal election. But caucuses are a different beast, and their rules have important implications for candidate choice and campaign strategies, and voter participation, representation, and turnout. Caucus rules make Iowa very different from the New Hampshire primary; one difference is the lower turnout that requires different campaign strategies.

In the real world of presidential nomination politics, candidate and media focus on Iowa is intense. However, the Iowa caucuses have drawn somewhat less direct scholarly attention. Only three books of which we are aware—Peverill Squire's 1989 edited volume, Hugh Winebrenner's historical perspective (1998), and a book by Christopher Hull (2007)—have the Iowa caucuses as their primary focus. Some other work, especially by Walter Stone, Alan Abramowitz, Ronald Rapoport, and Lonna Atekson in several articles (1989, 1992, 1995), Henry Brady's (1989) piece on strategy in the caucuses, and Adkins and Dowdle's (2001) examination of the importance of Iowa and New Hampshire, focuses specifically on Iowa. Abramowitz and his colleagues (2001) have also compiled a data set of political activism that, while not focused only on Iowa, contains several elections' worth of surveys of Iowa convention delegates.

We need to update our understanding of the Iowa caucuses. Most of the research that does exist is not based on Iowa survey data.[2] This book draws on a sequence of surveys of registered Iowa voters and likely caucusgoers conducted three times before the January 3 caucuses, a post-election survey of caucusgoers, and a unique in-caucus survey conducted in almost every precinct in the state. With these data we are able to paint a detailed picture of how Iowa caucus rules affect the outcomes, the participation, and the effectiveness of candidate campaigns in the caucuses.

Conventional wisdom maintains that Iowa caucus rules are archaic, complex, outdated, and even "Byzantine" (Wang 2007; see also Wine-brenner [1998]). This may in part be true, particularly in that the trans-lation of actual votes to delegates can be messy on the Democratic Party side. The Democrats do not report actual vote totals in the precinct cau-cuses, but only the number of delegates selected to represent each can-didate at upcoming county conventions. In addition, the Democrats use a realignment process whereby voters favoring a candidate who fails to reach a viability threshold (usually 15%) in a precinct can switch their vote to a candidate that has enough support to win delegates. Democratic delegates are awarded proportionate to their final vote share. The litera-ture argues that caucus participants are more strategic than primary vot-ers (Stone, Abramowtiz, and Rapoport 1992; Norrander 1989), and even though they represent more ideological extremes, they select moderate candidates that can win the nomination. (We should note, though, that Geer [1988] argues that primary electorates generally are not ideologi-cally biased.) As we detail in chapter 3, what is deemed a Byzantine pro-cess actually includes components that encourage the expression of true voter preferences. Because of the second round of voting and the pro-portional allocation of delegates by the Democrats, we actually find evi-dence of less strategic voting and more sincere voting in the Iowa cau-cuses compared to those who cast votes a month later on Super Tuesday.

One story the media tell is that caucuses are where grassroots, or re-tail, politics is at its best. Retail politics is often understood as personal politics, or small democracy with a small d. Retail politics provides op-portunities for learning by voters and a safety valve for political parties, as it allows communication between campaigns and voters with less reli-ance on mass media. Some contend that if the Iowa caucuses are won by grassroots political campaigns, which are often thought of as the health-iest form of politics, then Iowa has a legitimate claim to holding the first nominating event every four years (Hull 2007). On the other hand, if the caucuses are increasingly dominated by television ads and mass media campaigns, like many primary elections, then perhaps Iowa no longer is unique and should not have the privilege of voting first. Voter learning due to retail politics may result in a reduction of uncertainly not possi-ble via mass media campaigns. Hull (2007) finds evidence that the can-didate's use of old-style grassroots politics, especially days campaigning spent in Iowa, determines the winner of the Iowa caucuses.

Caucuses tend to have lower voter turnout than primaries, making mobilization efforts considerably more difficult for candidates. The organization required of them during a caucus tests their campaigns in ways that primaries just do not. Part of Obama's success in Iowa in 2008 has been credited to organization both offline (grassroots mobilization) and online, while Hillary Clinton's failure may be seen as a failure to use the right campaign strategies, given the low turnout in caucuses. Since there are fewer caucusgoers, they are harder to reach, and require a more personalized approach on the candidates' part.

As we will show, without resources, candidates find it much harder to reach potential Iowa caucusgoers, especially given the generally low turnout. We update the conventional understanding of retail politics here. Although Iowa has a reputation for grassroots politics, without financial resources one cannot win there—retail politics notwithstanding. While Huckabee won with substantially less money than Romney, he was by no means destitute in the context of the Republican campaign. Our surveys of actual caucus participants demonstrate the importance of resources and organization. People reported more contacts via live telephone calls from the Obama campaign than from any other Democratic campaign, and Obama had the highest level of e-mail contact among Democrats. His campaign also tied for the highest U.S. mail and in-person contacts. Moreover, Obama had the most contacts with actual caucus attendees, using grassroots mobilization methods. He also led his fellow Democratic candidates in television advertisements and generally outspent the Democratic field in Iowa. While money was clearly a factor in Obama's win in Iowa, we contend that his spending was successful because he used the money for grassroots mobilization as well as mass media campaigning.

How do Iowa voters respond to the candidate campaigns? They receive a lot of attention from the candidates, and in response they participate at high levels in both online and grassroots political activity. Some scholars maintain that party elites control the Iowa caucuses (Stone, Rapoport, and Abramowitz 1992). The literature also suggests that caucuses and primaries are both critical for party-building activities, but because caucuses are party meetings after all, the process may have advantages over primaries in mobilizing party activists (Stone, Rapoport, and Atkeson 1995). In drawing on our unique postelection survey of Iowa caucus participants, we reveal that almost half the 2008 caucusgoers were first timers. Ordinary citizens, not party elites, controlled the caucuses in 2008.

Conventional wisdom holds that because the caucuses have very low turnout, caucus participants are unrepresentative in terms of socioeconomic status, ideology and partisanship compared to ordinary voters. But in 2008 we find few socioeconomic or even partisan differences between Iowa caucus goers and registered voters. Even though turnout in the caucuses was less than most primaries in 2008 (16% of the eligible voter population; about 30% of party members), caucus participants were broadly representative of the state. Moreover, Lewis-Beck and Squire (2009) persuasively argue that Iowa itself is economically representative of the nation, even if it is not so demographically.

Part II. Conventional Wisdom: Sequential Voting Rules

For two decades after Jimmy Carter's success in traveling from Iowa to the White House, there was little evidence that the Iowa caucuses were kingmakers. In political folklore, the saying in New Hampshire has been "Iowa picks corn, New Hampshire picks presidents" (attributed to former New Hampshire governor John H. Sununu), and the evidence seemed to back that up. As the years progressed, early fund-raising became more important as the nomination calendar was frontloaded. Democrats also began to give greater primacy to "superdelegates," party leaders who comprised as much as 20% of national convention votes. Other than Gary Hart's short-lived surge after a surprise Iowa showing in 1984, there were no examples of candidates repeating Carter's trajectory out of Iowa. From 1980 until 1996, only three winners of the seven competitive Republican and Democratic Iowa caucuses became their party's nominee, and none actually became president.

Nevertheless, starting slowly with the McGovern campaign in 1972, candidates paid attention to Iowa and began to believe that winning—or more accurately, doing better than media expectations—was the key to gaining the nomination. Carter began the focus on Iowa when, as a little-known governor of a southern state, he staked it all on Iowa, and in coming in second to "uncommitted"—delegates who chose not to back any candidate—was perceived to have gotten the media bump that took him to the nomination (Squire 1989).

Since then, even though no other candidates seemed able to follow Carter's path, the Iowa caucuses nonetheless became more important and increasingly institutionalized (Hull 2007). Former California governor Ronald Reagan established himself as a force in the GOP in part by nearly defeating a sitting incumbent (Gerald Ford) in the 1976 Iowa caucuses. In the 1980s, Iowa propelled Gary Hart and televangelist Pat Robertson to national prominence in their respective campaigns. George W. Bush served as president for eight years after first winning in Iowa in 2000. In the week before the Iowa caucus in 2004, Howard Dean led Massachusetts senator John Kerry in a Gallup Poll of likely New Hampshire primary voters by a margin of 32 to 17%. In addition to this advantage, Dean also enjoyed a sizeable lead in fund-raising, entering January 2004 with nearly twice as much money as Kerry. By these standards Dean could be seen as favored to win the Democratic nomination (but see McSweeney [2007]). But following a surprising third-place finish behind Kerry and John Edwards in Iowa, Dean's national support flattened out, and he ended up losing New Hampshire and the nomination. Kerry thus provides an example—similar to Carter in 1976 and Obama in 2008—of a candidate building on a surprising victory in Iowa to steal the lead, and the eventual nomination, from candidates who had been seen as early front-runners. As the exception that proves the rule, in 2008 John McCain was the first major party nominee since 1992 who did not win in Iowa. Winners of the Iowa caucuses, particularly those who exceed early expectations, reap important dividends in terms of increased media attention.

This does not mean that Iowa is always a kingmaker. Scholars have argued that winning Iowa has been an unreliable predictor of primary vote share nationwide, and a poor predictor of winning the nomination (Adkins and Dowdle 2001; Mayer 1996, 2003). New Hampshire, not Iowa, is what is said to really matter in selecting presidential candidates. Yet other scholars examining opinion data in the 1980s and early 1990s found that voter perceptions of viability or electability—perceptions, we will show, that are shaped by who does better than expected in Iowa and New Hampshire—also shaped voting decisions in later primaries and caucuses (Aldrich 1980; Bartels 1987, 1988; Abramowitz 1989; Stone, Rapoport, and Abramowitz 1992; Norrander 1991, 1992, 1993; Kenney and Rice 1994; Squire 1989). How can these divergent findings, based on different levels of analysis, be reconciled? We seek to answer this question by relying on both aggregate election results over time and individual-level survey analysis in the 2008 contest.

The presidential nominating process is unique, as other U.S. elections do not occur in multiple places over time, offering multiple candidates where party identification has no bearing on an individual's voting decision.[3] Voters are often uncertain about candidate quality at the beginning of a campaign, so voters in later states may attempt to infer quality from the information provided by early states, especially by paying attention to the aggregate vote results in those states. Fairly extensive research has attempted to address the consequences of these sequential election characteristics for voter decisions. In one of the earliest and most important studies, John Aldrich (1980) contended that candidates' success depends mainly on a reciprocal relationship between resources (money, media attention, and popular support) and electoral outcomes (more specifically, exceeding or failing to meet prior expectations in a given contest). That is, greater resources spent in a given state will lead to a greater likelihood that the candidate will exceed electoral expectations. Exceeding expectations in a given contest subsequently leads to the increased ability to obtain resources. This reciprocal relationship ultimately leads to the winnowing of candidates as the nominating process advances. The model predicts that candidates will tend to spend resources in states where no one candidate has an advantage, will avoid contests where one candidate has a clear lead, and will spend resources in states that have elections early on in the process and/or have a large number of delegates at stake (Aldrich 1980). Aldrich's model clearly points to the importance of early nomination contests, such as the Iowa caucuses.

In another early account of how voters decide on candidates in nomination contests, Bartels (1987) argued that a conditional relationship exists between a voter's predispositions toward a candidate (favorability ratings) and the candidate's chance of winning the party's nomination (viability). Bartels thus showed that voters use candidate successes in early nominating events (evidence of viability) in making their choices. This again points to the fact that Iowa should matter. Others, however, argue that perceptions of whether a candidate can win the general election (electability) have greater predictive power than viability (Stone, Rapoport, and Abramowitz 1992; Abramowitz 1989; Norrander 1986a), casting doubt on the importance of early nominating events, which provide few cues about likely general election outcomes.

The literature on U.S. presidential nominations has thus focused on the importance of the "Big Mo," or momentum given to a campaign from winning the Iowa caucuses and New Hampshire's primary. This term was coined by Vice President George H. W. Bush during the 1980 presidential primary. After winning the Republican Iowa caucuses, Bush told a CBS announcer, "What we'll have, you see, is momentum. We will have forward 'Big Mo' on our side, as they say in athletics" (quoted in Bartels 1989, 123). Candidates clearly think momentum matters, which gives them another reason to focus on early states. But scholars are less certain, suggesting that a better understanding of the impact of the sequential nature of presidential nominations is necessary.

Punctuated Change: Candidate and Media Attention at the Iowa Caucuses

Iowa is a relatively small state, ranking thirtieth in population in the 2000 U.S. census. It is situated squarely in what is often called "flyover country," as movers and shakers fly over the vast American middle on their way from one coast to the other. Yet every four years Iowa becomes the center of the political universe. The result is intense candidate and media focus on a small Midwestern state where face-to-face politics dominates. Winning or losing the Iowa caucuses has made, reinforced, or more often broken the chances of many presidential candidates—both the well financed and those with little money. As Bartels (1989, 122) notes, "Small events in Iowa can have big effects on the rest of the presidential campaign." While the media focuses attention on the state, candidates, too, treat the caucuses as if they matter, spending large amounts of money. And while money matters to any campaign, the most precious resource is the candidate's own time. And much of it is spent in Iowa for up to three years before the next caucus.

Although much earlier research found that Iowa did not seem to exert much influence on the rest of the nominating process, there is evidence that the caucuses have become more important in the last few presidential election cycles. Since 2000, four of the winners of the five competitive caucuses have become their party's nominee, and in all three elections from 2000 to 2008, an Iowa winner has become president. Christopher Hull in *Grassroots Rules* (2007) shows that since 2000 (and especially in 2004) Iowa has grown in importance in the nominating process, arguing that this has happened in tandem with the rise of online politics. He notes there are few clear effects of Iowa in the 1980s and 1990s, but finds this suddenly changes in 2000 and 2004. The elusive Iowa momentum seems connected to the rise of electronic communications, as early successes or losses in Iowa are projected to future voters nationwide. As opposed to the traditional notion of momentum in a primary process (that is, a candidate's vote share in the caucuses), "e-mentum" is what Hull calls the increasing capacity of candidates to use online methods to bolster the effectiveness of their campaigns. He creates an index that consists of the candidates' Iowa vote share and a measure of their exposure via the Internet, and finds that primary vote share for presidential candidates over time is explained by Iowa e-mentum.[4] Drawing on the 2004 election, he argues that new Internet communications media (online fund-raising, candidate Web sites, e-mail mobilization) caused Iowa to have a "wired and wild" influence on nomination contests in other states.

Media attention was particularly intense in 2008, when for the first time since 1988 neither major party had an incumbent president running and as many as sixteen candidates made efforts to campaign there. The *Washington Post* recorded 2,025 candidate events in Iowa after January 1, 2007—twice the number of visits they paid to New Hampshire. In fact, candidates paid more visits to Iowa than to California, Texas, Florida, New York, New Jersey, Pennsylvania, Michigan, Illinois, and twelve other states *combined*. The *Des Moines Register* counted 233 candidate visits just in that city in 2007. Cedar Rapids enjoyed 87 visits. Ames had 73. Davenport, 65. The tiny town of Elkader (population 1,465) had 10 candidate visits in the run-up to January 2008—far more than what residents in many major metropolitan areas were exposed to. Thus, while the Iowa caucuses have long drawn media coverage, there is evidence of an increasing focus on that state in 2008.

A simple search in Google News shows that by 2008, there was more media coverage of the Iowa caucuses than for *any* other presidential nomination in history. An Internet search of "Iowa caucuses" on January 2, 2008, returned 42,240 articles in Google News. While this number may be inflated, as online media has generally proliferated, it gives us a clear sense of just how much focus there is on Iowa. A better measure of changes in media coverage of the Iowa caucuses can be found by tracking it in major print media outlets, such as the *New York Times* or the Associated Press (AP) (see fig. 2.1). The years with the greatest coverage were 1988, 2004, and 2008. From December 1975 until February 1976, there were eighteen stories related to the Iowa caucuses appearing in the *New York Times*, with no mention of the caucuses before to December 1975. By 1988, the attention the newspaper gave to Iowa grew in terms of both total coverage and a longer time horizon. From January 1977

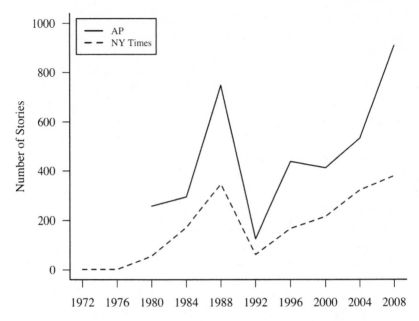

FIGURE 2.1. Media coverage of the Iowa caucuses, 1972–2008, in the major print media outlets.

through February 10, 1988, there were 160 *New York Times* stories about the Iowa caucuses. The *Times* published 190 stories mentioning the Iowa caucus between January 2007 and January 7, 2008, and even ran occasional stories on the 2008 caucuses in 2006. In 2008 in that newspaper alone, 379 articles related to the Iowa caucuses appeared.

Attention to the Iowa caucuses given by the Associated Press grew from 257 stories in 1980, the first year data was available, to 748 stories in 1988, 533 in 2004, and a whopping 907 stories in 2008. Consequently, both the AP wire and the *New York Times* show dramatic increases in the attention given to the Iowa caucuses over time. The national news media hype in the weeks leading up to the January 3, 2008, Iowa caucuses was intense, paralleling coverage of national disasters and international wars.

Of course, over the past thirty years television has become the dominant source of political news for most Americans. Relying on the Vanderbilt Television News Archive (http://tvnews.vanderbilt.edu/), figure 2.2 graphs coverage of the Iowa caucuses on ABC network news from 1972 through 2008 and on CNN from 1992 through 2008. ABC news coverage of the caucuses was slightly lower in 2008 than it was for the 1980 and 1988 nominations, but only by a fraction. The 2008 presidential nomination was one of the top three years for coverage of the Iowa caucuses in the past thirty years. In contrast, coverage of the Iowa caucuses on CNN shows a steeply rising curve, peaking in 2008. Roughly one-fourth of Americans get their news from CNN. In August 2006 at the Iowa State Fair, CNN asked one of us why so many potential presidential candidates were there seventeen months before the caucuses. The reason seemed obvious to us. "Media comes to Iowa. The candidates come to Iowa. The media comes to Iowa. There's sort of a back-and-forth symbiotic relationship."[5] The very fact that Iowa votes first in the current nomination schedule guarantees this media attention.

Squire (1989) shows that media coverage of the Iowa caucuses is related to the number of days candidates actually spend in Iowa campaigning. According to archival data from the *Des Moines Register*, 2008 broke all previous records for Republicans and Democrats in Iowa, with almost 1,200 campaigning days logged (see fig. 2.3). Candidate visits on the Democratic side were higher than in every previous campaign since

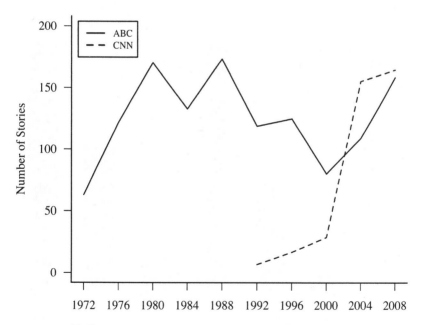

FIGURE 2.2. Media coverage of the Iowa caucuses, 1972–2008, in the major television outlets.

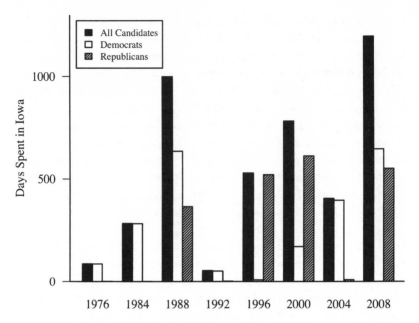

FIGURE 2.3. Total days spent in Iowa by all caucus candidates.

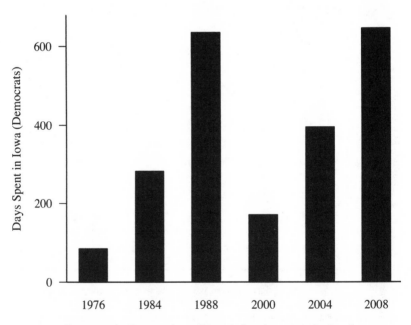

FIGURE 2.4. Days spent by Democratic candidates in Iowa in contested primaries.

1976, including the competitive 1988 election. Republican candidate visits in 2008 were higher than in every other year besides 2000.[6] Some have suggested that the Iowa caucuses may be more important for Democratic candidates (Norrander 1986), and in figure 2.4 we graph days spent campaigning in Iowa by Democratic candidates in contested primaries only. Again, 2008 broke all previous benchmarks with the most candidate visits to Iowa.

While compelling, these graphs are only suggestive of trends over time. Does Iowa really have a disproportionate effect on who wins each party's nomination, or does it not? We seek to update the literature on presidential nominations, now more than twenty years old.

Sequential Voting Rules: Updating Conventional Wisdom

Conventional wisdom holds that whereas winning New Hampshire may be a key to the candidate's receiving the nomination of his or her party, winning Iowa does little more than maybe influence New Hampshire (Mayer 2004; Adkins and Dowdle 2001). This wisdom is based on measuring election outcomes (candidate vote margins) from the Iowa caucuses and the New Hampshire primary. In this book we draw on pooled time-series data from 1976 through 2008 to test the hypothesis that *mass media expectations* pre and post Iowa affect outcomes in the primaries, not the election outcomes in early nominating events per se. The idea is that the media, a primary source of voter information, do not simply report who wins or loses a particular state. Instead, political reporters want to tell the most interesting story they can, which often leads to a disproportionate focus on those candidates who fare better or worse than initially expected. When a candidate exceeds or fails to meet these expectations, the media typically react with additional coverage of the "monumental win" or "devastating loss." Beyond vote share in the Iowa caucuses or the New Hampshire primary, media coverage of the candidates before and immediately after the Iowa caucuses significantly influences a candidate's overall performance in primaries nationwide, as we intend to show. Iowa matters because of media coverage of candidates in Iowa, and this effect is consistent over a thirty-year period.

The conventional wisdom is built on aggregate data used to study how election outcomes in Iowa and New Hampshire predict overall primary vote shares for each candidate. Since voting decisions occur at the individual level, we also seek to understand voting decisions and candidate choice using individual-level survey data. We explore the micro foundations of voting patterns, drawing on national opinion data collected both before and after Super Tuesday 2008. These data suggest knowledge of winners of the Iowa caucuses (a measure of exposure to media campaigns) increased perceptions that Obama would win the nomination (viability), which in turn increased the probability of voting for Obama. That is, Democrats who knew Obama won Iowa were more likely to believe Obama could win the nomination, and in turn these voters were more likely to vote for Obama in primaries and caucuses nationwide. Knowledge of which candidates won Iowa did not predict perceptions of candidate momentum (viability) for other Democratic or Republican candidates running in 2008. It is clear that media exposure of candidates can change rapidly over a short time. Additionally, under certain circumstances Iowa may matter independently of New Hampshire in terms of individual-level perceptions of candidate viability, and in turn vote choice.

Beyond vote choice, how does the sequential election process affect who is engaged in presidential nominations? There are not many studies of participation in primaries and caucuses (see Norrander [1989]; Atkeson and Maestas [2009] for exceptions). Normally, participation is high in early nominating events and then falls steadily throughout the nomination season. In 2008, turnout in primaries (at least for the Democrats) was high until the end in June, and actually increased slightly over time. Sequence again matters, as we find that the intense Iowa caucus campaign meant Iowans were more likely to participate both online and offline than registered voters nationally. Additionally, participation in the Iowa caucuses (the most competitive of the nomination contests) was less biased, with significant participation by lower-economic-status voters. Later voters benefited from information from early nominating events; voters from Super Tuesday states and the later Democratic primary in Pennsylvania were more interested in the nomination and were actually more likely than Iowans to follow campaign news. Online participation in caucus and primary campaigns nationwide mobilized the young, reducing age bias in the electorate. Competitive nominating events and online politics appear to reduce the bias of primary electorates. We suspect that if another state were exposed to the candidate campaigns and media attention that Iowa receives, we would find similarly high levels of online and offline political participation, given competition and media attention.

Part III. Changing the Rules

More than twenty years ago, Squire wrote, "There is little question about the importance of the Iowa caucuses in the nomination process. National media give the caucuses an enormous amount of coverage, and the candidates lavish the state with attention. The remaining question is whether Iowa, or any state, deserves this role" (1989, 6). Iowa's first-in-the-nation status is not only the product of history, but also the state's rabid defense of its place on the calendar. Its parties have secured rules from their national committees that preserve their right to vote early, state law puts the caucus in a special place on the calendar, and both parties have proved to be willing to reschedule the contest as early as needed to remain first.

Every four years, a chorus of critics raises a host of concerns: that Iowa and New Hampshire have an unjustifiably privileged position in the nomination schedule; media coverage of the Iowa caucuses is overblown compared with the number of delegates the state allocates; Iowa's demography is unrepresentative of the party or of the nation more generally (Iowa is 96% white, according to 2005 U.S. census data); Iowa favors midwestern candidates; low turnout in the Iowa caucuses leads to the choice of ideologically polarized candidates; Iowa is largely rural, and has an economy that is mainly agricultural compared with other states; and voters in states late in the process are denied a meaningful vote in choosing presidential candidates. One analysis of the 2004 election found that early states have up to twenty times the influence of late states in the selection of presidential candidates, and the preferences of Iowa voters were six times as influential as those of Super Tuesday voters (Knight and Shiff 2007). Critics such as Winebrenner (1998, 262) go further: "The public interest is not well served when manipulated and distorted nominating events like the Iowa precinct caucuses determine the viability of presidential candidates." Such critics contend that the selection of presidential candidates, one of the most important decisions that American voters make, should not be determined by Iowa. Because of the chaotic race among states to be among the earliest to hold a nomination contest (or aggressive frontloading) in 2008, the American public and the political parties may actually have the appetite now to revamp the nomination system.

One study suggests that if Iowa did not lead in the nominating process, the outcome of recent presidential elections would be different. Running simulations under different electoral rules, Knight and Shiff (2007) find that a national primary (or simultaneous election) in 2004 would have been more competitive and would have led to different party nominees, as would rotating which states went first in the process. If Iowa didn't lead in the nominating process, the choice of American presidents may have been different—not just in 2008, but in previous elections as well. If different individuals held the office of president, the course of American history would change, affecting the nation's war involvement, its economy, its foreign relations, and more.

Instead of having Iowa or any other state lead in a sequential election process, some have argued for a simultaneous election to nominate presidential candidates. If all states voted on the same day as in a national primary, the question of why Iowa or New Hampshire or Nevada or South Carolina would be moot. Former president Theodore Roosevelt offered to use a national primary in the 1912 Republican nomination, but incumbent president William Howard Taft declined (Altschuler 2008). Despite many years of polls indicating overwhelming support for a national primary, Congress and the parties have never seriously considered it.

Previous research discusses reform of the presidential nominating process, but does so generally without systematic empirical analysis (see Smith and Springer [2009] for an exception). We draw on our sequential state and national opinion surveys to show that support for reforming the nominating process has a lot to do with where voters live. While it's no surprise that Iowans oppose reform, nearly three-quarters of other Americans favor instituting a national primary, with somewhat lower support given for rotating state primaries. We also show that individuals from states that lose under current rules in terms of timing (late in the process) and population size (small states) are more likely to support reforming the nominating process.

As authors we ourselves have varying opinions toward reform. One of us has been active directly in the political process in Iowa, going so far as to serve as a county party chair during the 2004 caucuses and as an elected national convention delegate from Iowa in 2008. Two of us have written extensively on nomination reform in varying forms, and two have written extensively on election reform and election rules for over a decade. In examining our data and experiences, we propose a single reform of the process on which we can all agree at least in compromise.

Our Method: Sequential Survey Data

To answer questions about how the rules governing presidential nominations affect a whole variety of outcomes, we leverage a methodological innovation: sequential survey data mapped to a sequential election process. Our data come from repeated random-sample surveys of Iowa registered voters and caucusgoers over time, as well as national survey data of registered voters immediately before and after 2008's Super Tuesday on February 5. We also include a small survey of Pennsylvania Democrats, who voted late in the process. These data were collected between March 2007 and April 2008 through the University of Iowa Hawkeye Poll. We started with telephone surveys of Iowa voters fielded in March, August, and late October 2007, and added a telephone sample of actual caucusgoers collected immediately following the January 3, 2008, caucuses. The pre–Super Tuesday survey (fielded the week before the vote) included responses from registered voters in forty states that had not yet held primaries (respondents from states that had already voted were omitted, as were Alaska and Hawaii), while the post–Super Tuesday survey (begun immediately after) covered those states that remained afterward. The final survey of registered Pennsylvania Democrats was conducted just before the Pennsylvania primary (April 15–20, 2008). All the surveys share a common battery of questions, so they can be pooled or analyzed separately to model changes over time. The Iowa telephone surveys are supplemented by a statewide in-caucus pencil and paper survey randomly given to one participant in each one of Iowa's 1,784 precincts for both political parties. Individual chapters describe the nature of our data in greater detail.[7]

Many studies of U.S. presidential nominations have relied on descriptive statistics, case studies, historical analysis, or other methods of analysis that lack multivariate controls to untangle overlapping influences. These can be useful for understanding trends, as the graphs in this chapter show. In the rest of the book we continue to use such descriptive statistics, but also employ a number of sophisticated multivariate methods that allow us to explore the causes of trends, including the relative signif-

icance of overlapping influences such as income and education. Understanding the role of early nominating events in candidate selection and
political participation requires the use of methods that can better untangle cause and effect, such as multivariate statistical methods.[8] Despite
the advanced methods underlying the findings, we present the results
in a format accessible to readers having no background in statistics. We
use "what matters" tables and probability simulations (or predicted values) that are as easy to understand as simple percentages but based on
the regression coefficients, and thus show the findings' relative impact
on outcomes. A summary of methods is provided, but with more tech-
nical details contained in the endnotes of each chapter, so those wish-
ing to skip this discussion may do so. All multivariate regression tables
are included in appendixes for those who wish to examine our results in
greater detail.

Conclusion

This book has theoretical, practical, and normative implications. The attention received by Iowa is not because Iowa is in some way an excep-
tional state, but is instead due to its position in the nomination calendar. The Iowa caucuses are legally bound by Iowa law to be held before
any other nominating event in the United States. Sequential voting and
caucus rules are important aspects of the nomination season that shape
outcomes. Caucus rules shape outcomes because of proportional voting
rules for Democrats, lower turnout than primaries, grassroots campaigns
strategies, and more. We expose general patterns of how early nominating events, such as those at the Iowa caucuses, impact outcomes in presidential nominations. This is a pattern that has repeated itself in past decades and will continue in the future if the sequential election system is
maintained. As has often been assumed but rarely shown, Iowa may be
critical for underdog candidates who do better than expected, as Obama
ultimately did in 2008.

One of the interesting questions about 2008 is whether it represents
some departure from the "usual" nominating process that is essentially unique, or a series of events and process which, while resulting in
a unique outcome on the Democratic side, still represents more of a continuation than a departure. We argue that 2008, for all its unusual aspects, has commonality with the recent past and—unless significant rules

changes are made—is probably a pattern for the future. Our argument develops from an apparent reality, that front-running candidates simply cannot skip Iowa (or presumably any contest that is first in a sequential system). Clinton was rumored to have planned on avoiding Iowa, but in the end she was forced to run in the caucuses because of the way the media focuses on Iowa and then New Hampshire. Failure to run in Iowa would have meant failure to gain the level of media attention necessary to remain a front-runner. On the other side, while John McCain put fewer resources into Iowa than either Mike Huckabee or Mitt Romney, he did not avoid the state entirely, and in fact began running hard in the last few weeks. We believe that in these media-driven environments it is more and more the case that front-running candidates will not be able to afford to skip Iowa, assuming it remains first in the sequence of nominating events. Should some other state manage to leapfrog Iowa, then it will gain from the attention that has been Iowa's since 1976.

PART II
Caucus Rules

CHAPTER THREE

Iowa Caucus Rules

I have never understood the Iowa caucus. — Larry King, CNN

The Iowa caucuses are among the most commented-on political events in the world. Whenever there is a competitive presidential nomination for either major party, candidates, reporters, and pundits all leave their comfortable East Coast and West Coast haunts and begin camping out in Middle America, a place that many have never visited. And while Iowans (and some others) actively defend the caucus as a shining example of grassroots democracy, others charge that caucuses are archaic, arcane, and unrepresentative. The *New York Times* (2003) once called them "quaint." Others have been less kind. Over the years the Iowa caucuses have been characterized as "dominated by special interests" (Wilgoren and Swarns 2004, writing about Howard Dean), "indecipherable chicanery" (Lane 2008), and a "mind-numbingly complex system" (Fund 2007). In an article at Slate.com, commentator Jeff Greenfield (2007) takes the state of Iowa itself to task for suppressing turnout, since it requires participants to show up in person at a specific time of day and stay for a lengthy period of time. He also criticizes Democrats' caucus rules for violating precepts of one person, one vote.

As we begin our look at Iowa, we want to reiterate our basic point that the rules governing presidential nominations are important. In the case of Iowa, both the sequential voting rules that place Iowa first in the current nomination schedule and its use of a caucus process rather than a primary election matter by shaping candidates' campaign strategy, voter participation, and media coverage. And it is always important to keep in mind that the rules of the Iowa caucus itself differ by party. Republican candidates face a very different electoral environment compared to Democrats, as we describe in this chapter.

Whether criticisms of the caucuses arise as a matter of jealousy on the part of citizens in other states that do not get the attention Iowa does, or are sincerely argued positions about how a democratic process ought to work, the fact is that every four years Iowa gets its chance to shine, and every four years denunciation of the Iowa caucuses peaks. And yet the caucuses continue. Perhaps one of the most fascinating things about the Iowa caucus is how routinely people signal its death knell. Every presidential election cycle, the question is asked: is this the end for Iowa? In 2008, no less an Iowa caucus expert than political scientist Peverill Squire, for many years at the University of Iowa and editor of an important book on the caucuses (Squire 1989), felt compelled to write a eulogy of sorts to Iowa. While Squire's article means to challenge six "myths" about the Iowa caucuses, it is written in the past tense, suggesting that 2008 would be the last time Iowa would go first in the nominating process.

As we write this book, we do not know if Iowa will remain first in 2012, but Professor Squire may have come to bury the caucuses a bit too early. The 2008 caucuses broke all attendance records for both parties, and generated a level of citizen involvement in the nominating process never seen before. This may well protect their position for at least one more cycle. At its national convention in August 2008, the Republican Party adopted a tentative plan for 2012 that would leave the Iowa caucus and the New Hampshire primary intact; Iowa because the Republican straw poll is nonbinding on delegate selection, and New Hampshire because the plan specifically provides for that state and South Carolina to hold primaries before any other state (Deeth 2008). While the Democrats do not make their primary calendar decisions until late 2010, initial indications are that they will not disturb Iowa's position if the Republicans do not. With Obama winning the presidency, it is even less likely the Democratic Party will have an interest in moving Iowa, a state that was key to his nomination in 2008. Thus, it seems reasonable for us to provide the reader with a sense of the history of the caucuses and how they operate, with particular attention to the rules of the game that differ between Republicans and Democrats.

The Iowa Caucuses: A Little History and a Lot of Process

The primary purpose of this chapter is to provide an insider's understanding of how the Iowa caucuses operate.[1] Readers who have a solid understanding of the caucuses may feel free to skip ahead to our discussion of the 2008 Iowa campaigns. But for those for whom the caucuses remain a bit mysterious, or who would simply like to brush up on Caucus 101, this chapter should provide what you need to know. Iowa's political parties have used caucuses—which at their core are simply party meetings—to organize themselves since before Iowa statehood in 1846. With the exception of 1916, when a primary was employed but abandoned due to low turnout and high cost (Boots 1920), the caucuses have also been Iowa's starting point for choosing delegates to the national party conventions.[2] For most of that time, little outside attention was paid—and to be fair, little attention was paid by Iowans themselves. The precinct caucuses were the ultimate insider operation, held in homes and the back rooms of businesses but rarely out in public. They were used to elect precinct committee people who ran the county party organizations, and delegates to the biennial county conventions. Attendance was light, and efforts to bring people out minimal. For the most part, the only people who cared about the precinct caucuses were a few party activists.[3]

Everything changed in 1972, as one of the unintended consequences of the national Democratic Party's McGovern-Fraser Commission was to force Iowa Democrats to hold their caucus earlier in the year. The commission was formed after the disastrous 1968 Democratic National Convention. Among other things, it established rules intended to open up the nominating process to rank-and-file party members by making the selection of delegates more transparent (Shafer 1983; Ranney 1978). These rules required that delegates be selected within the year of the presidential election and that all party members be allowed to participate in the selection process. For Iowa, this meant that at least thirty days had to be allowed between each of the four steps in the caucus-to-convention process (precinct caucus, county convention, district convention, and state convention). As Squire (1989; 2008) notes, the Democratic National Convention was set for July 9, 1972, which required Iowa Democrats to move their caucuses to January 24 of that year, earlier than even the New Hampshire primary. But in the end this change did not play much of a role in the 1972 nomination. Even though there was a small amount of press coverage of the caucus after it happened, Squire (ibid.) also points out that South Dakota senator George McGovern spent only a day and a half on the road in Iowa to achieve his strong showing just behind Maine senator Edmund Muskie. But, as has become the stuff of political legend, the 1976 Jimmy Carter campaign saw the Iowa caucuses as an opportunity to make a splash and to get media attention for a little-known southern governor. When Carter did better than expected by coming in second to "uncommitted," his path to the presidency was launched, as was the mythology of Iowa as an important initial test of any would-be presidential candidate.

The point to be made here is that Iowa got its leadoff position not because anyone thought this state would be a good place to begin a presidential nominating process, but simply because its multistage delegate selection rules required the state's Democratic Party to change the timing of the 1972 caucus. Subsequently, the leaders of both major parties in Iowa recognized it would be to their benefit to remain first in 1976, and cooperated to ensure this was the case. But as Squire (1989) points out, this effort most likely would not have mattered but for the Jimmy Carter phenomenon. Once the leadoff position was established and Carter showed that it could matter, the legend of the Iowa caucuses was born.

While the story of Iowa becoming first to vote in the nominating process focuses on the Democrats, the Republicans were also affected by the decision to move the Democratic caucus earlier in the year. In addition to agreeing to share the January 19 date for their 1976 caucuses, the Republicans modified their existing procedures to ensure that data would be available for the media, instituting first a "poll" of those attending a few selected precinct caucuses (Squire 1989) and then moving to the ballot-based straw poll now in use. Both parties also worked together to enshrine the Iowa caucuses in state law. Iowa code states in part,

> Delegates to county conventions of political parties and party committee members shall be elected at precinct caucuses held not later than the fourth Monday in February of each even-numbered year. The date shall be at least eight days earlier than the scheduled date for any meeting, caucus or primary which constitutes the first determining stage of the presidential nominating process in any other state, territory or any other group which has the authority to select delegates in the presidential nomination. (Iowa Code 43.4, 2007)

Thus, the caucuses' status as the lead nomination contest for both parties is clearly laid out in Iowa law. The caucuses, then, are a hybrid of state law and party practice, defined by both the state and the national parties. Section 43.4 of the Iowa Code goes on to require that the state party central committees set the actual caucus date, as opposed to using a government-specified election date, which is typical in primary states.

Moreover, the party chairs in the ninety-nine Iowa counties are explicitly charged with issuing the "call" to caucus, setting up caucus locations, and identifying temporary chairs for each of their caucuses.[4] Unlike a primary election, the costs of the precinct caucuses are borne by the parties, not the state. One result is that one of the first activities of any precinct caucus is to "pass the hat" to raise funds for the county and state party. But also unlike a primary election, vote counting is done by the parties, not government officials. The Iowa Code specifies that

> When the rules of a political party require the selection and reporting of delegates selected as part of the presidential nominating process, or the rules of a political party require the tabulation and reporting of the number of persons attending the caucus favoring each presidential candidate, it is the duty of a person designated as provided by the rules of that political party to report the results of the precinct caucus as directed by the state central committee of that political party. (Iowa Code 43.4, 2007)

The first sentence of this Iowa Code section recognizes that the Democrats and Republicans operate under different caucus rules (see below), but nevertheless requires the parties to publicly report the results. In fact, another section of the code places criminal penalties on anyone willfully choosing to report inaccurate results or failing to report at all (Iowa Code, 39A.4[c] [2], 2007). So it is clear that while the caucuses may have become first by accident, and may have once been essentially party events, their importance in the nominating process has led to their codification and the requirement that the results be reported. Even so, room for variation exists so that each party can establish its own idiosyncratic rules.

The Purpose of a Caucus

Why caucus in the first place? Caucuses seem oddly out of step with the march of American progressive values and the move toward primary elections (which accelerated following Democratic Party reforms after 1968). Primaries were initially open only to party members, but over time many states have opened them by law to any eligible voter. More recent has been the rise of no-excuse absentee voting, letting any voter cast a ballot before the designated election day.[5] Yet in Iowa, caucuses older than the state itself persist into the twenty-first century. The main reason is that caucuses were not invented as a presidential nomination system; instead, they have always been about organizing political parties at the precinct level. Parties in Iowa still see value in this grassroots organizing and are unwilling to see it change. The fact that caucuses occur every *two* years rather than every four reinforces their basic purpose.

County political parties in Iowa are directed by a central committee whose members are chosen at the precinct caucuses, either in a fixed number or based on party strength in the precinct. The precinct caucuses are also used to elect delegates to the county convention (also held every two years), which is the governing body of the county party. Finally, county parties build their own platforms, again starting at the precinct caucuses where attendees introduce resolutions to be forwarded to the county platform committee, which then submits a platform proposal to the county convention for adoption. In addition to adopting a platform, the county convention elects delegates to the congressional district conventions and the Iowa state convention, both of which are also held every two years. The more this process is understood, the clearer it becomes that at their heart, the Iowa precinct caucuses are really about organizing both political parties from the grass roots up.

Grafting on a Nomination System

Every four years during the presidential nominating process, Iowa Democrats operate a "caucus to convention" system. At each level, from precinct caucus to state convention, delegates to the next level are chosen in rough proportion to the number of people supporting each presidential candidate at that level.[6] Iowa Republicans, however, do not couple their caucus and state convention process to the selection of their national convention delegates, no matter what it may look like to outsiders. The Republicans hold a presidential preference straw poll at their precinct caucuses, but there is no necessary relationship between the outcome of this poll and the election of delegates to the county convention. Likewise, at the Republican county convention there is no necessary relationship between delegate selection for the next levels and candidate preference. The same is true at the state convention, where national convention delegates are chosen; once more there is no requirement that national delegates be aligned to the preferences of the state delegates. Thus for Republicans, the straw poll results reported the night of the Iowa caucuses represent nothing more than the aggregated preferences of those attending the caucuses at that time. As Winebrenner (1998) describes, the Republican Party did not even hold an organized straw poll at its caucuses before 1976. It only established a voting process once it became clear that the party could benefit by feeding the media interest in Iowa.[7]

So while the Republican nominating process is not integrated into the caucuses, the Democrats do connect their national delegate selection to the precinct caucus results. However, this connection is not straightforward, though it does attempt to proportionally represent attendees' preferences. Beginning with the precinct caucuses themselves, Democrats apply a threshold requirement so that in most cases a candidate must have at least 15% support among those attending the precinct caucus to elect any county convention delegates.[8] This threshold also applies at the county, district, and state conventions. At each precinct caucus, following the procedure detailed below, candidate support is measured, and delegates are elected to the county convention. Those delegates are "pledged" to their candidate but not legally bound by the caucus results; they are allowed to change their mind at the county convention, which is usually held in March. Again candidate support is assessed, and any candidate preference group receiving 15% or more support at the county convention elects "pledged" delegates to the district and state conventions in proportion to their county convention support. Next, about two-thirds of Iowa's Democratic National Convention pledged delegates are elected at the congressional district conventions, usually held in April, again in proportion and subject to the 15% threshold. But delegates can once again change their allegiance at either subsequent convention. Finally, the remaining national delegates are elected at the state convention in June, also chosen in rough proportion to attendee preferences, recognizing that those preferences may not at all represent what happened five months before at the Iowa caucuses. So while the Iowa caucuses are the first nominating event, actual national convention delegates are not elected until April and June, at nearly the end of the nominating process.

It is worth noting that while the Republican Party process means campaigns need only focus on contesting the precinct caucuses, which have no real connection to national delegate selection, the Democrats' rules require that campaigns—at least those remaining active—organize and reorganize at every step if they wish to secure the national convention

delegates they presumably "won" on caucus night. It is also worth pointing out that the Democrats' proportional system with a 15% threshold
is quite similar to electoral systems that choose members of legislatures
through proportional representation. Democrats see the process as one
of "representing" voters throughout the steps of the nominating process
pyramid. Thus do Iowa Democrats (weakly) connect their January caucuses with their national convention delegates. In 2008, for example, media reports following the precinct caucuses said that Barack Obama won
16 of Iowa's 45 elected pledged delegates, while John Edwards won 14
and Hillary Clinton won 15. But no one had actually won *any* national
delegates at that point. By the time the final national delegates were selected in June—when only Clinton and Obama were still in the running,
and Clinton had "suspended" her campaign—the count was Obama 24,
Clinton 14, and Edwards 7, with 3 of Edwards's 7 actually elected by the
Obama delegates at the state convention as part of an agreement that
brought Edwards's pledged district delegates into the Obama camp. Ultimately, at the national convention on August 27, 2008, the final Iowa
vote was 48 for Obama and 9 for Clinton.[9]

One of the ultimate ironies of Iowa and the sequential nominating
process may be that Iowa votes both first and among the very last in the
nation. Its precinct caucuses, electing delegates to the county conventions, are first. But its state conventions, where the process of electing
national convention delegates is completed, are generally among the last
national events for convention delegate selection. In the unlikely event
of a competitive nomination going to the national convention itself, candidates may find themselves campaigning once again in Iowa in June—at
least for support from the three thousand or so state convention delegates who make the final decisions.

Inside the Caucus: How the Iowa Caucuses Actually Work

In the wake of the 2008 caucuses, there were numerous "insider" blogs
posted on caucus night providing varying levels of detail about how the
caucuses actually work.[10] But few of these gave detailed descriptions of
the actual process that occurs within the Iowa caucuses. Years ago a
group of political scientists attending a conference at the University of
Iowa around the time of the 1988 caucuses wrote about their experiences
in the journal *PS: Political Science and Politics* (22, no. 1 [March 1989]:

35–39). More recently, Fowler (2008) published a detailed report of the 2008 Democratic caucus in Iowa City Precinct 8, which was chaired by one of us authors, David Redlawsk. Our intent in providing the following description is to give a good sense of what happens in the caucus generally without getting down to the specifics of any particular caucus, for which either of the preceding sources is worth a look. We have already gotten some sense of the complexity of the Democrats' overall caucus process. Given this complexity, it will come as no surprise that it is much simpler to describe what happens inside a Republican presidential-year caucus.

First, a few things in common to both parties. The presidential-year caucus date has been the same for both parties since the agreement in 1976, and the parties start their precinct caucuses at about the same time, often in the same building. Voters sign in on preprinted forms listing all registered party members in their precinct. Those who are not registered with the party may register at the door, so caucus participants need not be registered voters ahead of time. This is different from primary elections in most states, with the exception of those few that allow election day registration. But no one is allowed to participate without becoming a registered party member. State law requires that anyone who will be of voting age on the date of the general election must be allowed to participate; thus, a number of seventeen-year-olds may join the caucus. And as described earlier, at the precinct caucus both parties elect county central committee members and county convention delegates, and debate and pass resolutions to be forwarded to the county platform committee. In all the above activities the two different caucuses are quite similar, and in fact in an off-year caucus they are virtually alike in procedures and results.

There are significant differences in the parties' presidential-year caucuses, driven by very different rules for national convention delegate selection. The Republican procedures are easy to describe, since there is no necessary link between presidential candidate preference and other parts of the caucus process. A presidential-year Republican caucus will be similar to that party's off-year caucus. In fact, the only difference is that the first order of business after officers are elected is the presidential straw poll. Once signed in as a registered Republican who lives in the precinct, the caucusgoer will generally be seated in a room—such as a library or school classroom—to wait for the caucus to be called to order by the temporary chair, appointed by the county party chair as the caucus convener. Following the call to order, a permanent chair and secretary are elected, with the temporary chair usually, but not always, getting the job.

At this point, the Republicans begin the presidential straw poll. In most precincts this will be carried out via a paper ballot (the state party's preference), which may be simply torn pieces of paper or a more formal ballot prepared ahead of time by the temporary chair. Those in attendance are asked if anyone wishes to speak on behalf of a candidate. Speeches are usually short, and are of the type "why I support candidate X and why you should too." Following the speeches, ballots are cast and then collected by the chair, who next assigns someone (perhaps the secretary) to count them, report the results to the caucus, and record them on a form provided by the state party. Given the media obsession with precinct caucus results, the caucus is temporarily suspended while the chair phones a special number to report the results to the state party. Significantly, those results are the actual number of ballots cast for each candidate. Typically the straw poll process takes no more than half an hour, after which the caucus moves on to electing county convention delegates and county central committee members at large, with all those still in attendance voting for these positions. Resolutions, if any, are offered up, possibly debated, and then voted on before forwarding to the county platform committee. The caucus then adjourns, probably about an hour or so after it began.

The Democrats, who are often across the hall, are almost always still in session when the Republicans adjourn. Will Rogers famously quipped, "I am not a member of any organized party—I am a Democrat," and to outsiders a Democratic precinct caucus appears to confirm this insight. Not only does it take longer than the Republican caucus, but the Democratic presidential preference rules are far more complex. This complexity comes because *national* party rules require proportional allocation of delegates at every level of a caucus-to-convention nomination system. The viability threshold requirement adds to this complexity, but the system may well end up giving more candidates a chance and more voters a choice, and bring about more sincere voting. Democrats begin their caucus the same way as Republicans do, by electing a permanent chair and secretary. Party rules require that "preference groups" not be formed until half an hour after the caucus opens, so the time is usually filled by reading letters of greetings from elected officials, and passing the hat to raise money for the local and state parties. Once the appointed time arrives, things shift into gear.

The first thing the chair must do is determine how many people are actually present. This sounds easy, and is when turnout is low; but when more than five hundred people crowd into a small elementary school gym, getting an accurate count is difficult. Some larger caucuses now issue cards with numbers to each person at registration, allowing the chair to determine the total count by simply looking at the next number once registration finishes. Why does this matter? Because the first step in determining the precinct results is to figure out the *viability threshold*: the minimum level of support any preference group must have to win even one county convention delegate. Assuming 200 people attend and the precinct is allocated 8 delegates, each preference group will have to have at least 30 members to be viable—that is, the group's preferred candidate will win at least one delegate.[11] Once the viability number is established, the chair announces the beginning of the "first alignment" period. During this time—usually thirty minutes—caucus attendees form preference groups by literally moving to different parts of the room (or even different rooms, at a large caucus) to show their support for their candidate. Candidate precinct leaders attempt to corral as many people into their corner as possible, using such enticements as food—cookies, cake, or even sandwiches, as the Hillary Clinton campaign provided in many precincts in 2008—and good old-fashioned efforts at debate and persuasion. This process is public—everyone in the room can see where their neighbors go. Most of the effort to bring people into a group happens in a friendly but slightly assertive manner. Still, there can be pressure to move in one direction or another as precinct leaders, friends, and neighbors argue and cajole. As our survey data reveal, most participants find this rare form of civic engagement fun and exciting.

After time is up, each preference group reports its number of members. The chair determines which groups have met the viability threshold and announces the result. Those who have joined nonviable preference groups (that is, pledged to support a candidate who has not received enough votes) now have one of four choices to make during what is known as realignment, lasting another thirty minutes.[12] They can move to some other viable preference group and add to that group's numbers; attempt to get people to come over to their group to make them viable; combine with another nonviable group to become viable either for one of the candidates or declare themselves "uncommitted"; or they can simply pack up and go home. For example, in the 2008 precinct caucus that two of us authors observed, two candidates, Connecticut senator Christopher Dodd and New Mexico governor Bill Richardson, were not viable after the first round in that they did not meet the 15% threshold. Those caucusing for either Dodd or Richardson realigned, and most joined the group caucusing for Edwards in the second round. Thus, the caucuses allow for a form of preference voting, where individuals can vote for their second-choice candidate if it is clear their first choice will not win any delegates (is nonviable). This is the part of the process that seems especially confusing and arcane to those who have never participated.

During the realignment period, precinct captains of viable preference groups work as hard as they can to bring over members of nonviable groups, while captains of nonviable groups may urge their supporters to move as a group in support of some other candidate. In one Iowa City precinct in 2004, supporters of Ohio representative Dennis Kucinich who were not a viable group were encouraged by John Edwards supporters to join them, since the two campaigns had announced that each would support the other in precincts where one was not viable. But the Kucinich captain was unhappy with what his campaign had told him to do, and he urged his supporters to go home. In the end, about half moved to Edwards and about half simply left. In the same precinct in 2008, the Edwards group was initially 11 people short of viability—only the Obama and Clinton groups were viable—so the Edwards precinct leaders worked hard to convince Biden, Dodd, and Richardson supporters—all nonviable—to join them. Supporters of Delaware senator Joe Biden came over as a group, while Dodd supporters split among the top three candidates and Richardson supporters mostly went to Obama. At the same time, the Obama group, in an effort to deny delegates to Clinton, sent some of its supporters to the Edwards group to ensure its viability. This kind of back and forth characterizes large caucuses, where there may be hundreds of people milling about as candidate precinct captains try hard to keep things under control and to the benefit of their candidate. In many cases during this process, the caucus is characterized by honest discussion and debate about the strengths and weaknesses of the candidates—a type of democratic deliberation that is often lost in modern American politics (Barber 1984).

Following the close of the realignment period, everyone is counted again to determine how many are now in each candidate's corner. If any nonviable groups remain—having failed to attract enough support— those people get one last chance to move to one of the viable groups. Then the final count is made and recorded on a form provide by the state party. Two important points are worth noting. First, there is no official record kept of the initial alignment; the first count in the caucus is not recorded anywhere. Second, the final alignment counts, although recorded, are never publicly reported. Instead, the raw counts for each candidate are translated into delegates, with delegates assigned as proportionally as possible. It is the delegate count in each precinct, not the actual number of supporters, which is phoned in by the precinct caucus chair. Once that count is known, caucus business is suspended while the caucus chair phones Democratic Party headquarters in Des Moines to report the delegate counts for the media.

Delegates are allocated through a process known colloquially as "caucus math" and often described by the media as some arcane calculation that no mere mortal can possibly do. In fact, the math is quite simple, though it may require a calculator. Given the number of participants, and given the final alignment support for each candidate, it is relatively easy to calculate the percentage of support for each viable candidate and to use that percentage to allocate delegates. If in a group of 200 caucusgoers there are 110 for Obama, 50 for Edwards, and 40 for Clinton once all alignments are made, then Obama will be allocated 55% of that precinct's county convention delegates, Edwards 25%, and Clinton 20%. In a precinct with 8 delegates, this translates to 4.4 for Obama, 2 for Edwards, and 1.6 for Clinton. However, since there cannot be fractions of delegates, basic rounding is used, so that the final numbers reported will be Obama 4, Edwards 2, and Clinton 2. What started as 200 people aligning themselves initially with 6 candidates and finally with 3 viable candidates becomes 8 delegates. Each preference group then elects its own delegates from among its members. Following these delegate elections, the caucus reconvenes as a whole to complete its business—electing the county central committee and debating resolutions. Democrats have spent anywhere from two to two and a half hours to get this all done.[13]

How the Rules Matter

Because nominations are decided through a sequential process, a major role Iowa plays is to signal to the rest of the country which candidates its voters think are potential presidents and which are not. This signal is given by the results of the precinct caucuses as reported by the parties. The Republicans report a vote count, whereas the Democrats report delegate allocations, but in both cases the media take this as a sign of a candidate's strength or weakness based on the "expectations game," as we discussed in chapter 2 and will cover in detail in chapter 7. Iowa voters know this, of course, which might cause them to vote strategically (also known as sophisticated voting; Abramson et al. 1992)—that is, support a candidate who they may like less but is more likely to actually win the nomination. Given the media environment, Iowans have a great deal of information on who the media think is viable, and are in position to act on it. Thus, Iowans might have a propensity to vote strategically, given their role in the process. In doing so they would be sending an invalid signal to later voters about their true preferences by simply reinforcing media expectations about viability. Alternatively, Iowans might vote sincerely; supporting the candidate they truly believe in, even if that candidate is not considered viable. If they were to do this, then Iowans would be telling later states what they truly believe about the candidates.[14]

Voters in later states should be able to take advantage of the information Iowans give them, and this information might well include a true measure of viability—the actual votes of sincere Iowa voters, rather than media expectations alone. We are well positioned to briefly investigate this point here. Our Iowa caucus and 2008 Super Tuesday surveys allow us to test both possibilities using Abramson and colleagues' (1992) estimate of voting patterns in the 1988 Super Tuesday event as a baseline and comparing them to our own surveys of 2008 Super Tuesday and Pennsylvania primary voters.

We show the comparison in table 3.1.[15] A sincere voter is one who casts a vote for the candidate he or she prefers over all others, while at the same time believing that some other candidate is more viable, that is, more likely to win the nomination. A strategic voter (sometimes called sophisticated voter) is one who casts a vote for a candidate he or she rates lower than another because that candidate is thought to be more viable. A strategic voter sacrifices general preference for a candidate in order to vote for one thought more likely to win. Finally, a straightforward voter is one who casts a vote for the candidate he or she rates the highest and that he or she also rates as the most viable, or likely to win the nomination.

In the 2008 Iowa caucuses, we see much *higher* rates of sincere voting and much lower sophisticated or strategic voting than expected from national samples based on either 1988 or 2008 Super Tuesday voters, with

TABLE 3.1. **Percentage of straightforward, sophisticated/strategic, and sincere voters: comparing national and Iowa samples**

	Time period 1: First nominating event—2008 Iowa Caucus (late October 2007)		Reference time period 2: National sample— 1988 Super Tuesday (from Abramson et al. [1992])		Time period 2: National sample— 2008 Super Tuesday (pre-/ post-Feb. 5)		Time period 3: Late nominating event—PA primary sample (April 2008)
Voter type	GOP	Dem.	GOP	Dem.	GOP	Dem.	Dem.
Straightforward (high rating and high viability)	53.5	55.6	52.8	43.8	49.6	65.9	77.8
Strategic/ Sophisticated (lower rating and high viability)	9.8	8.0	13.9	13.1	17.0	15.9	2.0
Sincere (lower viability and high rating)	28.2	29.9	10.3	14.3	24.4	13.7	17.2
Irrational	8.6	6.6	10.0	11.7	8.9	4.6	3.0

Note: Ties coded as missing following Abramson et al. (1992).

sincere voting in the Iowa caucuses 20 percentage points higher than in either of the other events. This suggests that Iowa's voting first in the sequential nominating process and the intensive grassroots campaigning we will document in the following chapters foster more sincere and less strategic voting. In other words, the rules matter. We also see higher rates of sincere voting among Democrats than Republicans, reinforcing our argument that the two rounds of voting for Iowa Democrats also have consequences. In fact, we strongly suspect that if first-round voting results were actually available, we would find even more sincere voting, since Democratic caucusgoers know they have a second chance. We see roughly the same percentage of straightforward voters nationally and in Iowa.

Iowa voters, at the beginning of a sequential election environment, create information for later voters, who then appear to behave more strategically in terms of candidate choice. We see roughly the same percentage of strategic voters in the Super Tuesday primaries in 1988 as in 2008, even though twenty years separate these two elections. The higher percentage of sincere voters nationally in 2008 on the Republican side (24.4%) may be because of greater overall dissatisfaction with the candidates compared to Republicans in 1988, or Democrats in either 1988 or 2008. Our surveys consistently showed Republicans less satisfied with their choices over the course of the 2008 nomination campaign.

Challenges to the Caucuses: Was 2008 the End of an Era?

The astute reader will have noticed that while the Republicans report actual straw-poll numbers, the Democrats do not. In our example above, Obama had 55% of all the supporters, but only got 50% of the delegates. Likewise, the precinct will be reported as a tie between Clinton and Edwards when Edwards actually had more supporters than Clinton. And any candidate who had up to 14.9% of the supporters (29 people in our example) received no delegates at all. These anomalies are not simply theoretical. They happen throughout Iowa for the simple reason that Democratic caucus attendees are choosing delegates, and the reduction necessarily requires rounding. Interestingly, this is not unique to the caucus. In all Democratic nominating events where delegates are selected, whether caucuses or primaries, rounding must and does take place, since no fractional delegates may be awarded. But in Iowa, the Democrats have chosen to withhold the actual vote counts and report only the delegate numbers, so it is impossible to know how candidates did in terms of actual support before the realignment period. For an event that has become so important, it seems odd not to provide the media and voters with full information about what happened. We return to this anomaly in the conclusion of the book.[16]

The Iowa caucus process has raised a number of questions from both media commentators and political scientists, often pertaining to issues of participation, fairness, and complexity. Conventional wisdom holds that the caucuses are archaic, arcane, and unrepresentative. Certainly events like caucuses that are mostly about party building seem archaic in a day when parties seem to be less important and states seem keen to open up nominations to all citizens, rather than just party members. And based on our description above, the rules may seem arcane to many, though to be fair this is only because rules governing all Democratic caucuses and primaries (like the 15% threshold for winning delegates) are simply spelled out more clearly for caucusgoers. And, of course, as we will consider in chapter 6, nomination contests of all types may be generally less representative of the public as a whole, since they typically attract those most interested in party politics.

Yet a closer look suggests something else. The Democrats' use of proportionality to allocate delegates may allow more candidates to have a chance, and their use of two rounds of voting, which encourages sincere voting over strategic voting, may lead to better translation of preferences and fairer outcomes. In effect, Democratic caucusgoers are given two votes, and if their first-choice candidate is not viable, they can vote for their second choice. Thus, even voters supporting a less than likely winner have a chance to vote for their favored candidate in the beginning, and then, having registered their initial preference, move to support a more likely winner. Primary voters do not get this chance (nor do Republicans in Iowa).

Defenders of the caucus process might also point to features that make caucuses even more open to participation than primary contests in most states. First, the caucuses have used same-day registration rules for many years, long before other states began adopting such processes for elections. They could do this because the caucuses are party events, and the parties can allow people to reregister right at the door if they wish—and they do. Unlike primaries, the Iowa caucuses also allow any person to vote who will be eligible to vote at the general election the following November. Young people who will not be eighteen until the November election day are eligible caucus attendees, unlike at primaries, where a voter must be at least eighteen on the date of the primary. The caucuses themselves, which used to be held in private houses and other not-so-accessible locations, have moved out into the open as the media attention increased. Thus, in most places caucuses are now held in public buildings—in fact, state law requires public buildings to be made available—and are increasingly in buildings accessible to the disabled.

In addition, caucus defenders can point to ways in which the caucuses involve voters in the grass roots of party organization (Squire 1989). As far as most people know, the Iowa caucuses are about presidential nominations—but they are also about identifying party supporters and bringing them into the system. Given the effort required to attend, voters may become more attached to their party organizations when they get involved in their caucus. Finally, election reform advocates have long called for revising the standard "first-past-the-post" system to allow voters to express something more than a single vote for one candidate. In particular, preference voting is often seen as a better process, since voters get to show not only their first choice, but also other preferences. In effect the Democratic caucus already does this, at least for those whose first choice fails to catch on with other voters. Realignment allows those voters to show their second preference, rather than be disenfranchised entirely, as is the case in standard primary elections.

At the same time, those who challenge the caucuses can make a strong case. Caucuses require that voters be present in person; there are no absentee ballots. People who are working, housebound, without transportation, or otherwise unable to attend in person simply cannot participate, especially since the caucuses are normally held on a weekday evening.[17] This is true for both parties. Moreover, Democrats who attend must be willing to be public about their candidate preference. There are no secret ballots in Democratic caucus (or convention) proceedings. And, of course, caucuses take time. Whereas voting may be a very quick process, caucusing can take at least an hour or two, effectively eliminating the participation of those who just do not have the time. And given the relatively low turnout, the caucus process itself may be subject to challenge as a representative activity, a point we will address in detail in chapter 6.

Given these strong critiques and the significant level of frustration expressed by party leaders in other states, pundits suggest every four years that the Iowa caucuses have had their last gasp. Yet four years later they rise again. So the debate over the fairness, representativeness, and appropriateness of the caucuses continues. We intend to contribute to the debate ourselves as we document the Iowa caucuses as a wellspring of grassroots participation and as more representative than conventional wisdom suggests. We do not, however, end the debate, leaving it to the reader to examine the evidence for 2008 and to ask whether the intensely competitive nomination contests that year represent a new Iowa caucus or simply the end of a tradition.

CHAPTER FOUR

Candidate Campaigns in Iowa

Grassroots or Mass Media Politics?

Every time I come home after visiting one of these two states [Iowa and New Hampshire] during a presidential campaign season, I can't think of a better way of doing it. — Charlie Cook, editor of the newsletter *Cook Political Report*; *Los Angeles Times*, January 14, 2004

We have already detailed in chapter 2 the explosion of media interest in Iowa in 2008, driven, of course, by the wide-open nature of the nomination contests for both parties. Here we look at what actually happened on the ground in Iowa during the year before the caucuses. In doing so we rely on our survey of Iowa caucus attendees, where we asked a series of questions about communications from the campaigns. Our results build on the work of Hull (2007), who examined the Iowa campaigns of 2000 and 2004. We will briefly sketch the campaigns for both parties, and then make use of our unique postcaucus data set of Iowa caucus attendees to examine voters' perceptions of the campaign ground games—the efforts campaigns make to contact and mobilize voters. In so doing we measure the extent of grassroots, or retail, politics in the Iowa caucuses compared with mass media, or wholesale, politics. In the next chapter we will turn to the voters themselves, and examine the extent of participation in the 2008 caucuses.

The 2008 campaign for president began as soon as the 2004 election ended, if not sooner, in what has been called the invisible primary (Aldrich 2009; Mayer 2009; Cohen et al. 2008). Once Massachusetts senator John Kerry and former North Carolina senator John Edwards became the 2004 Democratic nominees, with President George W. Bush and Vice President Dick Cheney running for reelection, potential 2008 candidates began to plot out their possible strategies, dependent, of course, on the 2004 outcome. Republicans knew that their 2008 nomination would be wide open no matter what, since Bush was term-limited and Cheney unlikely to run. Democrats had to wait and see whether they won or lost in 2004 before making much in the way of plans. But perhaps we can date the beginning of the 2008 race even earlier, to a CNN Poll report published online on December 21, 2002—"Poll: Hillary Clinton top Democratic 2004 choice." New York senator Clinton made it clear early on that she did not intend to run in 2004, but if Kerry lost, she could be expected to be a candidate in 2008. As it turned out, the Democrats did lose, and the 2008 race began almost immediately on both sides. Only two weeks after election day 2004, an item in the *New York Times* on the opening of the Clinton Library in Arkansas included this paragraph:

> But he [former President Bill Clinton] saved his strongest endorsement for his wife, Hillary Rodham Clinton, who has made clear that she will run for a second term as a senator from New York in 2006 but is also widely believed to be seeking the presidency in 2008. "She has the best combination of mind and heart, conviction and compassion I've ever encountered," he said. (Seelye 2004)

Pundits and political scientists both complain that U.S. presidential campaigns are far longer than those conducted in most other democracies—Americans seem to face "The Permanent Campaign" (Blumenthal 1982). Of course, the cause is quite simple to pinpoint. We know exactly when our next presidential election will be, and we know where the nomination campaign will begin. Parliamentary systems usually do not have set dates for elections; the government calls an election when it desires or is forced to do so, within certain parameters, and neither voters nor candidates know exactly when it will be until a short time before election day. But American politicians always know the date of their next election and can prepare accordingly. It should come as no surprise that rational politicians begin preparing for the next election as soon as possible, and that the next presidential election, beginning as it does in Iowa, comes to Iowa soon after the close of the previous election.

The Beginning of the 2008 Caucus

The first recorded 2008 candidate visit to Iowa was by Kansas senator Sam Brownback in December 2004.[1] Brownback returned in May 2005, and visits by a host of potential Republican candidates picked up steam by July of that year. For the Democrats, John Kerry visited Iowa in December 2004 to "thank supporters," while John Edwards appeared there at the end of March 2005, followed within months by former Virginia governor Mark Warner, New Mexico governor Bill Richardson, and Indiana senator Evan Bayh. In the end, the *Des Moines Register* counted over 2,100 candidate visits to specific Iowa communities in the run-up to the January 3, 2008, caucuses.

As the campaign began to fully develop following the 2006 congressional elections, Iowans faced a dizzying array of candidate choices. By November 2006 (about fourteen months before the 2008 caucus), eleven Democrats and fourteen Republicans had visited Iowa, spending about 232 days there between them. In the end, not all made it through, but on caucus night each party had seven candidates from which caucusgoers could choose. These candidates committed varying levels of resources to their Iowa campaigns, and while some were written off early by the media, there is no question that the 2008 Iowa campaign season was the most competitive ever. As we noted earlier, the media fascination with Iowa certainly gives Iowans (and the nation, if they choose to follow it) extensive information about the candidates—or at least about those whom the media designate as viable. The candidates themselves add to this information environment by opening campaign offices and hiring staff as well as by their own presence "on the ground." And, of course, there are the television ads that blanket the state.

Candidate Spending and Mass Media Campaigns in Iowa

According to campaign finance disclosures required by the Federal Election Commission, the 2008 candidates spent over $28 million in Iowa, though other estimates that include television advertising place the number much higher. Illinois senator Barack Obama led the Democratic field with $7.1 million (in the end, only a small part of Obama's $296 million spent nationwide and Clinton's $238 million), while Clinton and Edwards spent $4.6 million and $2.7 million, respectively. On the Republican side, former Massachusetts governor Mitt Romney outspent his competitors with approximately $4.3 million in Iowa. Colorado representative Tom Tancredo was second, spending around $2 million, and Texas representative Ron Paul spent just under $1 million. Former Arkansas governor Mike Huckabee, the Republican winner, spent well under $1 million.

Readers should keep in mind that these expenditure reports typically consist of candidate spending on staffing, travel, voter outreach, and other grassroots efforts, and often only represent a fraction of actual campaign expenditures. This is because media and staff spending can take place outside Iowa yet still reach Iowans—spending in Moline, Illinois, for example, reaches one of Iowa's major media markets, but is not reported as spending in Iowa. Considering this, one source estimates the total spent on the Iowa caucuses at upward of $51 million for all candidates (http://www.iowacaucus.biz/IA_CAUCUS_MONEY.html). This higher figure includes money spent on television and radio ads, which are difficult to track at the state level but can make up a large portion of candidate and issue group spending. CNN reported that Iowans were exposed to over fifty thousand political advertisements on television in the days leading up to the caucuses, costing nearly $40 million (http://edition.cnn.com/2008/POLITICS/01/01/iowa.ad.spending/).

According to CNN, Obama led his Democratic counterparts in television advertisements, spending at least $9 million on 11,000 ads. Clinton followed close behind, with $7.2 million spent on 8,000 spots, and Edwards aired 3,700 spots, costing him around $3.2 million. As for the Republicans, Romney was the top television advertiser in Iowa, expending approximately $7 million on 8,500 spots. Behind Romney were Huckabee with 1,800 ads, and former Tennessee senator Fred Thompson airing 1,100 spots, which cost about $1.4 million and $1.1 million, respectively. While early nominating events, such as the Iowa caucuses and New Hampshire primary, are known for retail (grassroots) politics, these very high expenditures on the mass media show that the ground game in Iowa is fought over the airwaves as well as in living rooms. As we show in this chapter, winning Iowa requires both money and time.

The Grass Roots in Iowa

While focusing on television advertising may be indicative of the "whole-sale" politics that took place in Iowa, many argue that it is the retail politics that make or break any given candidate. *Retail politics* refers to the grassroots, on-the-ground organizing that is thought to be at the heart of the Iowa caucuses. Whereas in chapter 2 we reviewed trends in the time candidates spent in Iowa during recent caucuses (see figs. 2.3 and 2.4), to understand how the candidates approached retail politicking in 2008 it is worth examining the total number of days each spent in Iowa. Beginning with the Democrats, Senator Joe Biden led the field with 120 days. Closely following Biden were Edwards with 110 days, and Senator Chris Dodd with 105 days on the ground. Obama personally campaigned in Iowa for 89 days, while Richardson devoted 77 days and Clinton spent 74 days in the state before the caucuses. The Republican candidates spent much less time in Iowa, with Romney's 76 days leading, just in front of Huckabee's 75 days and Tancredo's 71 days. Wisconsin governor Tommy Thompson was in Iowa for 65 days, while Sam Brownback and Arizona senator John McCain spent 61 and 43 days, respectively. It is worth noting that even candidates the media wrote off early (Dodd, Brownback) spent a great deal of time personally on the ground in Iowa.

Another aspect of effective grassroots campaigning is the development of a strong local operation. One way to get a feel for this is to look at the number of field offices the candidates established in 2008 in addition to the main state campaign headquarters, usually near centrally located Des Moines. Once again, we see a stark difference between Democratic and Republican candidates. Comparing the top five Democratic ground organizers with the top five Republicans, the Democrats combined for 117 field offices, while the GOP candidates combined for six. Not surprisingly, Obama led all candidates with 37 Iowa field offices, with Clinton trailing closely behind with 31 and Edwards with 24. Obama's experience as a community organizer in Chicago paid off in Iowa with strong local organization. Richardson, Dodd, and Biden had fewer campaign outlets with 13, 12, and 10 offices, respectively. As for the Republican candidates, Romney had only two field offices in Iowa, while former New York City mayor Rudy Giuliani, Tancredo, Brownback, and former New York governor George Pataki each had one office. Huckabee had no official field offices, though the campaign did have field staff working throughout the state.

Conventional wisdom about Iowa says that it is all about grassroots politics. Candidates who spend a lot of money on media but fail to develop a ground game are the stuff of legend. Most Iowa observers point to publisher Steve Forbes, who spent what was in 1995 and 1996 a very large amount of money on television advertising in Iowa, but whose campaign never got any traction, mostly because he did not build any kind of grassroots strategy. Other candidates—such as Connecticut senator Joe Lieberman in 2000 and General Wesley Clark in 2004—have simply skipped Iowa, in part because of the need there to develop a different style of campaign than in primary states. The 2008 results would suggest that the grass roots again mattered, given the perception that Obama in particular won on the back of community organizing and Huckabee upended Romney through grassroots politics.

But is this really the case? Do candidates who spend long days themselves in Iowa, build extensive volunteer organizations, and find ways to directly mobilize voters really have a chance against their better-funded opponents? Is there evidence that grassroots politics somehow makes up for a lack of financial resources? For grassroots campaigning to pay off, voters must be contacted through the efforts of the campaigns. While it may be that candidates with fewer financial resources can compensate for some of that gap through personal campaigning—and candidates operate in Iowa as if that were in fact the case—to date there has been little direct evidence available to tell us whether grassroots efforts reach voters, and in what ways they reach them (see Hull 2007 for an exception covering 2000 and 2004). Can candidates with fewer financial resources and media attention—say, a Joe Biden or a Mike Huckabee—make up for it by spending candidate time on the ground in Iowa and rallying the grass roots? At one level the answer must be yes, given Huckabee's win over much the much better funded Romney. But on the Democratic side, none of the underfunded candidates made progress.

Campaign Contact as Perceived by Iowa Voters

Our postcaucus telephone survey included a series of questions designed to learn how caucusgoers had been contacted by the campaigns. We identified five ways in which campaigns typically reach out to Iowa voters. First, they make great use of telephone banks. Virtually all campaign offices function as call centers, where volunteers spend many hours on the phone trying to reach as many potential caucusgoers as possible. Campaigns generally use a numbering system to code each person they reach as either a committed supporter, a leaner, an undecided, or a supporter of another candidate. This effort is, of course, very labor intensive. One way to overcome the need for labor is to move to automated dialing. These systems allow campaigns to send out recorded messages to large numbers of potential caucusgoers at a very low cost. The newest versions of these systems allow voters to respond by pressing the buttons on their phones, so campaigns can collect data using automated systems as well. Third, campaigns also spend a good deal of money sending out mailings to potential caucusgoers. U.S. mail pieces require little labor, but they do require more money than simply making phone calls using volunteers or automated systems. Fourth, we measure the amount of voter contact made in person by each campaign. Because Iowa is thought to be the epitome of personal politics, identifying the extent to which people are personally contacted at home by campaigns is important. Finally, with the rise of the Internet, campaigns have begun to use e-mail strategies to reach caucusgoers. E-mail is only one part of an Internet strategy, of course, but it was the part that the campaign could "push" out to voters in 2008, rather than waiting for voters to come to them (such as surfing for Web sites).

The survey asked caucusgoers to tell us whether they had received any of these five types of contacts from any campaign. But we went a step further and also asked respondents to tell us whether they had received any of these contacts from each specific candidate campaign. This allows us to examine not just the impact on voters of all the campaigns combined, but also the intensity and effectiveness of each individual campaign in its efforts to reach voters. Voter contact is the sine qua non of a campaign; campaigns that fail in this regard are doomed to fail. We should note that we did not ask voters if they had seen campaign commercials. As we pointed out earlier, massive amounts of advertising aired in Iowa throughout the caucus campaign. We have no doubt that virtually every caucusgoer saw numerous television spots; it would have been all but impossible to miss them if the TV was on at all. We also do not focus on television ads here because their frequency is relatively easily measured through campaign finance reports and organizations that track television advertising. What we are interested in are the campaign activities that both represent the grassroots campaign efforts and also often fly under the radar, either because they are carried out almost entirely by volunteers (and thus not reported as campaign expenditures) or because they are simply difficult to track (such as direct mail).[2] We

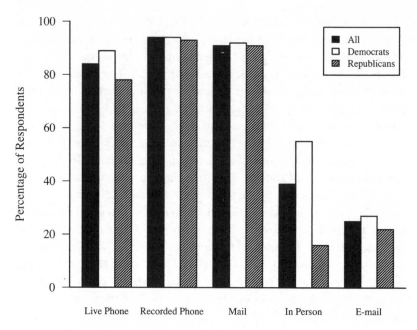

FIGURE 4.1. Campaign contacts in Iowa 2008.

should also note that these data are from people who actually attended a precinct caucus; we would expect that those who did not would report fewer contacts across the board.

Figure 4.1 displays the level of contact for each of the five contact methods overall and by political party. It is clear first of all that campaign exposure was ubiquitous among caucusgoers. Those who attended their caucus were responding to an amazing amount of contact: 94% reported being reached by a recorded phone message, 91% by mail, and 84% by a live phone call. Contact at people's homes was much lower, but still quite high, with nearly 40% of respondents reporting that at least one campaign had contacted them in person at their home. E-mail contacts fell behind the others, with 25% reporting these. Looking at this another way, respondents reported receiving an average of 3.3 of the 5 contact types, with only 2.4% reporting no contacts at all, while 11.3% reported receiving all 5 types of contact.

What is particularly interesting here is the difference in party strategies that appears in these data. Democratic campaigns clearly were more focused on individual contacts between campaign workers and caucusgoers. Whereas 89% of Democrats reported receiving at least one live phone call, only 78% of Republicans reported the same. On the other hand, efforts that do not require a significant staff or volunteer base— recorded phone calls and direct mail—show no difference at all between the parties. E-mail contact is also roughly the same for both parties. But the most dramatic difference comes when we look at in-person contacts. Only 16% of all Republicans in our sample reported *any* in-person contact at their home from *any* campaign, while more than half of all Democrats (55%) reported such "door-knocking" contacts. Clearly, Republican campaign strategy did not depend on personal contact in the way that Democrats did. This almost certainly reflects the key difference between the two parties' rules, where Republicans cast a secret vote and Democrats not only stand up in public, but also may change their mind. Thus, Republican campaigns appear to be more like those we would expect in a primary election, compared to the grassroots efforts of Democratic campaigns.

Candidate Contacts of Different Demographic Groups

It is instructive to look at these data by the common demographic breakdowns that campaigns use in targeting voters. Here we focus on voter age, gender, and first-time caucusgoers pooling Republicans and Democrats, since we will examine individual candidate campaigns below. Given the media focus on Obama's appeal to younger voters and the historical fact that caucusgoers tend to be a relatively old crowd, we first examine the amount and types of contact by voter age in figure 4.2. The clearest trend is that younger caucusgoers were significantly *less* likely to report any type of "traditional" campaign contact—by telephone, by mail, and even in person. But while there is a drop-off in such contacts for younger voters, this may be less than we would find in the absence of intense grassroots efforts, given that it is only a relatively small drop. In any case, while 84 to 97% of those aged thirty and over reported phone or mail contacts, only about 75% of younger voters reported being reached in these ways by any campaign. Other than those under the age of thirty, there are very few differences between age groups in traditional campaign contacts; the one exception was that voters 30 to 44 years old were the least likely to report in-person contacts, with only 28% saying someone had contacted them in person at home, compared with 34% of younger voters and over 40% of older voters. However, when we turn

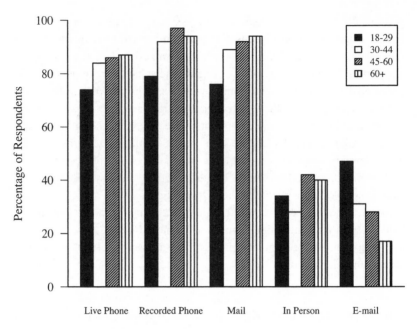

FIGURE 4.2. Campaign contacts by voter age.

to contacts by e-mail, we see a substantial shift. Voters under the age of thirty were far more likely to report hearing from a campaign in this way, with nearly half (47%) reporting e-mail contacts. The drop-off as voters get older is dramatic, so that less than one in five voters over the age of fifty-nine report any campaign e-mail contacts.

Of course, age was not the only demographic that campaigns focused on in Iowa. With Hillary Clinton running, a great deal of interest was placed on whether campaigns—especially Clinton's—were specifically reaching out to female voters. Figure 4.3, however, does not provide many clues as to whether this was the case. What we do see is that there is little gender difference in contacts made. Men appear slightly less likely to report contacts in person (36 versus 42% for women), but this difference does not reach statistical significance and probably reflects that men were more likely to attend the Republican caucus, and Republicans much less likely to report being contacted in person. There is also a small (again not quite statistically significant) difference in e-mail contact, with men more likely to report hearing from campaigns in this manner (28 versus 22%). This mirrors gender differences online, with men more likely than women to use the Internet for political information (Mossberger, Tolbert, and McNeal 2008).

Turning to first-time caucusgoers (fig. 4.4), we see what we might expect—across the board, first timers are less likely to report campaign contacts of any kind, except for e-mail. The biggest difference is in-person contact. Just over 30% of first timers reported someone contacting them in person at home, compared to nearly half of repeat caucusgoers. Likewise, first timers were significantly less likely to report any phone or mail contact, although to be fair, even "less likely" still represents a great deal of reported campaign contact. About 78% of first timers reported receiving live phone calls, compared with 90% of repeaters; 90% received recorded phone calls, compared with 97% of repeaters; and 85% got campaign mail, compared with 97% of repeat caucusgoers. Interestingly, the only contact that first timers are at parity with repeaters was e-mail, with about one-quarter of each group reporting the receipt of these. What differentiates e-mail is that for the most part it is "opt-in." Campaigns cannot make a contact unless the voter provides the e-mail address. Clearly, both first timers and repeat caucusgoers did this

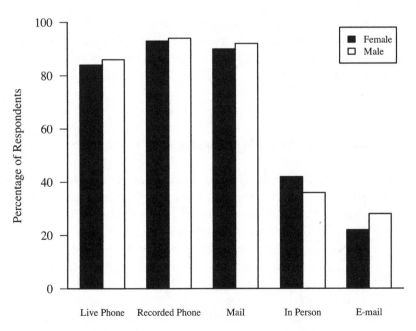

FIGURE 4.3. Campaign contacts by voter gender.

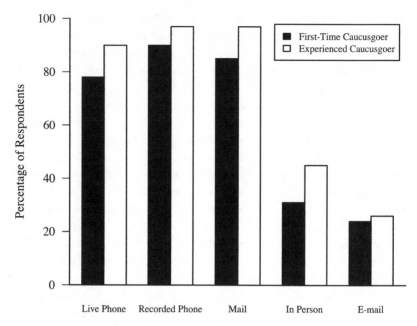

FIGURE 4.4. Campaign contacts of first-time versus repeat caucusgoers.

in equal numbers. But the more traditional contact methods rely heavily on lists that the campaigns themselves develop, usually from sources like voter registration records and lists of previous caucusgoers. First-time attendees are far less likely to be on those lists, at least at the beginning of the campaign.

Individual Candidates and Campaign Contacts in Iowa

We can drill further down into our data to look at reported contacts made by individual campaigns, likely the most important contribution of this chapter. We asked caucusgoers about 15 campaigns: 8 Democratic and 7 Republican. Respondents could indicate contact from none to all of the campaigns. Space precludes going through all these data in detail, but the overall pattern is easily seen, as shown in figures 4.5 (Democrats) and 4.6 (Republicans). The figures show the proportion of respondents in our postcaucus telephone survey who reported each type of contact. It is obvious that the candidates who had the most financial resources and the most media attention also made the most contacts. For the Democrats, reports of contacts made by the Obama, Edwards, and Clinton campaigns for the most part overwhelm contacts made by the remaining Democrats, with the difference in in-person contact especially stark. Those candidates who had the resources to do so sent a lot of mail and made a lot of phone calls. But those with fewer resources did not make up for their limited funds through the use of less expensive options, such as e-mail and door-to-door visits (usually carried out by volunteers). At the same time, the difference in levels of e-mail contact are far less than in other contact methods, suggesting that e-mail and other Internet-based approaches might have some potential to offset resource limitations in the future (see Bimber [2003]). But for the Democrats in 2008, it remains the story of those who had (attention and money) got more (contacts with voters).

Figure 4.5 also shows that Obama tied Clinton for the most live phone contacts, tied Clinton and Edwards for the most mail contacts, and ranked highest on in-person and e-mail contacts. This type of coverage requires money, and the Obama campaign outspent the other candidates

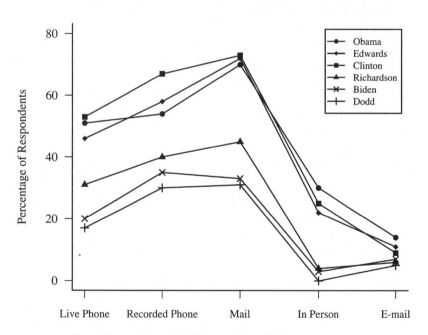

FIGURE 4.5. Campaign contacts made by Democratic candidates.

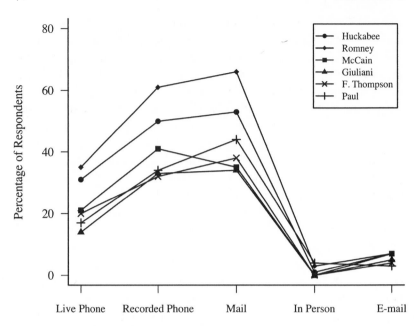

FIGURE 4.6. Campaign contacts made by Republican candidates.

(Clinton and Edwards) by a factor of at least 2 to 1, as we noted earlier. Clinton generally tied or trailed Obama in voter contacts, with the exception of recorded phone messages. The story we reveal here is that money is critical in winning Iowa, but how that money is spent matters. Obama chose to spend a great deal on grassroots efforts, which may have ensured his victory.

Republicans show a similar pattern, although with the exception of Romney the difference between the top-tier candidates and the others is not as extreme (see fig. 4.6). Our data show that Romney led the field of candidates in live phone, recorded phone, and mail contacts. He also led the Republican candidates in spending overall. Again, money translated into reaching voters in the Iowa caucuses. Despite winning the Republican caucus, Huckabee trailed Romney in all three forms of voter contact. In fact, considering that Huckabee was not viewed as a top-tier candidate before the August 2007 Republican straw poll, an argument could be made that for Republicans, some of the variations in traditional resources, like money and media attention, were offset by grassroots campaign activities like phone banking. However, there is little evidence that any Republican campaign did much in-person door knocking, since few Republican respondents indicated they had been contacted in this manner. On the whole, for all the conventional wisdom that Iowa gives a chance to less well-known, less well-funded candidates, evidence suggests that this was mostly not the case in 2008, as the relationship between the financial and the media resources we reported earlier and the contacts reported by caucusgoers is clearly strong.

Individual Campaign Contact by Demographic Groups

We think it is useful to look at the reports of campaign contacts by specific demographic groups for the individual campaigns. Given the nature of the Democratic campaign in 2008, it seems most reasonable to look at the top three candidates and their contacts by age and gender, while for the top four Republicans we will look at contacts with evangelical Christians, a key part of the Republican base in Iowa. For both parties we will also examine differences between first-time and repeat caucusgoer contacts by individual campaign.

Campaign Contacts and the Democrats

We begin with the Democrats. While the also-ran candidates were extremely active in Iowa through their personal visits (and Dodd's heavily reported move of his whole family to Des Moines for the last weeks of the campaign), caucusgoers reported relatively few of the contacts we measure here for those candidates. Thus, we focus on the top three finishers, Obama, Edwards, and Clinton, starting with contacts by respondent age. Age was a significant factor in the Iowa caucuses for the Democrats, with turnout among those under the age of thirty being much higher than in the past. Many of those young voters were strong Obama supporters. Do we see this reflected in campaign contacts? Figure 4.7 reports contacts by age group, focusing only on the youngest and oldest cohorts.[3] Most interestingly, respondents younger than thirty reported more telephone contacts from the Clinton campaign than Obama's—particularly recorded phone calls—but many more reported being contacted in person at their home by the Obama campaign than either of the other two. The difference with Clinton is particularly stark. Twenty-one percent reported an in-person contact from the Obama campaign, compared with 2% reporting such a contact from Clinton,

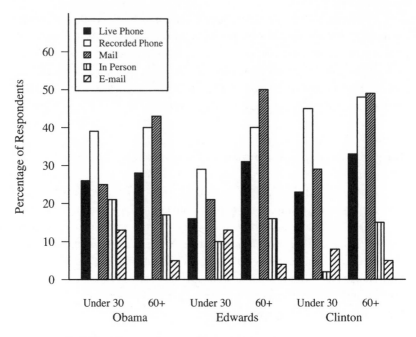

FIGURE 4.7. Individual Democratic campaign contacts by voter age.

and 10% from Edwards. Perhaps the Obama campaign took a page from political science research, which suggests that personal contacts are far more mobilizing than telephone contacts (Gerber, Green, and Larimer 2008).

On the other hand, among young people, Obama and Edwards made similar levels of e-mail contact, both well ahead of Clinton. But when we turn to the oldest age cohort, we can see where Clinton focused her efforts, with more overall contact among this group than either Obama or Edwards. These differences are concentrated on telephone and mail contacts. Obama more than held his own in contacting older voters at home or by e-mail. But the bigger story for the Democrats is that Obama did not limit his campaign's focus to younger voters, particularly in his door-to-door efforts. The evidence suggests that neither Clinton nor Edwards reached out much to younger voters at home, and even more strikingly, they had no advantage with in-person contacts of older voters either. Also striking is the extent to which Clinton did in fact reach out to younger voters by phone and mail, compared with Edwards, whose efforts were much more likely to be received by older voters.

While Obama was thought to be targeting mostly younger voters—something not really borne out in the data we collected—Clinton, of course, was expected to make her pitch heavily to women. Figure 4.8 looks at the Democratic contact data by gender. The quick story: for the most part, campaigns reached out equally to men and women; the only difference is with in-person at-home contacts. Here the Clinton campaign clearly did some gender targeting. While equal proportions of men and women reported in-person contacts by the Obama and Edwards campaigns, the same is not true for Clinton. Eighteen percent of women in our sample reported an in-person contact from the Clinton campaign, while only 13% of men did the same. And unlike her opponents, the proportion of male and female respondents reporting e-mail contacts from the Clinton campaign was the same, at about 6%. Both Obama (11% of men, 7% of women) and Edwards (8 and 6%) show some imbalance, favoring men. Still, it seems clear that the presence of a female challenger did not push either of the other campaigns to focus more on men.

As we saw earlier, first-time caucusgoers were far less likely to report

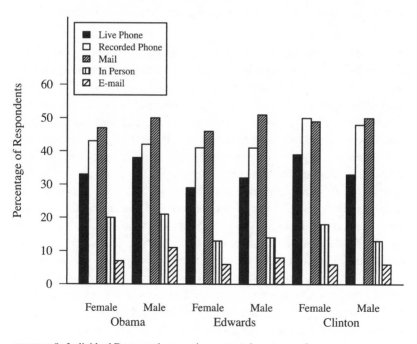

FIGURE 4.8. Individual Democratic campaign contacts by voter gender.

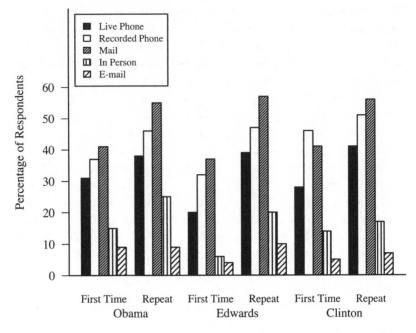

FIGURE 4.9. Individual Democratic campaign contacts by caucusgoer experience level.

any kind of contacts by the campaigns, with the exception of e-mail contacts. But here, too, Obama was reported to have made a special effort to get first timers out, and the explosion in turnout suggests that he was successful in doing so. The question for us is whether this increased turnout can be laid at Obama's door, at least in terms of the contacts that voters reported to us. Figure 4.9 reports campaign contacts by first-time versus repeat caucusgoers. Edwards is the clear outlier here; his campaign made fewer contacts to first timers than either of the other two. In particular, the Edwards campaign apparently failed to reach first-time caucusgoers when they knocked on doors. Both Obama and Clinton had more than twice as many in-person contacts as Edwards, with Clinton reaching both first-time and repeat caucusgoers in nearly equal proportions. But Obama had the most parity between the two groups across all the contact methods. Still, while the conventional wisdom suggested that Obama's outreach efforts with new caucusgoers was a key part of his win, the data suggest that those efforts were readily matched—at least in terms of what caucusgoers reported—by the Clinton campaign.

The Republicans: Evangelicals and First Timers

While Republican turnout among younger voters appeared to increase somewhat in 2008, the more interesting question has to do with the role of evangelical Christians, along with first timers. Evangelicals comprised as much as 60% of the Republican voters, according to CNN, with Huckabee presumably drawing many of them out to their first caucus. But do we see evidence of differential contact by Huckabee compared to the other campaigns? Figure 4.10 examines Republican campaign contacts of caucusgoers who identified as evangelicals. Note that given the extremely low level of in-person at-home contacts reported for the Republicans, we have dropped this category.

The evidence is that both Huckabee and Romney reached out to evangelical voters at a much greater rate than the other Republican candidates. But this difference is not anything that would be unexpected, given that both the McCain and Giuliani campaigns were far less intensive in Iowa than either Huckabee or Romney. In the end, the Iowa race came down to two men, and both were making at least some effort to contact evangelicals. But viewed another way, we see that Huckabee, de-

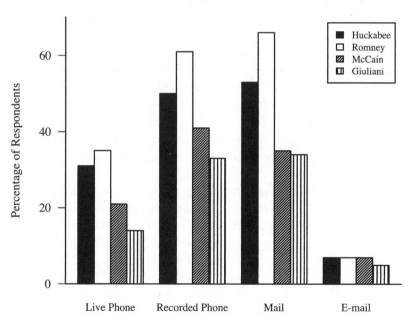

FIGURE 4.10. Individual Republican campaign contacts of evangelicals.

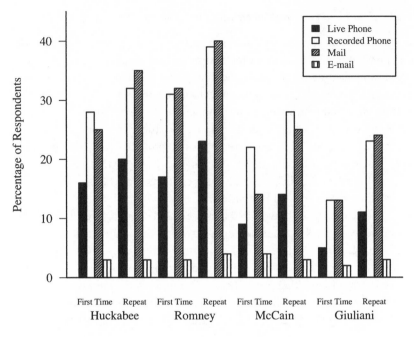

FIGURE 4.11. Individual Republican campaign contacts by caucusgoer experience level.

spite having far fewer financial resources than Romney, was able to effectively use grassroots efforts to reach his core constituency. Romney's financial advantage is clear in reports of mailing efforts, with 65% of all evangelical Republican caucusgoers saying they got mail from Romney, compared with only about 55% from Huckabee, in spite of evangelicals' general preference for Huckabee. But looking at volunteer-driven activities such as live telephone calls, the difference is eliminated; Huckabee clearly holds his own.

Finally, we look at Republican efforts to contact first-time caucusgoers in figure 4.11. The differences in contact between first-time and repeat caucusgoers do not appear as large as those for the Democrats, but of course the Republicans had far fewer contacts overall. The phone-banking strategies of all the candidates except Giuliani appear to have been pretty effective in reaching first timers relative to repeaters, especially by live telephone calls. At the same time, there is no evidence that Huckabee had any differential contact with first-time caucusgoers compared with his opponents. While first-time respondents were no less likely to report contacts from Huckabee (relative to the total contacts for each candidate), neither did Huckabee have any special advantage here.

Candidate Campaign Contacts: A Summary

Our data on campaign contacts are rich and complex. Here we have given a sense of what respondents told us they encountered during the campaign on the ground in Iowa. Perhaps what is puzzling is that for the most part, we do not see any effects that would suggest that the less well-funded candidates could somehow make up for their lack of finances by working harder on the ground, with, perhaps, the exception of Huckabee. Even in his case, however, Republican caucusgoers did not report more contact from Huckabee than Romney. But Huckabee—after being vastly outspent on television advertisements and in terms of other resources—was able to hold his own through mail, phone calls, and e-mail. On the Democratic side, Obama clearly outspent his competitors, and our data reveal he was able to reach more voters through party contacting methods.

One last commentary on campaign contacts. We asked all respondents to report contacts from all campaigns, so we also have some evidence about crossover efforts. We can look at those who attended a Republican caucus and the contacts they report from Democratic campaigns, and vice versa. In brief, what we find is that both Obama and Clinton had significant levels of these crossover contacts. Table 4.1 reports these numbers. It is not surprising that significant percentages of Republican caucusgoers would report receiving mail from the Democratic campaigns. After all, mail goes to a household, and everyone in the household may see it, regardless of their party preference. A similar thing happens with recorded phone calls. Yet it is still surprising that fully one-quarter of Republicans reported getting recorded phone calls from the Obama and Clinton campaigns. Live telephone calls are more carefully targeted by campaigns, who usually ask for a specific voter. Thus, there should be

TABLE 4.1. **Percentage of Republican caucusgoers reporting contacts by Democratic campaigns**

	Phone—live	Phone—recorded	Mail	In person	E-mail
Obama	12	25	18	7	2
Edwards	8	16	16	1	1
Clinton	11	24	17	2	2

TABLE 4.2. **Percentage of Democratic caucusgoers reporting contacts by Republican campaigns**

	Phone—live	Phone—recorded	Mail	In person	E-mail
Huckabee	9	16	14	0	0
Romney	10	16	15	0	0

much less spillover. Even so, more than 1 in 10 Republicans reported receiving such calls, suggesting they were specifically targeted by the Democrats. And looking at the reported in-person contacts, the Obama campaign must have made efforts to go after Republicans—in fact, more
Republicans reported in-person at-home contacts from Obama than
from any of the Republican campaigns! This is especially interesting,
since these reports are from people who ended up attending the Republican caucus despite these contacts.

Similar spillover effects appear for only two of the Republican campaigns: Huckabee and Romney. Table 4.2 reports those findings. Again
we see that those contact methods less in the candidate's control show
more spillover, while interestingly both campaigns seemed to contact
Democrats by phone about as often as the Democrats contacted Republicans. But unlike the Democrats, there are no e-mail spillovers, and
given the complete lack of in-person contact by Republican campaigns
to their own partisans, it is no surprise that there are no spillover effects
here either.

Conclusion: If 2008 Was the End of an Era, It Went Out with a Bang

Although it appears that sometimes a candidate with limited financial
resources can make contact with voters on par with better-funded opponents, for the most part these data from Iowa in 2008 suggest that both
wholesale and retail politics matter. It does, in fact, take resources to
compete in Iowa, and candidates who have little money, and even less
media attention, cannot easily make up for this by building some kind of
grassroots operation. Part of the reason, of course, is that even the seed
for grass roots costs money. It takes money to open offices, to hire staff
who then recruit volunteers, and to run operations on the ground. Iowa
cannot and does not even the playing field among rich and poor candidates, no matter what the conventional wisdom may say and no matter

the hope that springs anew each caucus season. Money, contacting potential voters, and organization are all generally needed to win Iowa. Our data clearly show that the Obama campaign excelled in each of these areas. His win in Iowa, in retrospect, should not be a surprise. Huckabee, on the other hand, benefited from both intensive contact efforts despite his lack of funds and, we suspect, the media fascination with him that developed as his poll numbers began to rise in October 2007. His win may be a bit more surprising, and evidence that grassroots campaigning can pay off.

Our review of the kinds of contacts campaigns made in Iowa is greatly influenced by the work of Christopher Hull (2007), who attempted something similar during the 2004 caucus. In that study Hull also asked voters to estimate contacts from previous caucus years, which is a rather tenuous way to develop the data, but given the lack of previous caucus studies may have been necessary. Our advantage is that we could collect these data during the most competitive Iowa caucus season in history, in which both parties were active and more than a dozen candidates crossed the landscape. With our improved survey data, we also tell a slightly different story from Hull's, one in which grassroots politics remains central, but also one in which a candidate without financial resources cannot compete as effectively in Iowa. We turn next in our examination of Iowa 2008 to the ways in which Iowans themselves responded to the campaigns, as we try to complete the picture of what happened in Iowa before examining the role the state played in the remainder of our sequential presidential nominating process.

CHAPTER FIVE

The Iowa Grass Roots

Participation in the 2008 Caucuses

When I told my family, they said, "Iowa?" And I said, "Yes, it's where it's at." — Jessica Love, 24, John Kerry Iowa campaign staffer (Associated Press, 2003)

Iowa is "where it's at" for young campaign staffers, not only because it is where everything begins for presidential candidates, but also because there are few other places that rely on old-fashioned grassroots politics like Iowa. As we saw in chapters 2 and 4, the candidates and the media both make huge investments of time and resources in Iowa, and in 2008 Iowa caucusgoers noticed, reporting a great deal of direct contact by the campaigns. But who exactly is caucusing? It seems very likely that as campaigns become more intense, and more voters pay attention, more potential caucusgoers find themselves actively participating in the campaign process. The question we ask in this chapter is, what did political participation look like for those who actually attended the 2008 Iowa caucuses? What kinds of activities did they engage in, and to what extent? We explore whether the campaigns in 2008 mobilized Iowans in ways that narrowed the expected gap between those who caucus and those who do not.

The single most influential study of Iowa caucus participants is by Stone, Abramowitz, and Rapoport (1989) (see also Stone, Rapoport, and Abramowitz [1992]), who used surveys of Iowa caucus attendees, delegates to the Iowa state Democratic convention, and caucus attendees in Michigan and Virginia, along with the American National Election Study in 1984, to examine who participated in Iowa, and to compare Iowa to other states. They established the conventional wisdom about participation in Iowa, arguing that those who attended the 1988 Iowa caucuses were party activists, unrepresentative of the state's rank-and-file party voters and the electorate as a whole. Not only were they strong partisans, but they were better educated, older, and in a higher income bracket. But this conventional wisdom was actually built on a narrow definition of the word *activist*. Stone and colleagues called their interviewees activists because they had attended a caucus and were convention delegates.[1]

While state convention delegates might easily be categorized as activists, caucus participants may not. What Stone and colleagues found was that caucusgoers—party activists, by their definition—were significantly more ideologically polarized compared with the ANES national sample of general election voters. Iowa polarization, though, was tempered compared with other caucus states that received little attention from candidates and the media. This is because the attention Iowa received presumably drove up turnout, and as turnout increases the caucuses (and any nomination electorate) become more representative of the party as a whole. While we have no disagreement with the basic logic of this argument, Stone and his colleagues never directly measured political activism (such as participation in previous caucuses) among Iowa caucusgoers due to survey question limitations. Thus, they simply assumed that those who were more ideologically extreme were more likely to be party activists. While we cannot go back in time to 1984 to measure party involvement of those caucusgoers, we can examine this basic question in the context of the 2008 caucuses, the best attended ever.

This chapter updates the arguments made by Stone and his colleagues. Much has happened in the twenty-four years since the first caucus year they studied; 1984 was only the fourth caucus year since Iowa's move to the front of the presidential nominating process. The caucuses that year, while competitive for the Democrats, were not for the Republicans, since Ronald Reagan was running for reelection. In the intervening years, the caucuses have become institutionalized, and have drawn greater and greater media scrutiny (Hull 2007). The 2008 caucus year is a good one for testing Stone and colleagues' major argument that as primaries and caucuses become more competitive and turnout increases, the nomination electorate becomes more like the general election electorate. Even a cursory look at 2008 data—whether from media entrance polls or our own surveys—shows that with half of all caucusgoers being first timers, activists are unlikely to have dominated the Iowa caucuses in 2008 the way they might have twenty-four years ago. While strongly suggesting that Stone and colleagues were correct in concluding that increased turnout broadens the caucus electorate, it also suggests that we need to look more deeply into just who it was caucusing in 2008.

In the pages that follow, we use comprehensive surveys of Iowa caucusgoers and primary voters in other states collected during the hypercompetitive 2007–8 campaign season to examine the participatory activities of caucusgoers. We consider in particular the differences between first-time and repeat caucusgoers, men and women, and those who claim to be active in their party compared to those who say they are not. Caucusgoing, for Stone and his colleagues (1989, 1992), was about supporting the party organizations, and given the very low turnout that defined the caucuses, the assumption that the majority who showed up were party activists might not have been unreasonable. But as we will show, in 2008 large percentages of Iowa caucusgoers were drawn not by a sense of party loyalty, but rather by candidates and issues, and nearly three-quarters of all who attended claimed they are not, in fact, particularly active in their party.

A Note about Our Caucus Survey Samples for This Chapter

We have two different samples of actual Iowa caucusgoers with which we can work. The first is a traditional telephone survey conducted immediately after the January 3 event, in which we reached 525 caucus attendees of both parties January 5–10, 2008. The second is our in-caucus survey, in which 2,611 respondents attending caucuses in all 99 Iowa counties completed a pencil-and-paper questionnaire before their caucus began. This latter survey asked fewer questions than the telephone survey, but had the advantage of reaching a wider base of caucusgoers, given the known problems of reaching some demographic groups by telephone. The in-caucus survey is, in effect, the best guide we have to the actual makeup of caucus attendees, because of its methodology (one randomly assigned survey in every precinct in Iowa) and its response rate (80.8% for Democrats and 65.6% for Republicans). Thus, we could weight the postcaucus telephone sample for the demographics in the in-caucus sample, but that would obscure some of the more interesting differences between the samples. An independent analysis of the two surveys based on different survey modes gives us more insight into what happened in Iowa. Because the telephone survey instrument was more comprehensive, we have chosen to focus primarily on the unweighted telephone survey, but we will also report interesting results from the in-caucus survey where these details might shed a different light.

The primary difference between the two samples is the extent to which younger participants were interviewed. While only about 7.5% of telephone respondents were age 18–29, just over 14% of the in-caucus sample was in this age group.[2] Older caucus attendees are significantly overrepresented in the telephone survey, making up nearly 42% of that sample, compared with only 34% of the in-caucus sample. This makes the most difference when we look at online and offline participation, where younger attendees are more likely to report using online participation modes, while older attendees are more likely to report using more traditional grassroots participation modes. Interestingly, however, both samples have the same percentage of first-time caucus attendees, about 46%, suggesting that while the telephone survey missed younger voters to some degree, it does not underrepresent those attending their first caucus.

Who Caucuses?

In chapter 4 we examined the ways in which the candidate campaigns reached out to voters during the long run-up to caucus night. But we did not provide much context about caucus participants. Here we examine in detail the demographics of our telephone and in-caucus samples. To our knowledge, these two surveys represent the most comprehensive look at actual Iowa caucus attendees in a long time, in terms of both the size of the samples and the sheer number of questions asked on a wide variety of topics (see Stone, Rapoport, and Abramowitz [1992] and Stone, Abramowitz, and Rapoport [1989] for other large samples of Iowa caucusgoers).[3]

Table 5.1 reports the frequencies for our samples by party for age, gender, religion, race, marital status, education, income, ideology, and party activism. While there are clear differences between the telephone and the in-caucus (pencil and paper) surveys, what we focus on here are the differences and similarities between the parties. In some cases (as will be true for the other tables), the party differences vary by survey, but in others the difference are consistent across surveys. These latter cases are of particular interest, since they suggest that what we are seeing really does represent basic differences between Republicans and Democrats, driven no doubt by the differences in the party rules and candidate

TABLE 5.1. **Caucus attendees, demographics by party, January 2008 surveys**

	Republican telephone	Democrat telephone	Republican in-caucus	Democrat in-caucus	Republican entrance	Democrat entrance
Age						
Under 30	9.0	6.3	16.5	16.2	11	22
30–44	18.5	10.7	19.2	15.3	15	18
45–59	32.2	40.3	40.9	39.7	46	38
60 and over	40.3	42.7	23.5	28.7	27	22
	N = 211	N = 300	N = 1,100	N = 1,357		
Gender						
Female	49.5	56.5	45.7	57.9	44	57
	N = 214	N = 301	N = 1,141	N = 1,400		
Religion						
Protestant	72.5	52.4	72.1	59.7		
Catholic	20.9	30.3	15.9	27.6		
Mormon	1.4	1.1	2.1	0.3		
Jewish	0.0	1.0	0.5	0.6		
Other	0.5	1.7	7.3	5.1		
None	4.7	14.6	2.1	6.7		
	N = 211	N = 294	N = 1,052	N = 1,247		
Born-again	40.9	17.6	48.2	16.7	60	
	N = 198	N = 239	N = 1,109	N = 1,338		
Race						
White	98.6	97.7	97.3	95.6	99	93
Black	0.5	1.0	0.5	2.4	0	4
Other	0.9	1.3	2.2	2.0	1	3
Hispanic	2.3	1.3	1.0	1.2		
	N = 214	N = 300	N = 1,140	N = 1,403		
Marital status						
Married	79.2	64.0	71.2	61.7		58
	N = 212	N = 300	N = 1,160	N = 1,419		
Education						
HS or less	23.4	30.7	19.4	23.8		
Some college	25.7	26.7	31.2	28.9		
College	34.1	21.0	35.7	29.1		
Postgrad	16.8	21.7	13.6	18.2		
	N = 214	N = 300	N = 1,237	N = 1,401		
Income						
Under 30,000	9.1	22.2				
30–49,999	25.1	24.6	42.0#	49.5#	37#	42#
50–74,999	26.2	22.2	58.0	50.5	63	58
75,000+	39.6	31.0				
	N = 187	N = 252	N = 1,160	N = 1,419		
Ideology						
Strong lib	1.4	16.8	1.1§	15.3§		18
Weak lib	0.5	17.4	1.1	35.8	1	36
Lean lib	2.3	22.8				
Center	9.9	29.9	13.2	38.9	11	40
Lean con	15.5	6.7				
Weak con	31.5	3.7	37.0	8.5	43	6
Strong con	39.0	2.7	47.6	1.5	45	
	N = 213	N = 298	N = 1,140	N = 1,395		
Active in party						
Not at all	35.0	35.6	21.6	24.0		
Not very	38.2	40.6	39.5	39.9		
Somewhat	23.2	18.5	29.8	28.6		
Extremely	3.6	5.3	9.2	7.5		
	N = 220	N = 303	N = 1,135	N = 1,413		

Source: Entrance polls from http://www.msnbc.msn.com/id/21228177 (Republicans, n = 1,600) and http://www.msnbc.msn.com/id/21225980 (Democrats, n = 2,136).

Note: Table entries are expressed in percentages.

In-caucus survey and entrance poll income measured as above/below $50,000.

§ In-caucus survey ideology measured as very liberal/conservative, somewhat liberal/conservative, or moderate/middle of the road.

campaigns (see chapter 3). Table 5.1 also reports the media entrance polls for Iowa in those demographic categories for which they were provided. Not surprisingly, our in-caucus sample matches the entrance polls more closely than does our telephone sample, which is significantly older and higher income. Differences in the samples are not surprising, given the very different methodologies used to collect all three.

Republicans versus Democrats

One of the most interesting and perhaps surprising differences between the parties is in the age of caucus participants. For all the media focus on young voters and the Obama bandwagon, the evidence is that Democratic caucusgoers, as a whole, were *older* than the Republican attendees. In fact, in the telephone survey, Democrats averaged 57.3 years old, compared with 54.1 for Republicans ($t = 2.24, p =. 02$). In the in-caucus survey, which captured many more younger voters, the average age for Democrats was 50.4 years, compared with 48.7 for Republicans ($t = 2.52, p = .01$). These differences in average age between Democratic and Republican caucusgoers are statistically significant regardless of samples used.

Some less surprising but consistent differences include that Democrats were much more likely to be women, with men representing only about 43%–44% of Democratic caucusgoers. Republicans were more gender balanced: 46%–49% of attendees were women. This tracks well with the national gender bases of the two parties. Iowa's religious diversity is mainly reflected in whether a respondent is more likely to be Protestant or Catholic. Again, no surprises here: more Democratic than Republican caucusgoers are Catholic. Democrats are also more likely to report no religious affiliation. Republicans, of course, are far more likely to call themselves "born-again" or evangelical. In fact, by our measures nearly half of all Republicans attending the 2008 caucuses were in this category, compared with about one-sixth of Democrats. While we do not have good historical data, there is some sense that evangelical turnout was up in 2008, motivated by the campaign of former Arkansas governor and Southern Baptist minister Mike Huckabee. Even so, evangelicals always comprise a large share of Republican caucusgoers. In 1988, televangelist Pat Robertson made a special appeal to this group and shocked the country with his performance in Iowa, beating Vice President George H. W. Bush and coming in second to Kansas senator Bob Dole.

Given Iowa's relative lack of racial/ethnic diversity (Hero 1998), our samples indicate no real differences between the parties on this dimension. Iowa does have a rapidly growing Hispanic population, but either they are not yet participating in significant numbers in the Iowa caucuses or we simply did not capture them in our surveys. Just over 1% of our total sample identified as Hispanic, though it is worth pointing out that given turnout in 2008, this would represent about four thousand actual Hispanic caucus attendees, no doubt a number that will grow in the future. We find that Republican caucus participants are more likely to be married, be better educated, and have higher incomes, all of which mirror national differences between the parties. And we find the Republican caucuses were more dominated by strong ideologues than were the Democrats in 2008. Between 40 and 50% of all Republican caucusgoers identified as strong (or very) conservative in our surveys, compared with only about 15% of Democrats, who called themselves "strong liberals." Democratic caucusgoers were far more likely than Republicans to place themselves in the middle of the ideology scale.

Finally, we look at the extent to which the Iowa caucuses are dominated by party activists, as Stone and colleagues found in the 1980s (Stone, Rapoport, and Abramowitz 1992; Stone, Abramowitz, and Rapoport 1989; Stone, Rapoport, and Atkeson 1995). Examining ideology in 1984, Stone and colleagues (1989) found that in the Iowa electorate, only 30% of Democrats thought of themselves as liberal, compared with 61% among those who caucused and 74% among state convention delegates. The assumption was that the more liberal the respondent, the more likely he or she was a party activist. Our advantage is that we actually asked people if they were active in their party, giving the options of "not at all active," "not very active," "somewhat active," and "extremely active." In the telephone survey, 25% of all respondents called themselves somewhat (20.5%) or extremely (4.5%) active, while the other 75% called themselves either not at all active (35.4%) or not very active (39.6%). And while the percentage of those somewhat and extremely active is higher in the pencil-and-paper in-caucus survey at about 37%, it is still well under half of all caucus attendees. In a low-turnout year, it may well be that activists are the only ones who show up, but in 2008 activists were outnumbered in both parties. Clearly, rank-and-file members were persuaded to participate in 2008.

To examine this phenomenon in more detail, we cross tabulated party activism with political ideology using our in-caucus survey, which has the higher estimate of activism. The results are displayed in figure 5.1.

Democrats

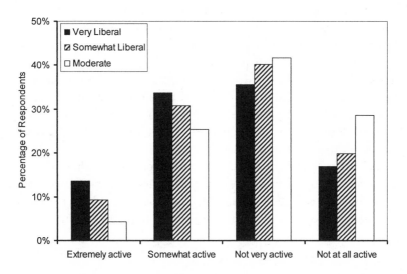

Republicans

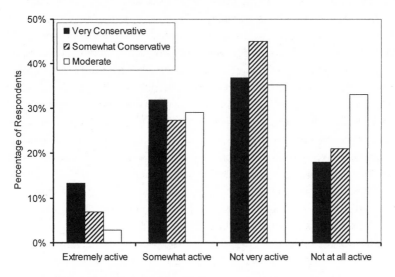

FIGURE 5.1. Party activism by respondent ideology.

As Stone and colleagues suggested, there is a clear relationship between political ideology and self-reports of party activity. For both Democrats and Republicans, those on the ideological extremes are more likely than those in the middle to say they are extremely active in their party. Likewise, moderates in both parties are much more likely to say they are not at all active in their party. So it appears that the basic assumption that ideology can predict party activism has some support. But a closer look suggests that it would be a stretch to say the 2008 caucuses were dominated by activists, even among the most ideological attendees. In fact, fewer than 50% of the "very liberal" Democrats said they were extremely or very active in their party, while nearly half the "very conservative" Republicans said the same. Given that voting for presidential candidates is a reflection of all those who attend, it would be hard to argue that in 2008 party activists controlled the Iowa caucuses.

First Timers versus Repeat Caucusgoers

One of the reasons that 2008 caucuses had a large number of nonactivists in attendance is that for both parties they attracted record numbers of first timers. As table 5.2 displays, these newcomers differed in significant ways from those who had attended before. They were younger—not terribly surprising on its face, since some first timers were simply not eligible to attend four years before. But the difference even among those who could have attended in 2000 or 2004 is quite significant. Only 7 to 12% of repeat caucusgoers were aged 30–44 years, compared with more than 20% of first timers. And in our in-caucus survey, which better captured younger caucusgoers, only 17.7% of repeaters were younger than forty-five years old, compared with 51.1% of first timers. First timers brought significant youth to the 2008 caucuses.

First timers were also less likely than repeaters to be married, and more likely to be female, no matter which sample we draw on. They were also slightly less likely to be white, though this difference is small, given the lack of racial diversity in the state. And not surprisingly given the age differences, first timers were also less educated and in a lower income bracket (at least in our in-caucus survey). Ideologically, they brought moderation to the caucuses, as they were more likely to place themselves in the "middle of the road" than were more experienced caucusgoers. But first timers were also slightly more conservative overall in both our surveys.

First timers also brought to the caucuses the perspective of the

	First time telephone	Repeat telephone	First time in-caucus	Repeat in-caucus
Age				
Under 30	14.0	1.8	28.5	5.1
30–44	21.7	7.3	22.6	12.6
45–59	37.5	36.7	32.4	47.5
60 and over	26.8	54.2	16.5	34.8
	$N = 235$	$N = 275$	$N = 1,129$	$N = 1,286$
Gender				
Female	57.2	50.4	56.8	49.2
	$N = 236$	$N = 278$	$N = 1,162$	$N = 1,337$
Religion				
Protestant	59.3	61.9	63.4	66.8
Catholic	28.1	24.9	21.7	22.9
Mormon	0.9	0.4	1.8	0.6
Jewish	0.4	0.7	0.4	0.7
Other	0.9	1.5	7.7	4.8
None	10.4	10.6	5.0	4.2
	$N = 231$	$N = 273$	$N = 1,040$	$N = 1,221$
Born-again	26.9	29.4	29.7	31.8
	$N = 201$	$N = 235$	$N = 1,108$	$N = 1,302$
Race				
White	97.0	98.9	95.4	97.5
Black	1.3	0.0	2.2	1.0
Other	1.6	1.1	2.3	1.5
Hispanic	2.1	1.4	1.6	0.7
	$N = 236$	$N = 277$	$N = 1,157$	N = 1,344
Marital status				
Married	67.5	74.7	57.1	74.1
	$N = 234$	$N = 277$	$N = 1,176$	$N = 1,361$
Education				
HS or less	35.3	21.2	26.3	17.8
Some college	28.5	24.5	32.9	27.1
College	24.7	27.7	29.7	34.4
Postgrad	11.5	26.6	11.2	20.7
	$N = 235$	$N = 278$	$N = 1,152$	$N = 1,344$
Income				
Under 30,000	14.8	18.3		
30–49,999	26.1	23.4	51.5[#]	40.9[#]
50–74,999	21.2	26.4	48.5	59.1
75,000+	37.9	31.9		
	$N = 203$	$N = 235$	$N = 1,176$	$N = 1,361$
Ideology				
Strong lib	9.4	11.2	8.7[$]	9.4[$]
Weak lib	7.7	12.6	17.7	22.2
Lean lib	15.0	13.7		
Center	23.2	20.2	32.4	22.8
Lean con	9.9	10.8		
Weak con	16.3	14.4	21.3	21.4
Strong con	18.5	17.0	19.9	24.3
	$N = 233$	$N = 277$	$N = 1153$	$N = 1340$
Active in party				
Not at all	44.4	27.9	32.1	14.9
Not very	36.4	42.0	43.8	36.1
Somewhat	15.9	24.4	20.3	36.7
Extremely	3.3	5.7	3.7	12.2
	$N = 239$	$N = 283$	$N = 1,180$	$N = 1,361$

Note: Table entries are expressed in percentages.

[#]In-caucus survey income measured as above/below $50,000.

[$]In-caucus survey ideology measured as very liberal/conservative, somewhat liberal/conservative, or moderate/middle of the road.

rank-and-file party member rather than the activist. It is not unexpected but still important to point out that first-time caucusgoers were far less likely to say they were active in their local party organization. Only 19 to 24% of first timers said they were somewhat or extremely active, compared with 31% of repeat caucusgoers in the telephone survey and 49% in the in-caucus survey. Had the first timers not shown up, the caucuses would have clearly been subject to greater influence by party activists, as Stone and colleagues (1989) argued was the case in 1984, though again it is important to note that about half of repeat caucusgoers did not call themselves party activists. And had party elites controlled the 2008 Iowa caucuses instead of so many first-time participants, these caucuses may not have had such an important influence on later nominating events, as we show in chapters 7 and 8.

Women and Men

Table 5.3 compares female and male caucusgoers. There is actually not very much to say here, and that in itself is instructive. Women and men were similar in most ways: age, religion, race, and education. Women were also about as active in their party organization as men, but women were slightly more likely to call themselves evangelicals in our telephone survey (this difference does not exist in the in-caucus survey). Women were more likely to be unmarried and report somewhat lower household incomes. And they were clearly more liberal, with far fewer women than men calling themselves conservative. In fact, women as a whole were solidly in the middle of the road. In our telephone survey, the mean ideological placement for women is 4.16 on a 7-point scale, compared with 4.43 for men ($t = 1.57, p = .11$). Still for the most part, male and female caucusgoers seem quite similar to each other. Another way of thinking about this is that women were just as likely to be politically mobilized by the Iowa caucus campaigns as were men.

Record Turnout in 2008, but Why Caucus?

As we have already documented, the Iowa caucus campaigns were both intense and lengthy. Candidate campaigns spent a great deal of money and even more time attempting to determine which Iowans to target and how voters could be convinced to "do politics" on a cold winter night.

	Women telephone	Men telephone	Women in-caucus	Men in-caucus
Age				
Under 30	6.2	8.8	16.3	16.7
30–44	12.5	15.5	16.2	18.0
45–59	35.3	38.9	40.5	40.2
60 and over	46.0	36.8	27.0	25.2
	$N = 272$	$N = 239$	$N = 1,278$	$N = 1,153$
Religion				
Protestant	60.1	61.5	66.4	64.1
Catholic	28.4	23.9	22.2	22.1
Mormon	0.4	0.9	1.3	0.9
Jewish	0.4	0.9	0.7	0.3
Other	1.1	1.3	5.4	7.1
None	9.6	11.5	4.0	5.4
	$N = 271$	$N = 234$	$N = 1,207$	$N = 1,070$
Born-again	31.6	24.0	30.2	31.0
	$N = 237$	$N = 200$	$N = 1,253$	$N = 1,162$
Race				
White	97.8	98.3	96.5	96.5
Black	0.7	0.4	1.7	1.4
Other	1.4	1.3	1.8	2.1
Hispanic	1.1	2.5	1.4	0.8
	$N = 276$	$N = 238$	$N = 1,321$	$N = 1,188$
Marital status				
Married	64.2	79.4	64.0	68.5
	$N = 274$	$N = 238$	$N = 1,333$	$N = 1,208$
Education				
HS or less	31.2	23.5	22.2	21.6
Some college	26.4	26.1	29.4	30.7
College	26.4	26.5	32.8	31.2
Postgrad	15.9	23.9	15.6	16.6
	$N = 276$	$N = 238$	$N = 1,317$	$N = 1,190$
Income				
Under 30,000	18.7	14.5	—	—
30–49,999	29.7	20.0	49.4[#]	42.3[#]
50–74,999	21.9	25.9	50.6	57.7
75,000+	29.7	39.5	—	—
	$N = 219$	$N = 220$	$N = 1,333$	$N = 1,208$
Ideology				
Strong lib	12.0	8.5	10.2[$]	7.6[$]
Weak lib	10.5	10.2	23.7	16.4
Lean lib	13.5	15.3	—	—
Center	23.3	19.5	28.8	25.5
Lean con	11.3	9.3	—	—
Weak con	13.5	17.4	17.9	25.3
Strong con	16.0	19.9	19.5	25.3
	$N = 275$	$N = 236$	$N = 1,315$	$N = 1,192$
Active in party				
Not at all	35.4	36.0	25.5	20.2
Not very	37.2	41.0	40.0	39.5
Somewhat	23.7	17.2	28.1	29.9
Extremely	3.6	5.9	6.3	10.4
	$N = 274$	$N = 239$	$N = 1,312$	$N = 1,171$

Note: Table entries are expressed in percentages.
[#]In-caucus survey income measured as above/below $50,000.
[$]In-caucus survey ideology measured as very liberal/conservative, somewhat liberal/conservative, or moderate/middle of the road.

These efforts apparently worked better than ever, as both parties experienced unexpectedly large turnout, in many cases overwhelming the spaces available for the precinct. In 2004, Democratic caucus participants numbered about 124,000, equaling the record turnout of 1988.[4] Most expectations for 2008 hovered around 150,000–160,000 for the Democrats and 80,000 for the Republicans. But when all was said and done, about 236,000 Democrats and 120,000 Republicans caucused, far exceeding previous records for both parties.

Obviously the intensity of the campaigns had something to do with this. But why do people caucus in Iowa? In both our postcaucus telephone and in-caucus pencil-and-paper surveys, we asked caucusgoers to tell us why they came to their caucus. Some reasons given were pretty obvious: to support a candidate, to oppose a candidate, or to support an issue, for example. Respondents could also indicate that they attended to be involved in their party, because they were asked to go by their friends, relatives, or union, or simply because it was "the right thing to do." Finally, we also offered "it is a fun social event" as a possible reason. People could pick as many of these as they thought applied to them. Given the conventional wisdom that defines caucusgoers as party activists, we expected party involvement to be a frequently cited reason for participation and perhaps the most important one.

Instead, we found that in the telephone survey, nearly all respondents (95%) said they attended the caucus because it was "the right thing to do." In one of the more fascinating differences between the telephone and in-caucus surveys, only about 59% of in-caucus respondents chose this same reason, a nearly 35-point difference between the samples. Given that the samples do not vary dramatically in demographics, this may well be a textbook example of a social desirability effect. Perhaps when talking to another person in an interview, caucusgoers were careful to give this normatively correct response—a sense of duty—but when filling out a survey privately by hand, they were simply less likely to make the same claim. Or it may be that the timing of the surveys mattered. The lower percentage occurred in the in-caucus survey, completed just before the beginning of the caucus. The higher percentage is in the telephone survey, completed several days later after participants had time to reflect on their experience and read the reports of massive turnout. Before the caucus started, it may have seemed questionable whether standing in long lines to sign in (some waited as long as an hour or more) and waiting in hot, crowded rooms had been the right thing to do to. But after participating, this perspective may have simply changed, reflecting the positive sense of being part of history that many may have felt.

At the same time, another factor may be at work. In the telephone interview it was absolutely clear that respondents could answer yes or no to every one of the choices, and thus could answer yes to as many as they wished. While the pencil-and-paper instructions attempted to make this clear as well, many respondents may have only chosen one answer, rather than as many as applied to them. An indication of this is that in the telephone survey the average number of reasons given for attending was 3.6 out of 8 (about 45% of the possible choices), while the in-caucus survey average was 2.3 out of 7 (about 33%). Even with these uncertainties, however, we are comfortable that these data provide real insight into reasons for attending caucuses. In fact, with the exception of the "right thing to do" reason, the rank order of the reasons is the same in both surveys, even if the magnitudes differ.

Figure 5.2 displays the responses from both parties to the "reasons" question in the telephone and in-caucus surveys. Beyond the sense of duty that many respondents indicated, the primary reason for attending

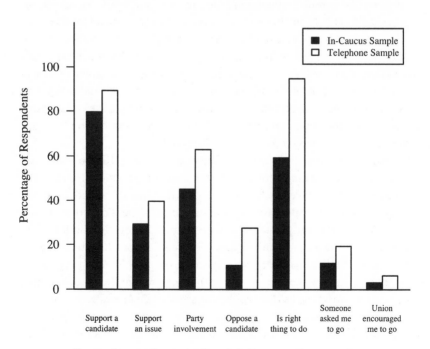

FIGURE 5.2. Reasons for attending caucus by sample type.

is to "support a candidate," not to be involved in one's party. A large majority of respondents in both surveys cited this reason (89% in the telephone survey and 80% in the pencil-and-paper survey); second was to be involved in their party organization (63 and 45%), and third was to show support for a particular issue (40 and 30%). It is clear from the participants' perspective that the reason to attend is simple—to show one's candidate colors, which may well reflect the growing reliance on candidate-, rather than party-centered, campaigns. All other reasons fall pretty far behind, despite the dozens of issue-oriented organizations that are on the ground in Iowa for every caucus, encouraging Iowans to take their issue to the floor for platform discussion (Redlawsk and Sanders 2000). These issue messages do, as it turns out, reach many Iowa caucusgoers and motivate their attendance, but it is the candidate campaigns that really bring people out. At the same time, it is clear that the campaigns themselves are connected to their parties, as caucusgoers also are very likely to indicate that they attend to be involved in their party organization.

While the other reasons for attending were much less likely to be given by the survey respondents, they remain important. A significant proportion (11% in the in-caucus sample and 27% in the telephone sample) said that they also attend to "oppose some other candidate." Given that there is little to no anticandidate public discussion during the caucus itself, this result seems a bit surprising. At the same time, 2008 may represent a unique situation, given the large number of candidates running in both parties, and the clear differences in their bases of support. Even so, for the large majority of Iowa caucusgoers, opposition to a candidate is not a driving force that gets them out.

There are some interesting differences between Republicans and Democrats concerning motivations for attending a caucus. Given the procedural differences between the two that we discussed in chapter 3—with Democrats literally standing up to be publicly counted and Republicans generally casting a secret straw ballot—Republican and Democratic caucusgoers might have different reasons for attending. In fact, of the eight possible reasons given in the telephone survey (seven reasons in the in-caucus paper survey), five show significant differences between the parties, as displayed in figure 5.3.[5] Democrats, not surprisingly, are much more likely to say their labor union encouraged them to go, though overall fewer than 1 in 10 Democrats gave this reason. They were also more likely to attend because the caucus is a fun social event

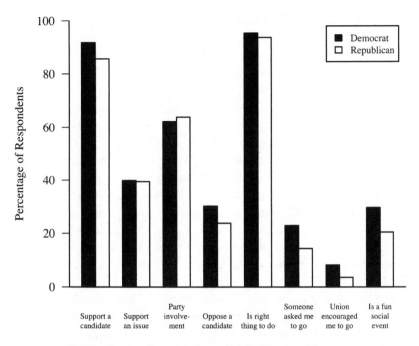

FIGURE 5.3. Reasons for attending caucus by party (telephone sample).

(30 versus 20%) and were more likely to attend because a friend or family members asked them to (23 versus 14%). Both of these responses reflect the social dynamics of a Democratic caucus, where attendees spend
much of the time milling about, talking to and trying to convince one
another to change their candidate choice during realignment (the quintessential social capital event). And, in fact, compared to Republicans,
Democrats are also more likely to say they attend to support a candidate, possibly reflecting this public aspect of the caucus.

Reasons to Caucus for First Timers and Young Voters

The 2008 caucuses were unique in their attraction of both first-time and
young voters. What could have motivated people to attend who are not
among those we usually think of as party activists? It turns out that first
timers as a group were not particularly different in their reasons for participating compared to repeat caucusgoers. In fact, the only significant
differences between the two are that first timers were more likely to say
they attended to show *opposition* to a candidate (32% of first timers,

23% of repeaters), and first timers were three times more likely to say that they attended because a friend or family members asked them to (30 versus 10%). The first of these differences may reflect that first timers may be somewhat more intense in their preferences, since getting out to a caucus requires a substantial commitment and, for those who have never been, some trepidation over what actually happens there. The second of these shows that it is the personal connection—someone other than a campaign—that also motivates first timers. Old Iowa hands tell anyone who will listen that one of the best ways to get people to caucus is to make sure their friends and neighbors ask them to go. Recent research on social desirability effects in voting behavior more generally supports this as well. Gerber, Green, and Larimer (2008) demonstrate that when people know their neighbors will be made aware of their participation, they are more likely to vote. A grassroots campaign in particular can take advantage of this—in fact, in 2008 the Clinton campaign explicitly worked a "caucus buddy" program into their outreach efforts, especially encouraging older women to bring a friend to the caucus. Our evidence suggests that this strategy may well pay off for first timers, but experienced caucusgoers do not need such a push to get them out.

Turning to age, caucus attendees under the age of thirty were far more likely in both our surveys to say they attended because a friend or family member asked them to go. In the telephone survey, 42% of our relatively small sample of this group said this was one of their reasons, while only 28% of those 30–44 years old, 17% those 45–59 years, and 14% of those 60 years and over gave this reason. Even in our in-caucus survey, where we captured a much larger group of younger attendees, we see the exact same pattern, although the percentages are significantly lower. About 25% of the youngest group said they attended because they were asked, while the percentages drop off rapidly by age, with only 12.5% of 30- to 44-year-olds, 9% of 45- to 60-year-olds, and 7.5% those 60 years and over giving this reason. But no matter how we measure reasons for attending, it is clear that the secret to getting Iowans to attend a caucus for the first time is as much about personal contact by people they know and trust as it is by direct campaigning.

Women and Reasons to Attend

One other unique feature of 2008 that had a direct bearing on Iowa was the presence of Hillary Clinton and her presumed appeal to women, especially older women. But as we saw in chapter 4, there are relatively few differences in the nature and amount of contacts reported by women caucusgoers compared with men, suggesting that while the media were focusing on Clinton's natural appeal to women, the Clinton campaign itself was reaching out to as many caucusgoers as possible—smart politics, of course. The data on why women attended their caucus bear this out; we see only a few differences between men and women here as well. Women in our telephone survey were no more likely to attend to support a specific candidate, nor were they more likely to go to the caucus because it is a fun social event. But they were more likely to say they attended to show opposition to a candidate (32% of women, 20% of men), and to be involved in their party organization (67 versus 57%). Even more interestingly, women were much more likely to say they attended because a friend or family members asked them to (22 versus 16%).

Of course, perhaps we would expect to find major survey response differences for Democrats, since Clinton was running in the Democratic caucus. Yet we find that there are only a few small dissimilarities between Democratic and Republican women. In particular, Democratic women were more likely than Democratic men to say they attended to support a candidate (92 versus 84%), and Republican women were a little more likely than Republican men to say they attended to be involved in their party organization (71 versus 65%). On the other hand, there is some evidence that Democrats did more to reach out to their female friends and family to get them out to caucus. Just over 25% of Democratic women said they attended because they were asked, compared with 17% of Republican women (and, as it turns out, only 11% of Republican men). Finally, reflecting the perception that the Democratic process is more social and more active, Democratic women were more likely to say they attended because the caucus is a fun social event, with 29% choosing this reason, compared with only 19% of Republican women.

Activists and Reasons to Attend

What about the activists? We have already seen that in 2008 they were actually outnumbered in both parties on caucus night by nonactivists. At the same time, because activists are generally experienced caucusgoers, they may well have a leg up on occasional and first-time attenders in understanding the rules and nuances of the event, especially in the case of the Democratic caucus. Here we are interested in whether ac-

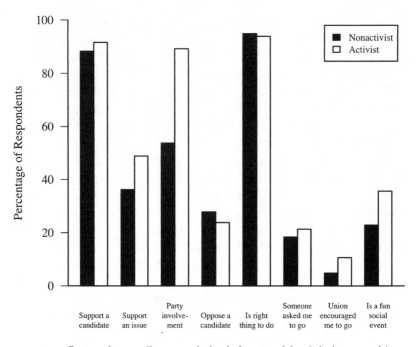

FIGURE 5.4. Reasons for attending caucus by level of party activism (telephone sample).

tivists have different reasons for attending a caucus compared to non-activists. Figure 5.4 displays the reasons to caucus by two levels of party activism—more active and less active—across all respondents. Most obviously and least surprisingly, activists were much more likely to say they caucus to be involved in their party organization, with nearly 90% of activists but only 54% of nonactivists giving this reason. They were also more likely to report that they caucus to support a specific issue (49 versus 36%). Thus, activists are more motivated to attend both by a sense of belonging to the party and by the issues that come in to play during the caucus campaigns. These issues are often seen as a sideshow to the candidate campaigns, pushed as they are by activists devoted to the cause, and not particularly connected to any candidate campaign. Two other reasons given by survey respondents show additional differences between activists and nonactivists. Activists were more than twice as likely to say their labor union encouraged them (11 versus 5%). Further, activists were more likely to cite the caucuses as a "fun social event" by a 36-to 23% margin. Both activists and nonactivists were equally likely to say they caucus because they want to support a candidate, because it is the right thing to do, or because a friend or family member invited them.

The differences between activists and nonactivists are especially stark in the Democratic Party and less so among Republicans, as shown in figure 5.5. Democratic activists were much more likely to say they attended the caucus to support a specific issue than either Democratic nonactivists or any Republicans. They were also much more likely to call the caucuses a fun social event: Democratic activists clearly attended at least in part because of the camaraderie and perceived excitement of the caucus process. They were also the ones who—in this time when organized labor no longer wields great political influence—were by far most likely to say that their union encouraged them to attend. The overall picture for activists is that they are in fact different from nonactivist attendees, at least in terms of the reasons that they go to caucus. Activists expect to support issues, to be involved in their party, and to have a good time at the event.

Grassroots Participation in Iowa Caucus Campaigns

We have looked at the 2008 caucus campaigns as perceived by the voters (chapter 4), as well as the reasons Iowans actually attended the caucuses. We turn now to participation in political activities by caucusgoers during the caucus campaign. The list of activities our surveys asked about covered both traditional grassroots and newer online, Internet-based activities. Grassroots participation included attending a campaign event; meeting a candidate; asking a question of a candidate; contacting an official; contributing money to a candidate (not online); and working on a campaign. Online activities included visiting candidate Web sites; sending or receiving political e-mail; reading political blogs; signing up online as a supporter for a candidate; watching a campaign video online; and giving money online to a candidate. These lists of activities represent both traditional activism, where Iowans get out of their houses to see campaign events and volunteer on campaigns, and online participation. We care about online participation in Iowa for two reasons: the general development of Internet-based politics (Bimber 2003), and the online activities in Iowa documented by Hull (2007). To get the full picture of voter participation, then, we must consider both grassroots and online activities.

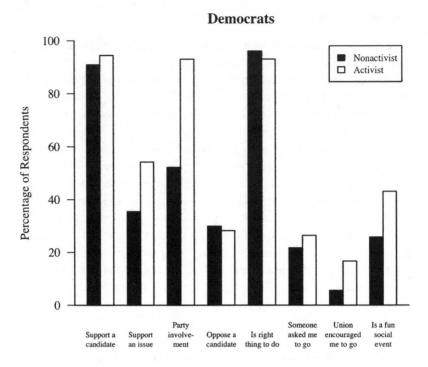

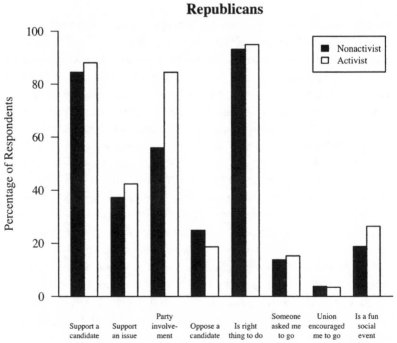

FIGURE 5.5. Reasons for attending caucus by level of party activism and by party (telephone sample).

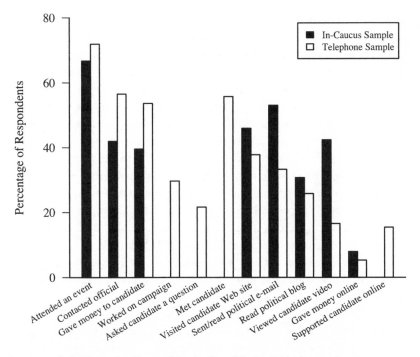

FIGURE 5.6. Offline and online participation in political activities by sample type.

Figure 5.6 presents a first cut on the participation data for caucus attendees. We immediately see the unique grassroots nature of the Iowa
caucuses. Across all respondents of both parties in our telephone survey,
72% reported attending a campaign event, 56% said they personally met
at least one presidential candidate, and 22% said they got to ask a question of a candidate. More than half contributed money and said they had
contacted an elected official, and nearly one-third reported working on
a campaign. Similar (but lower) percentages reported grassroots activities in the in-caucus survey, with 66% attending events, 39% contributing money, and 41% contacting an elected official. By either survey measure, Iowa caucusgoers were incredibly engaged in political grassroots
activities.[6]

Turning to online activities, we continue to find Iowa caucus attendees to be heavily engaged in the campaign. In the telephone survey, just
under 40% reported visiting a candidate Web site, while one-third said
they had sent or received political e-mail. Compared with 2004 as documented by Hull (2007), these are significant increases in online partic-

ipation. However, fewer reported other online activities, with only 5% saying they had given money to a campaign online. Compare this with the 54% who said they contributed to a campaign offline, and we see a significant disconnect. For all the online fund-raising in the 2008 general election, at least in the Iowa caucuses much of the money was donated in more traditional ways. Most likely these contributions involved making small cash donations at events, either through a nominal entrance donation ($10, $20) or via a pass-the-hat appeal, which seems to happen at nearly every political event in Iowa. Other online activities—reading political blogs (26%), watching an Internet campaign video (17%), and signing up online to support a candidate (15%), were less reported, but still obviously an important part of Iowans' participation in the caucus campaigns. When we look at our in-caucus sample, we find that 52% reported receiving or sending political email, 45% looked at a candidate Web site, and 30% reported reading political blogs, all higher percentages than the telephone sample, reflecting again that the in-caucus survey includes many more younger voters, who are more likely to pursue these activities.

Regardless of which sample we examine, several basic truths about Iowa caucusgoers in 2008 stand out. First, they were involved. People who caucus are generally personally invested in the campaigns that lead up to the caucus. Second, "grassroots rules," as Hull (2007) puts it. For as important as the Internet campaigns were perceived to have been, Iowa caucusgoers remained heavily engaged in the "real world" of politics. In fact, 89% of the telephone sample reported participating in at least one of the six grassroots activities we listed, with the mean number of activities at 2.88. Moreover, nearly 40% reported participating in four or more of the six activities. But the evidence also shows that online participation is becoming quite important, with 55% of respondents in the telephone survey reporting engaging in at least one of the online activities we asked about (the mean is 1.34 activities of the six listed).

These overall statistics most likely hide interesting differences between specific groups in our samples. In particular, given the major differences in the ways the two parties carry out their caucuses and in the nature of the campaigns they run, we must examine the participation data by party. And given the substantial increase in first-time caucusgoers in 2008, we should also see where differences lie between those who have participated in the past and those for whom 2008 was their first caucus, and whether men and women participate differently in Iowa. The remainder of this chapter examines participation by these groups in simple summary fashion. Readers looking for a more sophisticated analysis controlling for the various demographics of our sample can turn to chapter 9, where we will compare participation by Iowa voters to those in other states. Here we simply want to give the general sense of Iowa caucusgoers and their participation in the campaigns.

Democrats and Republicans: Different Strokes for Different Folks?

Figure 5.7 displays the grassroots activities of Republicans and Democrats who attended their party's caucuses as reported in our telephone survey. The only real differences are in the likelihood of giving money to a candidate, where 60% of Republicans indicated they had done so, compared with 49% of Democrats, and in contacting elected officials, where 62% of Republicans did so compared with 53% of Democrats. These findings are consistent with national party differences in political contributions. Otherwise, despite the differences in the basic nature of the two parties' caucus process and despite Republicans reporting fewer contacts by campaigns overall (chapter 4), there are no significant

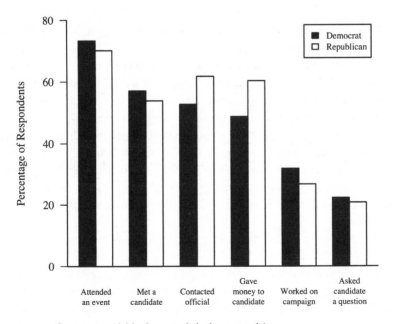

FIGURE 5.7. Grassroots activities by party (telephone sample).

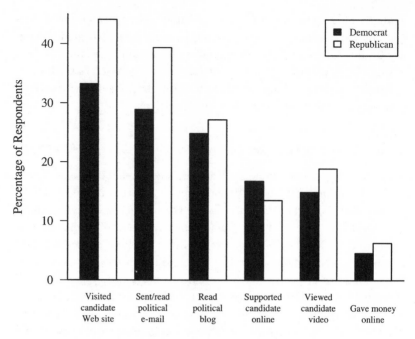

FIGURE 5.8. Online activities by party (telephone sample).

differences between the parties in traditional grassroots activities. Members of both parties were attending events, meeting candidates, asking questions, and working on campaigns in equal percentages. Of course, it is worth keeping in mind that about half as many Republicans as Democrats actually attended their caucuses, reflecting what was clearly a less active, less motivating caucus campaign on the Republican side. (The parties were fairly close to parity in terms of overall registration in Iowa before the caucuses.) Even so, Republicans who did attend were involved in the campaigns. When we look at our participation index, we find that Republicans on average reported 2.94 grassroots activities, while Democrats reported 2.85 of the 6 we surveyed, a nonsignificant difference.

Turning to online participation, figure 5.8 shows that for most activities, Republicans and Democrats are again quite similar, although Republicans were far more likely to say they visited a candidate Web site (44 versus 33%) and to say they sent or received political e-mail (39 versus 29%). Interestingly, even though Republican caucusgoers were more likely to give money to candidates in general, they were not more likely to give online. In fact, a very small percentage of both parties' caucus participants reported online donations—only 5% of Democrats and 6% of Republicans, likely reflecting the relatively older mean age of those who caucused. Online fund-raising, while important, still paled in Iowa compared with more traditional methods.[7]

Men and Women: Does the Caucus Lead to Participatory Equality?

Existing research on political participation has suggested a "partici-pation gap" between men and women when it comes to political cam-paigns. Verba, Burns, and Schlozman (1997) argue that women may be less likely to enjoy and have interest in participating in politics, though they also find that women become more politically informed and inter-ested when there are more women candidates and more women in of-fice. Similarly, Hanson (1997) finds women more likely to proselytize about political opinions when there are women candidates on the ballot in their states. Burns, Schlozman, and Verba (2001) find that education is the most important explanation for the small but persistent difference between women's and men's participation—better-educated women par-ticipate more than those with lower levels of education. Finally, women may discount their competence and participation in a variety of political activities at the mass (Huckfeldt and Sprague 1995) and elite (Kathlene 1994) levels.

However, both the extreme participatory nature of the caucuses and the presence of Hillary Clinton suggest that women who attended the precinct caucuses in 2008 may have participated in both grassroots and online activities at rates similar to men. Certainly we see that across both parties, about 54% of our telephone sample of caucusgoers is fe-male, while 46% is male, reflecting the overall Iowa population (50.9% female) fairly closely. And the in-caucus sample is even closer, compris-ing 52% women and 48% men. This suggests that in Iowa there is no par-ticipation gap, at least in terms of attending the 2008 Iowa caucuses. But what about participating in campaign activities during the run-up to the caucuses?

Figure 5.9 displays grassroots activities by gender. For the most part, with one really interesting exception, men and women reported equal levels of involvement. There are some small differences—more men

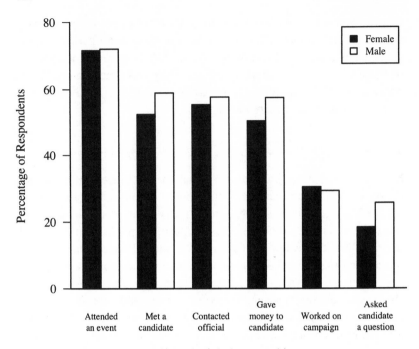

FIGURE 5.9. Grassroots activities by gender (telephone sample).

reported giving money (58 versus 51%), and more reported meeting a candidate (59 versus 53%); however, these do not reach statistical significance. In addition, women and men reported similar numbers of grassroots activities, with men reporting an average of 3.0 and women an average of 2.8, again an insignificant difference. But one difference is large and significant and perhaps telling. While 26% of men reported directly asking a question of a candidate, only 18% of women reported doing so. Another way of looking at this is the ratio between reported attendance at events, meeting candidates, and asking a question. While about 36% of men who attended any event reported asking a question, only 25% of women reported the same. And of those respondents who said they actually met a candidate, 44% of men said they asked a question, compared with only 34% of women. However we look at it, women were less likely to ask a question of a candidate. We can only speculate on why this might be, but it certainly could represent a tendency for women to defer to men at these events, or for candidates to call on men more often than women. Unfortunately, we do not have data that would develop this point further.

Turning once again to online activities, the differences are much more pronounced, as figure 5.10 shows. Men clearly have the advantage, consistent with national data on online political participation (Mossberger, Tolbert, and McNeal 2008). Our participation index shows that men engaged in an average of 1.47 online activities, compared with 1.25 for women. And when we look at specific activities, several clear differences stand out. While men and women are equally likely to say they visited candidates' Web sites, men are more likely to send or receive political e-mail (37 versus 30%), more likely to read a political blog (29 to 24%), and more likely to watch a candidate video on YouTube (19 to 15%). And while only 4% of women reported giving campaign contributions online, just over 7% of men reported this. The overall picture suggests that there is at least some participation gap between men and women when it comes to online activities, while there is little gap in the grass roots. Overall, the participatory nature of the Iowa caucuses seems to bring both men and women into the campaign process, especially through grassroots participation.

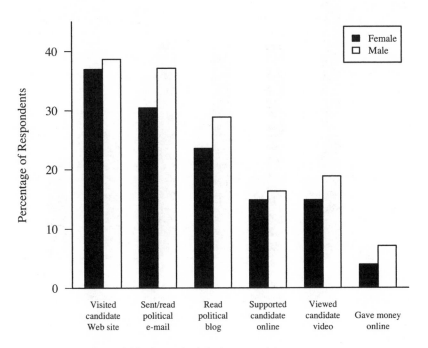

FIGURE 5.10. Online activities by gender (telephone sample).

First Timers versus Repeaters:
What's All This about Getting Involved?

We know that a substantial number of caucusgoers were first timers in 2008, well beyond anything observers anticipated. The intensity and competitiveness of the campaigns on both sides reached well beyond traditional caucusgoers. But did these first timers simply show up, having been convinced late in the game to attend, or were they involved in campaign activities all along? Our data suggest a mixed picture. As figure 5.11 shows, repeat caucusgoers were more likely to report every kind of grassroots participation, compared with first timers. In particular, most repeaters went to campaign events (83%), while fewer than six in ten first timers did (59%). Repeaters were also twice as likely to give money to a candidate (70 versus 35%). And while 30% of repeat caucusgoers said they asked a candidate a question, only 12% of first timers did the same. The evidence from our grassroots participation index

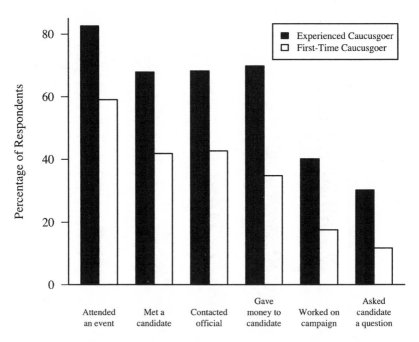

FIGURE 5.11. Grassroots activities by first-time and experienced caucusgoers (telephone sample).

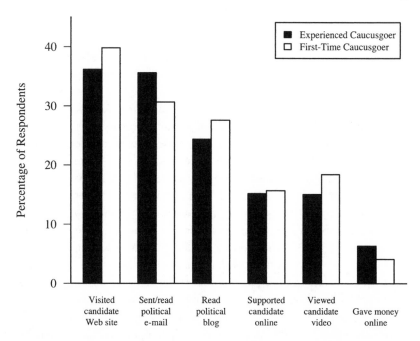

FIGURE 5.12. Online activities by first-time and experienced caucusgoers (telephone sample).

reinforces these differences. Those with caucus experience reported an average of 3.57 of the 6 activities, while first timers reported only 2.08 activities, a highly significant difference.

When we turn to online participation, the picture is entirely different. First timers are at least as likely as repeaters to report engaging in nearly every one of the online activities we asked about. Where differences appear in figure 5.12, they do not reach statistical significance. This is also borne out in the online participation index, where repeat caucusgoers reported 1.33 activities on average, while first timers reported 1.36 activities. Much of this is driven by the age of attendees. First-time caucusgoers were younger—on average, experienced caucusgoers were 61 years old, while first timers were 49. Moreover, 77% of those under the age of 45 in our sample were first-time caucusgoers, compared with 36% of those aged 45 and over. But in the end it is clear that first-time caucusgoers were much less likely to participate in grassroots activities, no matter what their age.

Are the Iowa Caucuses Dominated by Activists?

We close this chapter by returning to the question of the role of party activists in the Iowa caucuses. The caucuses have long been accused of being merely a forum for activists. But as we noted earlier, only about 25% of 2008 caucusgoers actually considered themselves to be very or extremely active in their party. More important, more than half the 2008 caucus participants were first timers, not experienced attendees. But we can go further than simply asking people how active they were by looking at our participation measures by levels of party activism. We find that activists are in fact quite different from nonactivists.[8] On every measure of activity, self-identified party activists do more than those who are not activists. This is true for both grassroots and online participation. The differences are particularly pronounced for working on a campaign (perhaps not surprisingly) and for asking a candidate a question. Those who say they are active in their party are more active in terms of interacting directly with candidates. Party activism brings with it an understanding of the process and an awareness of how campaign events work. For the most part, the differences in online participation are not quite as stark, except for giving money online. Nearly 1 in 8 activists reported doing so, by far the largest proportion of any demographic group, while only 3% of nonactivists gave money this way. But again, as with grassroots activities, those who are most active in their party overall are also most active in the campaigns online.

What lessons are there for the conventional wisdom that the Iowa caucuses are dominated by activists? First, if Stone, Abramowitz, and Rapoport were right at the time of their studies (the late 1980s)—and this is not a given, since they did not actually measure activism—things certainly changed by 2008. When asked, only one-quarter of caucusgoers in 2008 said they were active in their party organization, and across all caucusgoers, showing support for a candidate and attending out of a sense of duty were more frequently cited than attending to support the party itself. We would grant that in less competitive Iowa caucus campaigns, activists are likely to make up a larger share, since for the most part it is the campaigns that bring out voters, not the parties. And in a year when nearly half of all caucusgoers were first timers, it is almost axiomatic that activists would be in the minority. But this makes it all the more important to draw distinctions between caucusgoers. By asking about party activism directly, we find that activists really are active;

much more so than other caucusgoers. Calling voters who attend the caucuses "party activists" by definition is just not accurate. Many are, but in a high-turnout year like 2008, many more are not. As we will see in the next chapter, this high-turnout environment did exactly what Stone and colleagues suggested it would: bring a more representative electorate out on Iowa caucus night.

*   *   *

Over the last two chapters we have examined the nature of the 2008 Iowa caucus—the extensive participation, the intensive candidate campaigns, and the massive media focus. That makes it time to ask again, why Iowa? One obvious reason, as Stone, Abramowitz, and Rapoport note, is that "Iowa caucus attenders have a significant and disproportionate impact on the nomination process" (1989, 44). And, as they also point out, this would probably be the case for whichever state went first in a sequential nominating process. Unless candidates do not know where to start their campaigning until some time closer to election day, they and the media will undoubtedly flock to the first state deemed important.[9] What 2008 shows that neither 1984 nor 1988 could is the impact of dramatically increased competition when neither party has an obvious front-runner and following the twenty-year period during which the caucuses became institutionalized. The Iowa caucuses in 2008 were not dominated by activists as many assume they are. Large numbers of first-time attendees and relatively less active members of both parties attended, and in doing so made the Iowa caucuses something different than they might have been in the past. But an important question remains. Even in a high-turnout year like 2008, most Iowa voters did *not* caucus. We know that those who did were involved in many participatory activities that those who did not go probably missed. We also know that the high turnout meant that the caucuses were not necessarily dominated by activists. But before we can fully justify Iowa's role—if we can at all—we still need to consider the extent to which caucusgoers in 2008 adequately represented voters throughout the state of Iowa. For that we turn to the next chapter.

CHAPTER SIX

Decided by the Few

Are the Iowa Caucuses Representative?

With Daniel C. Bowen

Caucus attenders and other nomination activists are not typical of the larger populations they may be presumed to "act for." They are better educated, older and have higher incomes. They are more committed to and active in their party than the average citizen. They are less likely to be indifferent on the issues and are more "extreme" in their ideological commitments. These ideological preferences do have an impact on their candidate support, which may result in candidates facing a tension between their nomination supporters and those they must satisfy in the general electorate. — Stone, Abramowitz, and Rapoport (1989), p. 44

After a year (and in some cases several years) of campaigning by more than a dozen Democratic and Republican presidential candidates, a record number of Iowa voters trudged to schools, community centers, and other public buildings on January 3, 2008, to participate in a process some have called a scam (Hitchens 2007), others have dismissed as arcane and difficult to understand (Kurtz 2007), and still others have attacked as unrepresentative due to low voter turnout (Wang 2007). A Google News search of "Iowa caucuses" on January 2, 2008, returned about 42,240 articles, including those bearing headlines such as "Politicians Love, Loathe Iowa Caucus System" (Kiely 2008a), "The Trouble with Caucuses" (Webb 2008), and "Not Caucusing? Most of Iowa Won't Either" (Rainey and Mehta 2008). It seems at times as if the only people who defend the Iowa caucus process are Iowans—and sometimes even they wonder about its vagaries (Yepsen 2008a, 2008b).

In the last three chapters we have seen that the rules governing the

Iowa caucuses matter because they condition the candidates' campaigns and the voters' responses. We have also learned that in 2008 the Iowa caucuses were a hotbed of candidate activity, and that voters responded in kind to this competitive environment. There is a real sense among candidates that Iowa matters. In a speech in Des Moines four days before the general election, Illinois senator Barack Obama credited his nomination to Iowa, saying, "On the day of the Iowa caucus, my faith in the American people was vindicated. What you started here in Iowa has swept across the nation" (Gavrilovic 2008). And while Arizona senator John McCain might not have seen it the same way, former Arkansas governor Mike Huckabee's victory over former Massachusetts governor Mitt Romney no doubt played an important role in his nomination as well.

The problem is that, by many accounts, the Iowa caucuses are a questionable way to start the presidential nominating process. Arguments against Iowa come in several flavors. One of the most salient is simply that "no one" caucuses; that turnout in Iowa is astoundingly low. Many point out that few eligible voters in that state actually brave a cold winter night to show up at their caucuses, and that some who would do so cannot because they must work or take care of children, or are otherwise occupied on a weekday evening. The raw numbers would seem to support this. By one estimate, only 6.1% of the voting eligible population (VEP) caucused in Iowa in 2004, down slightly from 6.8% in 2000 (McDonald 2008a).[1] But 2008 saw a dramatic increase, with a VEP turnout of 16.3% (McDonald 2008b.) Even so, this turnout rate is much lower than McDonald recorded for 2008's early primaries, including New Hampshire (52.5%) and South Carolina (30.4%).

Why this low turnout? Wang (2007, 2) argues that "campaign workers know that only the most avid partisans will go through the tribulations of a caucus, and these avid partisans are likely to be people who have voted consistently in the past. Thus as a political calculus it makes no sense for them to reach out to infrequent or potential new voters." Her comment has certainly been the conventional wisdom in the past, although, as we saw in chapter 5, nearly half of those attending in 2008 were first timers—evidence that campaigns did go after new voters. But our data also show that first timers were less likely than repeat caucusgoers to be contacted by campaigns, even in 2008. Campaigns have limited resources, and it may just make sense for them to focus mostly on those voters they believe will actually show up to caucus. Thus, those who are less likely to show up do not hear much from campaigns, reinforcing their tendency to stay away. This, of course, is true to some degree of all political campaigns.

Conventional Wisdom: Iowa Caucuses Are Unrepresentative

As noted in the opening excerpt from Stone, Abramowitz, and Rapoport (1989), scholars examining earlier competitive Iowa caucuses found that those who attended were not typical of the larger population for whom they are presumed to act. In addition to being better educated, older, and in a higher income bracket, they were more committed to and active in their party than the average citizen (Stone, Abramowitz, and Rapoport 1989; Norrander 1989; but see Geer [1988]). Caucusgoers were also found to be more ideological than those who did not participate—more liberal (Democrats) or more conservative (Republicans) (Stone, Abramowitz, and Rapoport 1989). One key reason those who attend are different might be that the apparent complexity of the caucus system in Iowa and other states can deter participation, especially by those who are less committed to their candidate or party. It also takes considerably more time to attend a caucus than to cast a vote in a normal election.

Wang (2007) has an even stronger critique, as she condemns caucuses in general as antiparticipatory:

> Caucuses, as opposed to primaries, by their very structure violate fundamental principles of voting rights. Their time-consuming, inflexible, Byzantine procedures discourage broad participation, presenting substantial barriers to the right to vote. It is not that the caucuses violate the Constitution—they are run by the parties, not the states, and do not violate voting rights as a matter of law. Rather, because of their exclusionary nature, they go against some of the core values we express when we talk about voting rights, such as the fundamental nature of the right, equality of opportunity to participate in the process, and fair access to the ballot. (Wang 2007, 1)

The conventional wisdom about the Iowa caucuses is that they are unrepresentative of Iowa's registered voter population, and Iowa is in turn unrepresentative of the nation. It is not just that Iowa is 96%

white, but also that it has no large cities, and agricultural issues are of great importance (Winebrenner 1998; Hull 2007). The problem of representation is linked to the issue of turnout. With low turnout comes the distinct possibility that those who do show up will be highly unrepresentative of the larger population. As other research on nomination contests shows, those who do participate are typically the strongest partisans (Norrander 1989; Squire 1989; Stone, Abramowitz, and Rapoport 1989; Stone, Rapoport, and Abramowitz 1992), leading to the fear that they are more likely to reflect extremes rather than a presumed partisan middle ground. The concern over this possibility of nominating a candidate too liberal to be elected in the general election was one reason Democrats created "superdelegates." (Kamarck 2009). Superdelegates attend the convention but are unpledged to any candidate. In 2008 they comprised 20% of all Democratic National Convention delegates. In theory, superdelegates would be able to "fix" errors made by unrepresentative primary electorates.[2]

That those who participate in nominating events are different from those who do not seems almost obvious, so it is no surprise that evidence of the unrepresentativeness of the Iowa caucuses appears readily available. Wang (2007), for example, cites media sources reporting that the caucuses are primarily populated by older voters, and claims that 64% of 2004 Democratic caucusgoers were over the age of fifty.[3] And while detailed historical data on who turns out is difficult to come by, one study of the Iowa caucuses from 1984 through 2000 puts the mean age of attendees at 51 years, with a standard deviation of 15.5 (University of Northern Iowa 2008), which is roughly the same as reported in our post-caucus telephone survey in chapter 5.[4] Stone, Rapoport, and Abramowitz (1989) used extensive survey data from the 1984 Iowa Democratic caucus to show that participants had higher socioeconomic status than statewide registered voters—as noted earlier, they were older and better educated, and had higher incomes. Both Democrats and Republicans who attend the caucuses are more likely to have graduated from college than their respective counterparts from Iowa or the national electorate (Squire 1989). They are also more committed to and active in their party than the average citizen.

In chapter 5 we took great pains to show that at least in 2008, those who attended the Iowa caucuses were much more likely to be rank-and-file members of their party rather than activists. But even if we were to show that Iowa caucusgoers were an exact match for those who stayed home, critics would continue to complain about Iowa's role, using the broader point that Iowa itself is unrepresentative of the entire nation (see Hull [2007] for a summary of this argument). As is well known, Iowa is much more racially homogenous than the country as a whole and is more reliant on an agricultural economy. Yet it has a rapidly growing Latino population (almost 4% of the population in 2008), which has increased 27% since 2000. In fact, Iowa is one of the top five states in Latino population growth.[5] Even so, it is hard to argue that the state "looks like" the country as a whole. But on the other hand, it is hard to argue that any one state looks like the country as a whole, even a state as large and diverse as California, which perhaps ironically has a much higher Latino population than the national average. While allowing that Iowa may be demographically unrepresentative of the nation, economically it has been shown to be one of the most representative states in the Union (Lewis-Beck and Squire 2009).

In the end, these claims about representativeness matter because of the outsized effect Iowa plays in the nominating process, as we will detail in chapters 7 and 8. Accepting that no one state can be perfectly representative of the nation, given the sequential structure of the presidential nominating process, it remains important to understand the extent to which the Iowa caucuses are skewed in ways that make it an inappropriate starting point. And given that turnout is clearly related to representativeness, we need to start by taking another look at the conventional wisdom on Iowa caucus turnout.

Turnout at the Iowa Caucuses

Turnout and representativeness are related because lower turnout generally implies a less representative electorate. So if turnout at the Iowa caucuses is truly as low as 6% (in 2004), those who do show up are likely to be only the most active of the activists, the most extreme of their parties. The question of measuring turnout would seem to be a simple empirical one based on the number in attendance and the number who could potentially show up on caucus day. Yet standard turnout statistics like McDonald's (2008a) 16% turnout in 2008 may be misleading where nominating events are concerned, because the proper baseline is not a state's voting eligible population (VEP) or even total registered voters, but members of the political party holding the event. Caucuses are run by parties and are party affairs. As we discussed in chapter 3, they are used not only to nominate candidates for elected office but also to take care of party business.

Calculations such as those by McDonald, which have been widely cited in the media, are thus only one measure of turnout. The VEP simply may not be the relevant base. Because caucuses are political party activities, we should expect that it is primarily partisans who participate in them. In particular, although the Iowa caucuses are open to all voters, one must be willing to actually register with a party before being allowed to enter the caucus. Thus, the caucuses are at best a semi-open event.[6] Using VEP as the base for turnout calculations in nomination contests fails to recognize that many voters (like independents, who represent one-third of the Iowa electorate) choose to disassociate themselves from either major party. Second, and perhaps more important, the 6.1% turnout figure generally cited for 2004 ignores the fact that there was no competition on the Republican side, since President Bush was unchallenged for the nomination. To include all voters as the turnout base when only one party holds a nominating event depresses reported participation and understates the true involvement of voters in the nominating process.

We are by no means the first to make such a point about nomination electorates. Geer (1988) traced the arguments about the representativeness of primary electorates and pointed out that the appropriate comparison is not the general electorate but those who actively "follow" the party, and who are likely to support it in the general election. In a similar vein, we argue that the base for calculating nomination contest turnout should include only party members. By this standard, 2004 Iowa caucus turnout was about 23% of registered Democrats.[7] What about Republicans? Even without a nomination contest, about 11,000 Republicans showed up to carry out the other party business Iowans conduct at their caucuses. While the Iowa VEP in 2008 was approximately 2.2 million people, the total population of registered Democrats was 644,690, of whom about 239,000 participated in Democratic caucuses (Grose and Russell 2008). More than 1 in 3 registered Democrats (37%) participated, as did 20% of registered Republicans. Combined, about 30% of all Iowa partisans caucused in 2008.[8] Whether one sees turnout at the Iowa caucuses as miserably low or acceptable has a lot to do with the baseline used for the eligible population, and whether citizens who are not registered with either party (independents) are included.

The Question of Representativeness

But even 37 and 20% partisan turnout seems low, compared with what we might expect given the importance attached to the Iowa caucuses. And low turnout may lead to our second problem—an unrepresentative group of voters may make choices that do not reflect their party's mainstream. While arguments about the appropriate base for turnout calculations may be in the eye of the beholder, the question of whether those who do turn out are representative of their parties is one we can test empirically.

Given that candidates spend months in Iowa implementing tradi-tional retail politics and that the media pay an inordinate amount of at-tention to them, we have some positive expectations about Iowa caucus attendees. While they may be more partisan than registered voters as a whole, caucusgoers are also likely to be better informed, more aware of political issues, more involved, and in general much more likely to be the kind of citizens political scientists always want to find—"homo politicus" (Dahl 1961.) However, few scientific studies of caucus attendees exist in the literature.

Why does it matter whether the Iowa caucuses are representative at least of Iowa voters in general? To presage later chapters in this book, re-sults of these caucuses affect the overall nominating process, not just in 2008, but over the last thirty years as well. Hull's (2007) recent analysis of Iowa's impact suggests that its influence is growing, as the state gen-erates a new kind of momentum based on the Internet resources candi-dates develop and exploit during the caucus campaigns (see Haynes and Pitts [2009]). And there is no doubt that whatever impact Iowa might have for those candidates who win or at least beat expectations, it clearly winnows the field, eliminating those who do not do well and structuring the choices faced by later states in the nominating process. If Iowa does in fact matter for later contests, then we should hope that its caucusgoers represent their own party well.

We may indeed have some hope in this respect, at least when we look at the competitive 2008 nomination. Most of the existing system-atic research on the Iowa caucus dates from the 1988 caucuses, which were competitive for both parties. A lot has happened since then. The increase in turnout in 2008 should mean, if nothing else, that those who showed up were more representative of their parties as a whole than may have been the case in the past. This is what we explore in the remainder of this chapter.

Surveys of Iowa Caucus and Registered Voters

What follows is drawn from our three Iowa statewide random-sample telephone surveys, conducted at the University of Iowa during 2007. Each was conducted ahead of the caucuses: one in March, another in early August, and the third in late October.[9] These surveys offer snapshots of the Iowa electorate and the evolving differences between registered voters and likely caucus attendees. The first survey was in the field March 19 through 31, 2007, with a sample of 1,290 registered voters. It included 1,170 registered voters and 489 self-identified likely caucus attendees. The second survey was conducted from July 29 through August 5, 2007. This survey utilized a split-sample format, with a 907-respondent registered voter sample and a 555-respondent likely caucus attendee sample. The third survey was conducted October 17 through 24, 2007, again with two samples: a 564-respondent registered voter sample and a likely caucus attendee sample of 550 respondents.[10] In addition, as we described in chapters 4 and 5, a fourth telephone survey of those who actually attended a caucus was conducted immediately after the January 3, 2008, caucuses. We use this survey—rather than our pencil-and-paper in-caucus survey—as the reference point, because its mode of collection is the same as all the precaucus surveys.

Who Caucused in 2008? Are Likely Caucus Attendees Representative of Iowa Voters?

Pundits and scholars have accused the Iowa caucuses of being undemocratic and unrepresentative of the nation as a whole and even of Iowa itself. Consequently, we examine four areas of comparison between registered voters and those who reported as being likely to attend a caucus: partisanship, basic demographic and attitudinal characteristics, and candidate choice.[11]

Partisanship and Caucus Attendance in 2008

Table 6.1 presents the distribution of the registered voter and caucus samples by party identification, using a standard 7-point scale. We provide the registered voter samples for comparison, though of course we do not expect much change in those over time except for random

TABLE 6.1. Partisan strength: Comparing Iowa registered voters and caucus attendees (likely and actual)

	% of registered voter sample			% of all likely caucus attendees			% of all actual caucus attendees	% of own party sample			% of own party likely caucus attendees			% of own party actual caucus attendees
	March 2007	August 2007	October 2007	March 2007	August 2007	October 2007	January 2008	March 2007	August 2007	October 2007	March 2007	August 2007	October 2007	January 2008
Strong Democrat	24.1	22.4	22.0	36.2	35.4	34.4	28.52	45.7	43.6	45.1	58.2	61.6	60.0	49.35
Weak Democrat	12.6	12.5	10.6	13.7	10.0	11.6	9.94	24.3	24.3	21.7	21.8	17.3	19.0	17.21
Independent lean Democrat	15.2	16.5	16.2	11.8	12.1	14.1	19.32	30.0	32.3	33.2	20.0	21.1	21.0	33.44
Independent	6.3	9.3	5.0	1.5	2.4	1.5	n/a	n/a	n/a	n/a	n/a	n/a	n/a	n/a
Independent lean Republican	10.3	10.2	11.0	6.4	6.4	7.6	8.82	24.9	26.0	23.9	17.8	15.9	18.4	20.89
Weak Republican	12.9	11.7	12.3	9.0	11.4	8.9	9.94	30.6	29.9	26.6	21.3	28.5	20.7	23.56
Strong Republican	18.6	17.4	22.9	21.4	22.3	21.9	23.45	44.6	44.1	49.6	60.9	55.6	60.9	55.56

Source: Results from the University of Iowa Hawkeye Polls.
Note: For March survey, N = 1,170 for registered voters sample. N = 489 for likely caucus sample. For August survey, N = 907 for registered voters sample. N = 555 for likely caucus sample. For October survey, N = 564 for registered voters sample. N = 550 for likely caucus sample. For January survey, N = 533 for caucus attendee sample.

sample error, and possibly small movements one way or the other by voters. Overall, the partisan makeup of each registered voter sample remained fairly constant over all three precaucus surveys, with the exception of some increase in strong Republicans by October 2007, offset by a
decline in the pure independent group. These small changes are clearly
a matter of sampling.

In contrast, the likely caucus attendee samples show some interesting patterns when compared with registered voters. Even a quick glance
at table 6.1 shows that strong partisans made up a disproportionately
large share of the likely caucus attendees. Strong Democrats, for example, comprised on average about 22% of the Iowa's registered voter population in the three surveys, but represented about 35% of all likely caucus attendees surveyed. In comparison, while strong Republicans made
up about 20% or so of the registered voters on average, they were about
22% of our likely caucus attendee sample. Thus, while strong Democrats
appear to significantly overrepresent their share of their party's caucus attendees, strong Republican likely caucus attendees appear by this
measure to track closely to their representation in the registered voter
samples.

Pure independents, although allowed to vote at a caucus after reg-
istering on the spot for the party of their choice, are underrepresented
among likely caucus participants, accounting for less than 2.5% of that
group in all three surveys, compared with 5 to 9% among registered voters. This is not surprising, since the caucuses are partisan events and
pure independents are unlikely to see themselves going.[12] But in looking
at independents who claim they "lean" in one direction or the other, we
see the same pattern. Both independent Democrats and Republicans are
significantly underrepresented among those who say they plan to caucus. Thus by these measures, the caucuses do appear to represent those
who are strong partisans much more than those who are weaker in their
party support.

But all of this is about people who say they plan to caucus. What about
those who actually did? Between our October survey and the actual caucus in January, the intensity of the 2008 caucus campaigns did nothing but grow. Candidates made more visits, campaigns contacted more
potential voters, and the media wrote many more stories. Perhaps this
level of intensity has implications for those who earlier were less likely
to caucus. Our January postcaucus survey reveals two very interesting
patterns. First, and foremost, the strong partisan bias (especially for

Democrats) of the likely caucus samples is virtually eliminated by caucus night. Strong Democrats represent about 28% of actual caucusgoers, compared with about 22% of registered voters. And strong Republicans are likewise not so different overall: just 23% of our total sample, almost exactly what they represent in the October registered voter sample. Moreover, the representation of independents improves significantly in both parties, actually exceeding their percentage for Democrats in the registered voter sample. The evidence appears to suggest that on caucus night 2008, those who attended were not all that much different in terms of partisan strength from those who did not.

Even more interestingly, our data show clearly what happens when a caucus campaign increases in competitiveness and intensity, and thus in turnout. Across all three precaucus surveys, the percentage of likely caucus attendees who said they were independent "leaners" grows substantially for the Democrats (from 11.8% of the full sample in March 2007 to 14.1% in October) and then jumps to over 19% on caucus night. The growth for Republicans is more muted, as befits the fact that their campaign was less intense and only half as many people showed up. The result is that by the caucus, over 27% of those attending initially call themselves independents when asked for their party preference, compared with just over 32% of registered voters in October 2007. Clearly, the increased turnout and intense competition led the 2008 caucus to be much more representative of registered voters as a whole than many commentators and researchers would have anticipated. In contrast to previous literature (Stone, Abramowitz, and Rapoport 1989), we find that actual caucus attenders may be not only party activists (or strong partisans), but also a large proportion of independents or nonpartisans.

The second half of table 6.1 shows the percentage that each partisan category occupies of its own party's samples. While the numbers differ, this analysis actually makes it even clearer that caucusgoers in 2008 were not overly likely to be strong partisans. In October, while strong partisans made up between 45 and 50% of their own party sample, among likely caucus attendees they were at 60% for both parties. But between late October and January 3, those with weaker partisan ties clearly became mobilized, so that on caucus night all partisan groups were represented in rough proportion to their prevalence in the Iowa registered voter population. So while there is evidence in the literature that both primaries and caucuses exaggerate the influence of strong partisans over independents and moderates (Fiorina, Abrams, and Pope 2004;

Donovan and Bowler 2004), in Iowa in 2008 this influence was greatly muted.

Demographic and Attitudinal Characteristics

We see that as the caucus campaigns heated up throughout 2007, they appear to have mobilized not only strong partisans, but also those who were much more moderate in their partisan preferences. The nature of a competitive campaign of any type is that it reaches more people than a noncompetitive campaign. As more money is spent on voter outreach, more potential voters are brought into the fold. The remaining question is whether in increasing interest and turnout, these competitive campaigns also improved representativeness in other ways. Table 6.2 reports a number of demographic and attitudinal measures from the earliest precaucus survey (March), the later one (October), and the actual caucusgoer survey.[13] Thus we can track changes, if any, in the nature of those who said they were likely to caucus and those who actually did.

EDUCATION.   The greatest difference in demographic characteristics between likely caucus attendees and registered Iowa voters is educational attainment, as seen in table 6.2. Those with only a high school diploma or less are underrepresented in the likely caucus sample in both March and October, and among both Democrats and Republicans. The greatest disparity exists in the Democratic Party sample from the October survey. Here those with no education after high school accounted for 37.2% of the registered voter sample but only 24.9% of the caucus sample—a difference of 12.3 percentage points. Among our respondents, those who told us in March or October 2007 that they were likely to caucus were clearly better educated than the registered voter population as a whole. Yet by caucus night things had changed as more voters became mobilized. Those with only a high school diploma accounted for 30.7% of actual Democratic caucus attendees, closing the gap by about 5 points. Still, a gap remained, as college-educated respondents made up a greater percentage of the caucus sample than they do the registered voter sample in all instances examined, particularly among the Democrats, even by caucus night. The Republican subsamples are surprisingly similar on education, with no difference between the registered voter sample and the caucus sample reaching 5 percentage points. This may be accounted for by the greater homogeneity within the Republican Party in the first place.

TABLE 6.2. Demographics and issue salience: Comparing Iowa registered voters and caucus attendees (likely and actual)

	All respondents					Democrats					Republicans				
	March 2007		October 2007		January 2008	March 2007		October 2007		January 2008	March 2007		October 2007		January 2008
	Registered	Likely caucus	Registered	Likely caucus	Actual caucus attendees	Registered	Likely caucus	Registered	Likely caucus	Actual caucus Attendees	Registered	Likely caucus	Registered	Caucus	Actual caucus attendees
Education															
H.S. diploma or less	34.1	27.8	32.9 (39)	24.6	27.6	33.8	26.7	37.2	24.9	30.7	33.0	29.2	28.0	23.9	23.4
Some college (4-year or technical)	27.9	26.2	38.9 (34)	29.2	26.3	26.8	23.7	30.1	27.9	26.3	27.2	27.9	27.6	30.3	25.7
Bachelor's	23.5	25.5	25.2 (19)	30.4	26.5	21.9	24.4	17.7	28.9	21.0	27.5	27.9	33.3	33.5	34.1
Postbachelor's	14.5	20.5	13.0 (9)	15.8	19.7	17.5	25.1	15.0	18.4	21.7	12.3	15.2	11.1	12.2	16.8
Total	100	100	100	100	100	100	100	100	100	100	100	100	100	100	100
Income															
Less than 30k	20.4	15.2	24.0 (26)	21.4	16.6	24.4	16.3	28.5	22.6	22.2	15.9	14.2	19.5	19.6	9.1
30k to under 50k	28.2	24.8	19.3 (23)	20.3	24.8	28.1	26.8	19.2	21.9	24.6	27.0	21.4	19.0	19.0	25.1
50k to under 75k	18.4	20.2	22.8 (22)	23.5	23.9	14.9	16.0	23.3	24.2	22.2	21.9	24.4	22.1	22.2	26.2
75k and up	33.0	39.9	34.0 (29)	34.8	34.6	32.6	41.0	29.0	31.3	31.0	35.2	40.1	39.5	39.2	39.6
Total	100	100	100	100	100	100	100	100	100	100	100	100	100	100	100
Gender															
Female	52.7	50.6	58.5 (54)	56.4	53.3	57.1	58.6	64.3	60.3	56.2	46.8	38.3	53.4	52.1	50.7
Male	47.3	49.4	41.5 (46)	43.6	46.7	42.9	41.4	35.7	39.7	43.8	53.3	61.7	46.6	47.9	49.3
Total	100	100	100	100	100	100	100	100	100	100	100	100	100	100	100
Marital status															
Not married	24.1	23.7	29.6	31.3	28.7	28.7	28.3	31.0	32.3	34.3	17.9	17.3	29.1	30.0	20.8
Married	76.0	76.3	70.4	68.7	71.3	71.3	71.7	69.0	67.7	65.7	82.1	82.7	70.9	70.1	29.3
Total	100	100	100	100	100	100	100	100	100	100	100	100	100	100	100

Age															
18–29	4.9	6.4	5.3 (16)	6.2	7.4	5.1	6.8	5.3	6.6	6.3	5.3	6.5	5.0	5.4	9.0
30–44	17.1	13.9	17.0 (23)	15.3	13.9	16.4	11.2	16.4	15.8	10.7	18.6	15.8	18.3	13.0	18.5
45–59	34.3	34.7	33.4 (31)	34.5	35.2	38.6	39.8	34.1	33.9	37.7	33.9	32.6	32.0	36.2	31.8
60 and up	43.7	45.1	44.3 (29)	44.0	43.4	40.0	42.2	44.3	43.8	45.3	42.2	45.1	44.8	45.4	40.8
Total	100	100	100	100	100	100	100	100	100	100	100	100	100	100	100
Religion															
Protestant	68.3	69.4	63.7	59.9	60.8	62.62	63.1	57.0	53.5	52.4	75.5	81.8	68.4	71.7	72.5
Roman Catholic	20.1	17.5	23.1	24.9	26.3	22.24	19.5	24.4	27.6	30.3	16.5	12.1	23.2	17.7	20.9
Other	11.6	13.1	13.2	15.3	12.9	15.14	17.5	18.6	18.9	17.4	8.0	6.1	8.4	10.7	6.6
Total	100	100	100	100	100	100	100	100	100	100	100	100	100	100	100
Born-again															
Yes	31.2	28.7	29.7	24.9	28.2	19.98	16.8	20.1	13.2	17.6	43.5	43.6	36.6	42.4	40.9
No	68.8	71.3	70.3	75.1	71.9	80.02	83.2	79.9	86.8	82.4	56.6	56.4	63.4	57.6	59.9
Total	100	100	100	100	100	100	100	100	100	100	100	100	100	100	100
Issues (% who say issue is "very important" for their presidential vote)*															
Immigration	47.8	49.1	50.3	46.1	37.3	41.3	40.1	39.8	34.4	23.8	56.0	63.1	58.8	66.3	44.0
Iraq	26.6	29.2	26.3	27.5	19.3	38.5	42.2	36.7	34.9	26.5	44.4	41.6	19.1	15.8	9.3
Abortion	36.8	36.6	37.1	36.5	32.6	29.9	32.2	34.2	31.4	22.3	38.9	41.6	40.8	44.1	47.0
Gay marriage	25.2	25.3	25.2	22.5	19.5	14.5	15.0	13.2	13.6	9.9	19.2	26.7	35.8	38.2	33.0
Economy	11.5	10.5	15.0	15.0	21.4	11.4	9.7	11.6	15.8	19.9	13.2	11.8	15.9	14.1	23.7
Terrorism	9.6	12.5	10.7	9.6	8.9	2.1	2.6	2.3	1.7	.3	12.4	10.0	19.1	23.4	20.9

Source: Results from the University of Iowa Hawkeye Polls. Figures in parentheses are from the 2006 Current Population Survey of Iowa registered voters. These are used for comparison only.

Note: For March survey, $N = 1,170$ for registered voters sample, $N = 489$ for likely caucus sample. For August survey, $N = 844$ for registered voters sample, $N = 555$ for likely caucus sample. For October survey, $N = 564$ for registered voters sample, $N = 550$ for likely caucus sample. For January survey, $N = 533$ for caucus attendee sample.

*Issue marginals (last six rows) are the result of multiple questions, thus the categories do not add up to 100%. Immigration, abortion, and gay marriage percentages are the result of two questions and should not be compared directly to totals on Iraq, economy, or terrorism. All cross-tabs are statistically significant, with a 95% confidence interval using a chi-square test.

INCOME.   Perhaps the most surprising finding presented in table 6.2 is the similarity between the proportion of respondents from each income group in the registered voter samples and the likely caucus attendee samples as well as those who actually attended on January 3. Further, income differences appear to have decreased as the campaign went on, for samples from the October survey show greater similarity than do those using the March data. On the Democratic side in the October survey, the poorest category (those making less than $30,000 a year) accounted for about 6% less in the caucus sample than in the registered voter sample; this is twice the size of any other difference. On the Republican side in the October survey, no difference between the two samples is greater than 1 percentage point. The overall message here is one of surprising consistency. The 2008 caucuses simply do not appear to be unrepresentative of lower income groups. Even our sample of postcaucus attendees appears to show that in terms of income groups, caucus participants closely matched the registered voter population.

GENDER.   The gender makeup of the likely caucus samples and the registered voter samples is also surprisingly similar. Only the Republican Party sample from March shows evidence of substantive skewness: men accounted for 8.4% more of the likely caucus sample than the Iowa registered voter sample. Yet the January postcaucus telephone sample shows that both men and women accounted for roughly 50% of Republican caucus attendees. Other than that, however, all the differences between the caucus samples and the registered voter samples fall well within the margin of error for each survey and subsample.

MARITAL STATUS.   A similar story can be told regarding marital status. Married respondents made up roughly the same percentage of registered voters as likely caucusgoers, for both surveys and both parties as well as in terms of actual turnout in January.

AGE.   Another often-used critique of the Iowa caucuses is that they are biased toward older voters. Our data, however, contradict this claim and the Century Foundation's recent report (Wang 2007). While over 40% of all respondents who said they were likely to attend a caucus were over the age of sixty, and the same percentage showed up on caucus night, this number matches the share of the registered voter sample that is over sixty. This similarity is also found in both party subsamples. In other words, if voters in Iowa are skewed to the elderly, it is a skew that affects the entire group of registered voters who responded to our survey and is not due to the particulars of the caucus system.

RELIGION.   Likely caucusgoers do differ from registered voters on religion, particularly in the Republican subsample. Caucusgoing Republicans were more likely to be Protestant and less likely to be Roman Catholic in both the March and October surveys. Also, likely Republican caucus attendees were 5.8% more likely to say they are born-again Christians in October, an increase over the March results. This overtime increase may be attributable to the emergence of former Arkansas governor and Southern Baptist minister Mike Huckabee, the eventual Republican winner in Iowa. Likely Democratic caucus attendees, on the other hand, were less likely to be born-again Christians than were the registered Democrats. By the time the caucus happened, these effects were smaller, so while more born-again Christians actually caucused compared with their share of Republican registered voters, the share declined a bit to 41% from October.

ISSUES.[14]   How Iowans viewed the importance of a series of issues during the caucus campaign does reflect some polarization in the likely caucus sample, particularly on the issue of immigration. In the October survey, likely Democratic caucus attendees were over 5% *less* likely than registered Democrats to say that immigration was important to them. Republicans, however, show the opposite effect, with likely Republican caucus attendees over 7% more likely than registered Republicans to stress the importance of immigration. There was also a trend for likely Republican caucusgoers to care more about social issues like abortion and gay marriage than did Republican registered voters on a whole. Trying to make comparisons on issues by the time of the January caucus is somewhat problematic, since we do not have a registered voter sample to compare in January. While we would not expect significant demographic changes among registered voters between late October and early January, it is quite certain that opinions regarding which issue was most important and even which issues were very important changed over that time. National surveys over the period show, for example, that the condition of the economy became increasingly important to voters over the course of both 2007 and 2008, while issues such as the Iraq war became somewhat less so.

In summary, we find few significant differences between likely caucus attendees and registered Iowa voters in terms of socioeconomic status or attitudes, with some exceptions, most clearly education and religious preference. Caucusgoers were in fact better educated than registered voters overall, and in that way the caucuses are unrepresentative. But the big picture for 2008 is that those who attended the Iowa caucuses looked (demographically) and thought (in terms of partisanship) remarkably like those who were registered voters but did not choose to attend.[15] What differences do show up in the March sample are mostly gone by the time of caucus day in January. We suggest that this has a lot to do with the competitiveness of the 2008 campaigns on both sides of the aisle.

Candidate Support

Table 6.3 presents support for the major candidates of both parties by registered voters versus caucus attendees. The key point is that not surprisingly, likely caucusgoers from both parties were much more likely to support a candidate than were the registered voters, who were more likely to respond "don't know." The result is that nearly every candidate did at least somewhat better among likely caucusgoers than among registered voters. In fact, only Hillary Clinton fared worse among the caucus samples than among the registered voter samples, perhaps because her support was very strong among those with the least education, who were less likely to caucus (Redlawsk, Bowen, and Tolbert 2008). In contrast, by October former North Carolina senator John Edwards, Huckabee, and Romney all received more support among those saying they would be likely caucus participants than among registered Iowa voters.

While there is no point comparing actual results in January with registered voter preferences in October, the January results show how hard it is to do head-to-head polling in Iowa, given that there is no clear definition of a likely caucusgoer, and that in 2008 all the traditional expectations of who would caucus seemed inoperative. It is especially interesting that our postcaucus survey results for the Republican caucuses are quite close to what actually happened, while our Democratic caucus results significantly overstate support for Edwards and understate support for both Clinton (by about 4 points) and Obama (by about 7 points).[16] The reason, we believe, has everything to do with the fact that Iowa Democrats do not report actual vote totals (as we described in chapter

TABLE 6.3. **Candidate support by Iowa registered voters and caucus attendees (likely and actual)**

	March 2007			August 2007			October 2007			January 2008	
	Registered	Likely caucus	difference	Registered	Likely caucus	difference	Registered	Likely Caucus	Difference	Caucus attendee	Official results
Democrats											
Edwards	23.1	35.3	+12.2	16.3	26.7	+10.4	9.5	20.0	+10.5	37.3	30.0
Clinton	24.4	28.7	+4.3	29.9	24.7	−5.2	32.9	28.9	−4.0	25.1	29.0
Obama	16.6	21.2	+4.6	20.7	21.6	+0.9	21.7	26.6	+4.9	31.0	38.0
Richardson	1.6	1.1	−0.5	5.6	9.6	+4.0	3.5	7.2	+3.7	3.0	2.0
Don't know**	27.6	11.9	−15.7	22.8	14.4	−8.4	25.1	8.9	−16.2	0.0	—
Others	6.8	1.8	−5.0	4.8	3.0	−1.8	7.4	8.5	+1.1	3.3	1.0
Republicans											
Giuliani	15.9	21.6	+5.7	9.3	11.9	+2.6	10.3	13.8	+3.5	4.1	4.0
Huckabee	0.8	1.9	+1.1	2.2	1.9	−0.3	3.7	13.8	+10.1	33.6	35.0
McCain	14.5	21.2	+6.7	2.2	3.3	+1.1	2.9	4.3	+1.4	15.0	13.0
Romney	9.9	18.1	+8.2	20.4	28.4	+8.0	23.4	36.7	+13.3	26.4	25.0
Thompson, F.	—	—	—	5.1	8.1	+3.0	6.3	10.6	+4.3	12.7	13.0
Don't know**	40.0	23.5	−16.5	36.3	27.6	−8.7	38.5	14.4	−24.1	0.0	—
Others	18.9	13.7	−5.2	24.6	18.9	−5.7	15.3	6.4	−8.9	8.2	10.0

Source: Results from the University of Iowa Hawkeye Polls.

Note: For March 2007 survey, $N = 1,170$ for registered voters sample, $N = 489$ for likely caucus sample. For August 2007 survey, $N = 844$ for registered voters sample, $N = 555$ for likely caucus sample. For October 2007 survey, $N = 564$ for registered voters sample, $N = 550$ for likely caucus sample. For January survey, $N = 533$ for caucus attendee sample. For January official results, source is Iowa Democratic and Republican Parties, respectively.

**Caucus attendees of both parties less likely to say don't know. Edwards, Romney, and Huckabee have higher support among likely caucus attendees that registered voters. The other gaps are within the margin of error.

3) but instead the number of delegates each candidate wins to the county conventions, whereas Republicans report the results of a straw poll of all caucus attendees. Convention delegates are apportioned ahead of time based on Democratic voting strength in the precinct as defined by the previous two general elections, and not based on the attendance at the precinct caucus itself (as we detailed in chapter 3). Thus, more turnout does not result in a larger number of delegates being elected.

Conclusion and Implications for Reform

Despite conventional wisdom, published media reports, and previous research arguing that the Iowa caucuses are unrepresentative, we find that the socioeconomic status of likely and actual caucus attendees and registered Iowa voters was surprisingly similar in 2008. Even the partisanship of actual caucusgoers and registered voters was more similar than we expected from previous research (Squire 1989; Stone, Abramowitz, and Rapoport 1989). Although caucus attendees are somewhat more partisan, other research suggests this does not lead to significant divergences in candidate choice due to strategic voting, where participants seek to elect a candidate most likely to win their party's nomination regardless of their own preferences (Norrander 1989; Geer 1988). It may be that the relatively intense Iowa campaign mobilizes a less committed and more "typical" citizen than nomination campaigns in other states. The reason for the different candidate preferences between likely caucus attendees in March and October 2007 and registered voters overall as reported in table 6.3 must be the results of campaign effects and increased political interest and engagement among caucus attendees. Chapters 2 and 9 of this book and Hull (2007) describe the intensity of the media and online information campaign in Iowa in 2008 and 2004. The 2008 caucuses clearly broke records in many categories, including candidate spending, attention paid by candidates and the media, and, of course, attendance. Figure 6.1 shows that likely caucus attendees responded to this media campaign, and were much more engaged and interested in politics than were the average voters. Seventy percent of those planning to attend the Democratic caucus had "thought a lot about the campaign," and 70% had watched a debate, while over 40% were "very excited" by the election in the late October survey. If another state had experienced the campaign and media attention of Iowa, we might expect similar

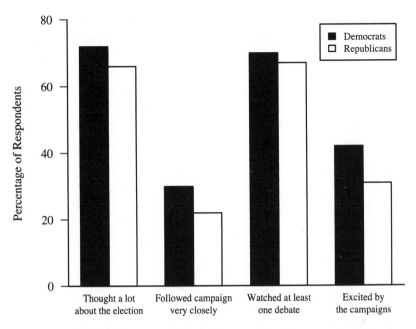

FIGURE 6.1. Iowa caucusgoers' campaign involvement, late October 2007 survey.

awareness of the political campaign and similar choices among party candidates.

Iowa may not look like the rest of the country, but those who attended the 2008 caucuses well represented Iowa voters in general (more than 80% of Iowans are registered to vote) and its partisans in particular. Moreover, recent research suggests that while Iowa may differ demographically from the "mean" of all states, economically it may be the median state. Lewis-Beck and Squire (2009) show convincing evidence that on a wide variety of economic measures, Iowa is essentially the most average of states, which may be particularly important in presidential elections, where the economy itself is often a key factor in voters' decisions (Lewis-Beck and Paldam 2000; Lewis-Beck 1988).

Of course, the reality is that nomination electorates are *nearly always* more liberal or conservative than the population as a whole (although see Geer [1988] for a counterargument on ideology). They are never "representative" of all voters. After all, caucuses and primaries are not general elections—they are elections to choose who will represent the party in the general election. Our results are surprising in that we find the socioeconomic status of Iowa caucusgoers and registered voters were quite similar in 2008, a unique year with high turnout which significantly dampened distortions between those who caucused and registered voters overall. While the caucuses are relatively low-turnout affairs, in contrast to previous research we find they appear to be fairly representative of the Iowa electorate, at least when both the competition between candidates and the intensity of the media spotlight are at the levels they were in 2008.

PART III
Sequential Voting Rules

Effects of Iowa and New Hampshire in U.S. Presidential Nomination Contests 1976–2008

With Rob Hunsaker

[Iowans] pick corn . . . New Hampshire picks presidents. — New Hampshire governor John Sununu, 1988

U p to this point we have focused on Iowa and the rules of its caucuses. We have shown that in 2008, Iowa caucus attendees looked a lot like Iowa registered voters overall. We have described how the caucuses run and considered how the 2008 campaigns worked to mobilize Iowans and resulted in record turnout. All this is interesting in its own right, especially for Iowans, but the broader impact of Iowa is yet to be shown. So now it is time to focus on the second set of important rules governing American presidential nomination campaigns, those that define the sequential nominating process. Iowa would not have the importance that it does if it were not the first in a string of caucuses and primaries that occur across the nation over several months. The candidate and media focus on Iowa means that voters in later states have access to information that Iowa voters do not. If they make use of this information in making their own decisions, then Iowa's role certainly goes beyond the objective results of the first-in-the-nation caucuses.

Some have argued that despite what candidates think and despite the media attention given to Iowa, Iowa does not really matter very much. Almost as many candidates have won Iowa and gone on to lose their party's nomination as have won Iowa and the nomination. If winning or at least beating expectations in the caucus matters, it may only matter in a limited way, at best exerting some influence on the results of the next contest, the New Hampshire primary. But any effects after that quickly wash out, according to some scholars (Adkins and Dowdle 2001; Mayer 1996, 2003, 2004; Winebrenner 1999). Yet, in this media-driven campaign age, it is simply difficult to imagine Iowa's effects being so limited. Moreover, Hull (2007) gives us reason to doubt this conventional wisdom. So we use this chapter to better explore the question of how Iowa matters, and to see whether former New Hampshire governor John Sununu was right to dismiss its influence on presidential nominations. We do this by systematically examining how results from Iowa affect outcomes in subsequent nomination contests. Our results show strong and robust effects over time, and we demonstrate that the consequences of Iowa do go beyond simply conditioning how voters in New Hampshire respond.

How Iowa "matters" may be determined, at least in part, by how voters and the news media assess whether or not candidates meet or exceed expectations there. The news media appears to use results from Iowa to determine whether candidates deserve its increased or decreased coverage in later states. Voters in these states may form evaluations about candidate viability and electability based on results from the early states, such as Iowa or New Hampshire. Using aggregate election results data from 1976 through 2008, we find that changes in media attention given candidates that are associated with outcomes in Iowa affect candidate performance in the New Hampshire primary. Further, similar shifts in media attention due to results in New Hampshire help predict a candidate's overall vote share across all primaries.

As we have noted, American presidential nomination contests are unique in that they make use of a sequential process in which voters participating in later contests have information about the results of earlier contests. The potential effects that this sequential voting has on information used by voters has been recognized, and a theory of sequential voting associated with this process has been developed and tested with laboratory experiments (Morton and Williams 2001). These elections are also characterized by the fact that they are intrapartisan, or de facto nonpartisan contests. Thus, voters are selecting from a number of candidates within the same party. This lowers the range of policy differentiation across candidates for voters to assess (relative to a partisan contest) and removes major decision cues. Nomination contests with no incumbent remove the two dominant vote cues (party and incumbency) that voters regularly rely on in candidate contests. In this regard, presidential nomination elections may be seen as a relatively low–information, multicandidate choice setting where voters must rely on readily available cues when making decisions (for example, Lupia 1994; McDermott 1997, 1998; Lau and Redlawsk 2001).

Furthermore, scholars have recognized that choices in presidential nomination contests and other electoral settings may be affected not only by preferences for candidates (based on either policies or general likeability), but also by expectations about a candidate's chances of success (viability). Voters and donors may assess candidates in terms of expectations about their prospects for winning the nomination, being elected in November, or both (for example, Abramowitz 1989; Abramson et al. 1992; Mutz 1995). There is also a rich, cross-national literature that provides systematic evidence of "strategic" or "sophisticated" voting in many multiparty (multicandidate) choice settings (for a review see Cox [1997]). For example, we have evidence from elections in Canada, Great Britain, New Zealand, Japan, and elsewhere that some voters may defect from their most preferred choice and vote for a lower-ranked option if they perceive their first option has little chance of winning (Cain 1978; Blais and Nadeau 1996; Karp et al. 2002).

One causal mechanism driving this behavior is voter response to information about a candidate's electoral prospects. This information can come in the form of facts about a party's historic strength in an electoral district, candidate standing in recent opinion polls, or other sources. Some voters are known to adjust their vote intentions strategically in response to information obtained from opinion polls (Bowler and Lanoue 1992; Johnston et al. 1992). Supporters of candidates or parties at the margins of viability may be particularly attentive to, and responsive to, information from these polls (McAllister and Studlar 1991). In sequential nomination elections, voters may also utilize information from early electoral events, adjusting their voting intentions in response to changes in perceptions of candidate viability (Abramson et al. 1992; Bartels 1985).[1]

Strategic voting and "bandwagon" effects are likely to be part of a broader phenomenon referred to as momentum—the advantage gained by candidates because they are perceived to be leading or gaining ground. Scholars are divided as to what momentum means; whether it reflects learning, rational behavior, or irrational behavior (Mutz 1997;

Bartels 1988; Brady and Johnston 1987). That said, the primary way of learning about candidate viability is likely to be the mass media.

Early States and Expectations

Existing research helps us to understand how, and why, early election events can have critical effects on the final outcomes in presidential nomination contests. Here we are interested specifically in how (and why) the Iowa caucuses and New Hampshire primary affect subsequent results in the nominating process, even when these two states play a trivial direct role in the allocation of national convention delegates. Put differently, how do early events in these very small states contribute to candidate momentum in later states' nomination contests?

We propose a model of outcomes in which early events "matter," in part, because news about outcomes in early states serves as a major source of information about candidate viability in a relatively low-information-choice setting. Early nominating events receive disproportionate media attention (relative to their share of delegates), and much of that media attention relates to expectations about a candidate's performance in early contests. The former claim here is uncontroversial, and the latter has been noted elsewhere (Brady and Johnston 1987). In this model, the role of the media can be seen as somewhat analogous to the process in which share-market analysts set corporate earnings expectations. In share markets, when a firm exceeds its earnings expectations, its share price may rise. If it fails to meet expectations, its share price may fall. Likewise, more media attention may be earned by candidates who exceed expectations. Those who fall short of expectations may see their share of news coverage shrink.

In this model we grant the media substantial discretion in setting and adjusting expectations. Reporters, editors, and pundits define the criteria for determining whether a candidate scored an "easy win" or an "upset," was "far behind" or suffered "defeat." There is substantial discretion in framing whether 25% is a "comfortable second" (Bill Clinton, New Hampshire 1992) or 23% is a "strong second" (Pat Buchanan, Iowa 1992); or whether 26% is a "flat tire" (Bob Dole, New Hampshire 1996) or 26% is an "overwhelming defeat" (Howard Dean, New Hampshire 2004).[2]

"Horse-race" coverage of campaigns involves the media handicapping the candidate pool—with a substantial proportion of their coverage focusing on who the front-runners are expected to be, who the under-dogs are, and who beats or fails to meet expectations. Initially, the decision to even report on one particular candidate rather than another, and the amount of attention granted, can be seen as the expression of media expectations. Candidates who are not expected to be players in a contest will receive less media attention—if for no other reason than media resources (column inches, minutes of news time, availability of reporters to cover events, and so on) are finite. Attention must be rationed in favor of candidates who are expected to place relatively high, especially if there are many candidates.

Voters thus receive substantial information about media expectations of candidate viability, and the media's interpretation of whether candidates met, exceeded, or failed to meet expectations. If some voters choose based on expectations about who is viable or electable, election results from early contests and changes in media treatment of candidates associated with these results are likely to be a major source of readily available information for voters in subsequent contests. Although this argument is not wholly original, few (if any) studies have estimated outcomes in U.S. presidential nomination contests as a sequential process that includes adjustments of media expectations associated with results from initial contests.[3] Instead, conventional accounts of outcomes in nomination contests emphasize the role of (1) candidate national opinion standings at the start of the process, (2) candidate financial resources at the start, (3) home state advantages (Norrander 1993), and (4) campaign visits to the state (Hull 2007). But previous studies do not account for how media expectations might be set, nor have many previous studies considered how alterations in media attention given to a candidate associated with an early outcome affect the candidate's prospects in subsequent contests.

Although much of this book relies on our unique series of voter surveys conducted during the 2008 Iowa caucuses and the Super Tuesday primaries, data for this chapter come from nomination contests from 1976 through 2008, providing a longitudinal view of the effect of early nominating events on later voters. These data are used to model initial media attention to candidates, candidate performance in Iowa and New Hampshire, and aggregate performance, including Gallup Poll opinion measures of each candidate's national poll standing as measured before the Iowa caucus, and measures of candidate fund-raising (inflation adjusted) in the year before the caucus. Campaign visits are measured as the candidate's proportionate share of the total days that all candidates from a party spent in Iowa in the year before the caucus. Measures of national media attention to candidates include attention to candidates two weeks before and in the days immediately after the Iowa caucus, and in the week before and immediate days after the New Hampshire primary. A total of ninety-one candidacies are in the data set. Two incumbent presidents who had serious primary challenges (Gerald Ford 1976 and Jimmy Carter 1980) are included, while other incumbents who lacked serious challenge (George H. W. Bush 1992, Clinton 1996, George W. Bush 2004) are excluded, since our chief interest is in competitive nomination contests.[4]

Modeling Expectations: How Iowa and New Hampshire Matter

Given that there is no readily available measure of "media expectations about front-running candidates," we make use of a relatively straightforward surrogate. Information about media expectations for each candidate is represented by the number of times a candidate's name appeared in *New York Times* stories about Iowa and New Hampshire that ran before voting in each state, and in stories that ran after voting.[5] Mentions of candidate names in campaign-related stories were coded, while mentions of candidates in stories about governing were omitted. We make the reasonable assumptions that candidates mentioned the most frequently across several stories are expected to be front-runners.

Total attention to Iowa and New Hampshire is uneven across time. Media attention to individual candidates is measured in a manner that is comparable across time by calculating the proportion of all candidate mentions of each Democrat, and each Republican, respectively. Table 7.1 lists the top candidates for both parties on this measure based on *New York Times* stories about the Iowa caucus that ran two weeks before Iowa. Thus, the table illustrates who received the most Iowa-related media attention before the Iowa caucuses, which we assume to reflect initial (pre-Iowa) media expectations of candidate viability in the state.

We also calculate how media attention to these candidates shifted in the days immediately after Iowa and New Hampshire, respectively, by comparing each candidate's coverage in stories about each state that ran before voting to coverage in articles running after results were known. Table 7.2 lists the candidates with the largest net change in how much they were mentioned in stories about Iowa after the caucus, compared with mentions before voting took place. Table 7.3 lists the same infor-

TABLE 7.1. **Most frequently mentioned candidates in Iowa stories (precaucus)**

	Democrats		Republicans	
1976	Carter	.24	Reagan	.52
	Bayh	.16	Ford	.48
	Udall	.10		
1980	Carter	.60	Regan	.34
	Kennedy	.30	G. H. W. Bush	.31
			Connelly	.11
1984	Mondale	.43	n/a	
	Glenn	.20		
	Askew	.10		
1988	Gephardt	.31	Dole	.42
	Dukakis	.21	G. H. W. Bush	.27
	Simon	.19	Kemp	.15
1992	Harkin	.71	n/a	
	B. Clinton	.11		
1996	n/a		Forbes	.40
			Dole	.22
			Gramm	.13
2000	Bradley	.54	G. W. Bush	.55
	Gore	.46	Forbes	.22
			McCain	.15
2004	Dean	.47	n/a	
	Gephardt	.19		
	Kerry	.14		
2008	Edwards	.33	Romney	.36
	Obama	.28	Huckabee	.29
	H. Clinton	.28	McCain	.15

Note: Cell entries are the candidate's proportionate share of all candidate mentions, within party.

mation for New Hampshire. For example, televangelist Pat Robertson was mentioned quite infrequently in stories about Iowa before the 1988 caucus, but his share of references to all GOP candidates increased by 21 points (from just 10 to 31%) in stories about Iowa published in the days immediately after his second-place finish.

This measure of change in media attention serves as a surrogate measure of how media expectations of candidate viability adjust after Iowa votes. Before the 1988 GOP caucus, expectations (and attention) for Kansas senator Bob Dole, Vice President George H. W. Bush, and New York representative Jack Kemp were higher; after Iowa caucused, expec-

TABLE 7.2. **Largest change in press attention to candidate, 1976–2008: Before and after the Iowa caucus**

Biggest gain		Biggest loss	
B. Clinton, 1992	+24%	Harkin, 1992	−39%
Robertson, 1988	+21%	Edwards, 2008	−21%
Huckabee, 2008	+21%	Forbes, 1996	−19%
Buchanan, 1996	+17%	G. W. Bush, 2000	−18%
Obama, 2008	+17%	Ford, 1976	−12%
Tsongas, 1992	+15%	Gephart, 2004	−10%
Reagan, 1976	+12%	G. H. W. Bush, 1988	−9%
Hart, 1984	+10%	Humphrey, 1976	−9%
Harris, 1976	+9%	Kemp, 1988	−8%
Kerry, 2004	+9%	Dole, 1988	−8%
H. Clinton, 2008	+9%	Gephardt, 2004	−8%
Keyes, 2000	+9%	McCain, 2008	−8%
Forbes, 2000	+8%	McCain, 2000	−8%
Gephardt, 1988	+7%	Mondale, 1984	−7%
Baker, 1980	+7%		

Note: Percentage point change in candidate's share of references among candidates from the same party.

TABLE 7.3. **Largest change in press attention to candidate, 1976–2008: Before and after the New Hampshire primary**

Biggest gain		Biggest loss	
Hart, 1984	+27%	Ford, 1976	−24%
Reagan, 1976	+24%	Forbes, 2000	−21%
McCain, 2000	+19%	Simon, 1988	−12%
Reagan, 1980	+17%	Shriver, 1976	−12%
Carter, 1980	+16%	J. Jackson, 1984	−12%
Carter, 1976	+16%	B. Kerry, 1992	−11%
Paul, 2008	+12%	Bradley, 2000	−10%
B. Clinton, 1992	+11%	Glenn, 1984	−10%
Buchanan, 1996	+11%	Forbes, 1996	−9%
Gore, 2000	+10%	Clark, 2004	−9%
Dole, 1988	+9%	McCain, 2008	−9%
G. W. Bush, 2000	+9%	G. H. W. Bush, 1992	−9%
Buchanan, 1992	+9%	Gephardt, 1988	−9%
Udall, 1976	+8%	Kennedy, 1980	−8%
Kerry, 2004	+8%	Harkin, 1992	−7%
H. Clinton, 2008	+8%	Brown, 1980	−7%

Note: Percentage point change in candidate's share of references among candidates from the same party.

tations about Robertson shifted, and he enjoyed greater media attention before New Hampshire. As another example, Colorado senator Gary Hart received relatively little notice before Iowa (10% of mentions of Democratic candidates in 1984). However, after posting a "surprising" second-place finish there (with just 16%, 32 points behind former vice president Walter Mondale), his share of media attention in postresult coverage of Iowa more than doubled (increasing 10%, to 20% overall), while Mondale's share of attention declined relative to his rivals. Hart's 1984 victory in New Hampshire corresponded with another 27-percentage-point bounce in attention. Political commentator Pat Buchanan enjoyed a similar phenomenon after collecting a mere 22,000 Iowa caucus votes in his "surprise" second-place finish in 1996. Looking from before Iowa to after New Hampshire, in terms of beating initial media expectations, Hart (1984, a 37-point increase in attention), California governor Ronald Reagan (1976, 36 points), Arkansas governor Bill Clinton (1992, 35 points), Buchanan (1996, 28 points), President Jimmy Carter (1976, 20 points), Mike Huckabee (2008, 19 points), New York senator Hillary Clinton (2008, 18 points), Massachusetts senator John Kerry (2004, 17 points), Robertson (1988, 17 points), and Barack Obama (2008, 16 points) rank highest in the net gain in attention from before Iowa to immediately after New Hampshire.[6]

How, then, are initial media expectations set, and how might they predict voting in early events? More important, how do changes in expectations produced by the Iowa results affect voting in a subsequent nominating event (New Hampshire)?[7] Logic suggests several factors that drive the press to give some candidates more early attention: fundraising, poll standing, incumbency,[8] and home state advantages.[9] We expect candidates who raised more money before Iowa, those with higher national poll standings, those from Iowa, and incumbents to receive more initial media attention in the Iowa caucus campaign. We measure campaign fund-raising as total funds raised the year before the Iowa caucus in terms of inflation-adjusted (to 2000) dollars. We also expect that candidates who spent more time in Iowa may generate more media attention in their coverage of the caucus. These factors are used to estimate a candidate's share (proportionately) of total news mentions of candidate names before Iowa. Although some of these items are well correlated, the correlations are by no means perfect.[10] For readers who are interested in the details of our models, they can be found in appendix A. Here we will describe the results, referring to the tables in appendix A.

Table A.7.1 reports results of our model of candidate share of media attention (our surrogate for expectations) in the weeks before Iowa. We find that about 75% of the variance in candidate share of media attention can be explained by fund-raising, poll standing, and share of time spent in Iowa, along with two candidate-specific factors, incumbency and home-state advantage, the latter of which applied in 1992 when Iowa senator Tom Harkin campaigned for president in Iowa. Each additional 10% in opinion standing is associated with 5% greater media attention, and $10 million in fund-raising adds an additional 4.8% share. An additional 10% share of candidate days spent in Iowa leads to an additional 3.2% increase in attention. These results are not surprising, but they do illustrate that money, poll numbers, and days campaigning in Iowa are not perfect predictors of media attention given to candidates in Iowa.

Part of media coverage likely involves setting expectations by interpreting if a lesser-known but well-financed candidate is deserving of as much attention as a well-known officeholder. Indeed, these nomination contests are often frequented by well-financed candidates who gain little traction with voters (former Texas governor John Connelly, $19 million in 1980; Ohio senator John Glenn, $11 million in 1984; Texas senator Phil Gramm, $22.3 million in 1996; Rudy Giuliani, $51 million in 2008), and well-financed candidates who were relatively unknown quantities early on (Robertson, $24 million in 1998; publisher Steve Forbes, $20 million in 1996; Mitt Romney, $74 million in 2008).[11] What, then, are the potential effects of media attention/expectations, independent of candidate poll standing and fund-raising? Or, forgetting pretense to causal arguments, does media attention predict something that fund-raising, campaigning, and poll standing might not?

Table A.7.2 reports estimates of Iowa caucus results from 1976 through 2008, using the standard variables included in models estimating nomination outcomes (Norrander 1993; Mayer 1996, 2003). When standard forecasting variables are used (column 1), money, poll standing, and time in Iowa appear to have substantial power predicting vote share in Iowa. In contrast, when press attention to candidates is used to estimate results, the effects of money and poll standing disappear (whether we model vote share or candidate place of finish), and any effect of time spent in Iowa is greatly truncated. Iowa vote share is also estimated here with an instrumental variable, where press attention predicted by the model reported in table A.7.1 is used to predict Iowa vote share. Again, we see that press coverage of a candidate (predicted by the candidate's fund-raising, polling numbers, and campaigning) outperforms models that use polling, finance, and time spent to predict outcomes in Iowa. How should these results be interpreted? Why would media attention predict as adequately (or better) as direct measures of money, poll status, and days spent in Iowa?

Clearly, media attention to candidates covaries with fund-raising, and there is no easy way to sort out the alternate causal processes that may be at work here. Reporters and editors may be particularly savvy at using information beyond national poll numbers and candidate time spent in Iowa to anticipate who will succeed in Iowa, and thus direct more of their attention to those candidates. After all, there is a qualitative difference between Mory Taylor spending 92 days in Iowa before the 1996 caucus, and Barack Obama spending 89 days there before the 2008 caucus. These results are consistent with a process whereby candidates who receive more media attention gain electoral advantage beyond that associated with their time spent in Iowa, their fund-raising, and their national standing in opinion polls.

The potential effects of Iowa on nomination contests in subsequent states is a more important matter. As good as reporters, editors, and pundits may be at anticipating outcomes in Iowa, they often find their initial expectations were off. One of the primary political functions of the news media is interpreting and framing events—that is, defining the meaning of such things as "victory," "second place," or "26 percent." Expectations are then adjusted, with increased attention directed at candidates who exceeded initial expectations (Hart in 1984; Robertson in 1988; Buchanan in 1996; Kerry in 2004) or were not expected to do well anyway (Bill Clinton and Massachusetts senator Paul Tsongas in 1992).

Table A.7.3 reports estimates of New Hampshire primary results from 1976 through 2008. Candidate vote share (and place) are estimated as a function of the standard variables (early poll standing, finances, time in Iowa, state of residence), along with two independent variables representing the potential effects of Iowa: the candidate's vote share in Iowa, and the change in media attention directed at the candidate immediately after Iowa.[12] Again, the underlying assumptions here are that some voters opt for candidates they expect to be more viable, and that they make use of election results, and media interpretation of results, to assess viability.

Results in Table A.7.3, while estimated with aggregate data, are consistent with such a process. We see a robust association between a candidate's performance in Iowa and performance in New Hampshire. Iowa vote share and Iowa place of finish (not shown) are significant predictors of New Hampshire vote share, the likelihood of winning in New Hampshire, and place of finish in New Hampshire. This result holds when we control for the candidate's fund-raising and initial standing in national polls. Independent of these effects, we also see that change in media attention to a candidate post-Iowa also has a significant effect on support in New Hampshire. Candidates like Hart, Robertson, Buchanan, and Kerry may have had an additional edge in New Hampshire because of the shift in media attention they earned from their "surprise" finishes in Iowa. Although there is no relationship between the shift in media attention to a candidate and winning New Hampshire, the potential importance of the media bounce coming out of Iowa on the overall nomination contest should not be underestimated.

As Table A.7.4 shows, performance in New Hampshire is a strong predictor of aggregate primary vote (and thus delegate share), with Iowa having a more muted effect (depending on specification). But results in table A.7.4 demonstrate that *change in media attention* after Iowa and after New Hampshire have important substantive effects on how much support a candidate receives throughout the nomination contest. Increased attention to a candidate immediately after Iowa, and again immediately after New Hampshire, is significantly related to increased vote share across the nomination contests. When tables A.7.2 and A.7.3 are considered together, the results suggest that changes in news about candidates due to results in Iowa affect how well a candidate does in New Hampshire. Candidate performance in New Hampshire then produces additional adjustments in media attention to candidates (and expectations about viability), and this is associated with how well a candidate fares overall. One need not win Iowa to win New Hampshire, nor must one win New Hampshire to win a nomination (although it clearly helps). However, additive models in table A.7.4 suggest that performance in Iowa had less effect on overall primary vote share than performance in New Hampshire did; but it is important to remember that the nominating process is sequential. Success in New Hampshire corresponds with earlier electoral success in Iowa and the media bounce associated with beating expectations in Iowa. Beating early expectations may determine whether a candidacy ends quickly or whether it lasts longer.

Estimates from the first model in table A.7.4 were also produced using data from 1976 through 2004 (omitting 2008) in order to test how the model predicted the 2008 outcomes. These predictions are listed in

TABLE 7.4. **Actual and predicted 2008 overall primary vote share**

	Actual	Predicted
Republicans		
McCain	47.2	41.5
Huckabee	20.1	25.3
Romney	21.7	23.4
Giuliani	2.8	12.1
Democrats		
Obama	48.3	42.6
Clinton	47.1	47.4
Edwards	2.7	8.6

Source: Table A.7.4, column 1.

table 7.4. Table 7.4 illustrates that the model performs fairly well in predicting the overall vote share for the main candidates, although underpredicting Obama's and McCain's vote share. Of course, vote share is not the same as winning the nomination. Results in table A.7.4, and the predictions in Table 7.4, suggest that a model based on pre-Iowa poll standing, results from the earliest contests, and shifting media attention does a good job explaining a candidate's vote share (which corresponds highly with how long a candidate remains in the contest). These results also demonstrate that such models have less utility in distinguishing which candidates actually win.

Nomination contests are sequential, and thus the stage is set for early events to have important effects that cascade over time. Early results can alter media assessments of a candidate's viability, with the change in news attention breathing new life into some candidacies while leaving others all but forgotten. From 1976 through 2008, media expectations about which candidates were viable were set before Iowa voted. Iowa's results then led to altered media expectations about who the front-runners were. New Hampshire's results further altered media expectations about candidate viability, and these shifts in attention to candidates then shaped the context voters faced in subsequent states.

Media Expectations and Sequential Elections

The patterns shown here present some important questions: about the role of the media in setting and shifting expectations about candidate viability, and about the effects early states such as Iowa and New Hampshire have on the eventual outcome. The analogy here between share market analysts and the media is obviously imperfect. In the market, the analyst sets expectations, and the market responds. In an election context, the media set their own expectations and then voters *and* the media respond to how candidate performance matches expectations. But where share market analysts face repercussions if their analyses are flawed (that is, their clients suffer financial loss), there is no such mechanism policing the accuracy of media analysis. The news media exercises substantial discretion in defining who is viable, and there are no strong incentives for the press to set expectations "correctly" (if that were even possible).

News media interpretation of whether the same number of votes is a "comfortable" second place for one candidate or a "crushing defeat" for another; or whether being a senator from a nearby state should be used to discount the importance of support for one candidate in New Hampshire (for example, Paul Tsongas in 1992) but not another (John Kerry in 2004) may combine with interpretation of random moments in early states to amplify the effects that early states have by altering mass perceptions of candidate viability in subsequent states. Models reported in this chapter cannot account for such effects. But as an extreme example of an Iowa event having effects in New Hampshire and on the eventual nomination outcome, consider Howard Dean's 2004 caucus night speech in Iowa. The information flow from Iowa to New Hampshire was not simply that Dean placed third and failed to meet expectations, and that Kerry became more viable (and received more attention). It was that Dean had made a speech in which he seemed to be out of control, and screaming. A CNN Poll conducted before the New Hampshire primary estimated that 90% of respondents in New Hampshire saw or heard the speech before they voted. Forty-eight percent saw or heard it at least six times, with many saying they saw or heard it at least a dozen times.[13] Events such as Dean's "scream," Maine senator Edmund Muskie's "crying," Ronald Reagan's "I paid for this microphone," or Bill and Hillary Clinton's being anointed "comeback kids" in New Hampshire combine with interpretation of objective outcomes to affect which candidates remain viable to voters—or become more so—in the remaining contests.

In short, the sequential nominating process places substantial discretion with the news media. Media response to margins of a handful of votes in early states—and interpretation about whether someone exceeded expectations based on these narrow margins—may be enough to leave a better-financed (or simply better) candidate stuck in third place with no perception of viability. Consider the fate of Tennessee senator Lamar Alexander, and the media bounce that culture warrior Pat Buchanan enjoyed after Iowa in 1996. It is likely that Buchanan was unelectable. Yet Buchanan beat Alexander by a scant 5,000 votes to secure a "surprise" second place in Iowa. The media boost associated with that may have helped Buchanan beat Dole (by a mere 2,000 votes) and Alexander (by 9,000 votes, 18% versus 23%) in New Hampshire. A few thousand votes in Iowa was the difference between a headline-grabbing second place versus an ignored third-place finish for Buchanan, and it may have doomed Alexander. Increased media attention after Iowa propelled Buchanan to New Hampshire, and New Hampshire drove media attention away from Alexander.

Or consider the fate of General Wesley Clark's candidacy in 2004. Clark opted to ignore Iowa. He placed third in New Hampshire on January 27, just ahead of Edwards (behind Dean and Kerry). The next nominating event deemed most worthy of reporting on was the South Carolina primary on February 3. Edwards, being born there, was expected to do well, and he did, winning 45%versus 30% over Kerry. That was Edwards's only win in the seven contests conducted that day, along with two second-place finishes. Clark won one (Oklahoma), placed second in three states (Arizona, New Mexico, and North Dakota), and beat Edwards in most February 3 states. Yet media attention to Clark had already begun to wane immediately after New Hampshire. Despite beating Edwards in New Hampshire and on February 3, news-media focus was on South Carolina and Edwards. In 2004 and other years, news expectations were based on Iowa, New Hampshire, and South Carolina; not New Mexico, Oklahoma, and Arizona. Clark didn't contest Iowa, and he did well in the wrong states, in the wrong time zones. The disproportionate attention directed at South Carolina in 2004, and the effects it may have had on voter perceptions of candidate viability, was driven by media discretion.

It is probably impossible to say what the "correct" news stories about expectations and candidate viability should have been in these cases, or what they should be in any year. The point is that outcomes in early contests generate information about viability in the form of press attention granted to some candidates and denied to others. The U.S. news media does not have consistent criteria for determining how outcomes in early contests should be interpreted. Lack of transparency in Democratic caucus rules (discussed in chapter 3) may give the media even more discretion in interpreting early nominating events, further amplifying the effect the media have (unintentionally or not) on changing the course of elections by affecting perceptions of candidate viability based on a very small number of votes.

A two-candidate contest between a "front-runner" and a "surprising" opponent is a hard story for reporters, editors, and producers to resist, because it is an easy story. It is easier, and more exciting, to report that a candidate had a "surprise second" place or that someone failed to meet expectations than it is to explain how Iowa actually works. The reality of Iowa—for Democrats, but not for Republicans at least—is that (1) actual voter support for candidates is not reported, and (2) the statewide apportionment of precinct-level delegates is based on general election results from previous years and is unrelated to the number of people who show up to vote at the precinct nominating caucuses. Thus, rural areas may be given a disproportionate share of delegates. Because there is a weaker link between the actual voter aggregate support a candidate receives across all the precinct caucuses and the "delegate totals" elected to the county level that the media use to report how a candidate placed in a close contest, it is possible that the candidate who wins the most delegates will not be the one who received the most first-preference votes, given the fact that the mobilization of voters does not pay off directly in terms of additional delegates in the precincts with higher turnout.[14] But there must be a story, and in it, someone must win, place, and show; and the story will likely be that someone met, exceeded, or failed to meet media expectations.

Regardless of how the media may frame candidate performance, the assumption here is that voter response to information about candidate performance is the causal engine that drives the aggregate process described in this chapter. That is, candidates perform better (or worse) in New Hampshire, in part, because New Hampshire voters make choices based, in part, on perceptions of candidate viability. We assume they adjust these perceptions of viability in response to information they receive about results in Iowa. Likewise, voter decisions in states holding contests after Iowa and New Hampshire are expected to be affected by perceptions of candidate viability formed by results in New Hampshire and Iowa. In the next chapter, we examine public opinion data to test if this dynamic is at work, and to assess the impact that results from the first stage of the sequence (Iowa) may have later in the process.

CHAPTER EIGHT

The Micro Foundations
of Momentum

I've got the "Big Mo." — George H. W. Bush, after winning the 1980 Iowa caucus

The last chapter illustrated how candidates for a party's presidential nomination benefit from beating media expectations in early nomination contests. Using aggregate measures of performance in Iowa and New Hampshire, we showed that change in media attention to a candidate predicts how well that candidate will do in subsequent contests. Early expectations, as measured by the share of media attention a candidate receives before Iowa, are set by the media's interpretation of the candidate's fund-raising and standing in opinion polls. Failing to live up to these expectations in an early state like Iowa or New Hampshire can lead to less media attention, and less voter support. When a candidate performs better than expected, media attention to that candidate increases, which has a positive effect on his or her performance across subsequent caucuses and primaries.

Of course, media attention is not the only engine driving this process. We assume that voters use information about candidate performance to set or adjust their own perceptions of candidate viability and electability. We, and many others, suggest that voter perceptions are important in determining candidate choice in nomination contests. For this to be the case, however, several things must occur. First, voters making choices in states holding later primaries need to actually be aware of who won the contests in the earliest states. The discussion in chapter 7 suggests that media coverage of "surprise" upsets and defeats in Iowa and New Hampshire can have important consequences for a candidate's fortunes, but how many people are actually paying attention? Second, we would expect to see that awareness of outcomes from early states explains something about how voters perceive the viability and electability of candidates. Third, if perceptions of candidates are affected by results from early states, and perceptions help us understand the dynamics of candidate choice in nomination contests, we should also see that perceptions of electability and viability move in predictable ways in response to early election results. Finally, if such perceptions have something do with the dynamics of momentum in presidential nomination contests by affecting how well candidates do in the later contests, we should see that such perceptions affect voter intentions in states that vote later.

In this chapter, we use the data from our series of 2008 presidential nomination surveys to assess the following multistage process:

Awareness of earlier results → Perceptions of viability/
electability → Vote

This process illustrates the individual-level basis of momentum. Most studies detail momentum only in terms of the second and third elements of this process. Bartels (1988) describes how some candidates might benefit from momentum because people make strategic decisions when evaluating multiple candidates. Although some voters may be most attracted to one particular candidate, they may opt for a less-preferred alternative that is seen as having a better chance of winning their party's nomination—so as not to waste their vote on a candidate who may have no chance. Voters may also make strategic assessments about who to support based on their perceptions of who might have the best chance of winning the general election.

Several studies have identified one or both of these forms of strategic voting in presidential nomination contests (Abramowitz, McGlennon, and Rapoport 1981; Bartels 1988; Abramowitz 1989; Abramson et al. 1992; Kenney and Rice 1994). There is also a large literature documenting strategic voting in other settings (for example, Cain 1978; Alvarez and Nagler 2000; Blais et al. 2001; Karp et al. 2002). We suggest that some version of this process has been in operation since American parties gave rank-and-file voters the task of electing the majority of delegates to their national nomination conventions. One question, however, is, where do voters gain the information they use to assess candidates' electoral prospects in nomination contests?

Our data come from a unique national survey we conducted before and after the February 5, 2008, Super Tuesday primaries. Although it is difficult to generalize from opinion data collected from a single year, the 2008 contests featured the same basic structure that has been in place since 1972. Most delegates for each party were selected in a series of events that began with early contests in Iowa and New Hampshire, with the majority of voters making choices weeks and months after Iowa. Clearly, 2008 was somewhat different, given that both parties had wide-open contests for their nominations, with the Democratic contest lasting into June. Furthermore, in any given presidential election year, rules structuring campaign finance, the sequence of caucuses and primaries, the interval between events, and the proportion of delegates selected directly by voters may change. But the sequential nature of the nomination contests that has long structured the process remained in place in 2008. Below, we assess how results from early in this sequence of contests affected voter choices later in the process. We do this to enrich our understanding of how voters reason, and of how the results in Iowa and New Hampshire affect the trajectory of nomination contests.

Conventional Wisdom: Momentum and Early Nominating Events

Despite a few well-known cases of candidates building momentum from early success in Iowa, many scholars argue that *winning* Iowa is an unreliable indicator of primary vote share nationwide or of who will win the nomination (Adkins and Dowdle 2001; Mayer 1996, 2003, 2004; Winebrenner 1998). However, as we showed in chapter 7, winning Iowa may not be as important as beating expectations and shifting perceptions of viability. Jimmy Carter (1976), Ronald Reagan (1976), Gary Hart (1984), Pat Robertson (1988), and Pat Buchanan (1996) each lost in Iowa, but our aggregate analysis suggests that increased media attention associated with their Iowa performance propelled their candidacies into New Hampshire, and in some cases beyond.

What, then, is momentum, and how does it build? What role do early election results from places like Iowa play in generating momentum? Some of the earliest studies of the nomination contests attempted to unpack these questions by examining the importance of the voter's perception that a candidate could win the nomination (viability) or win the general election (electability), two different candidate attributes

(Aldrich 1980; Bartels 1987, 1988; Abramowitz 1989; Stone, Rapoport, and Abramowitz 1992; Norrander 1991, 1992, 1993; Kenney and Rice 1994; Squire 1989). Perceptions of viability and electability might play an important role in structuring vote choice, because the presidential nominating process is a decision context in which party identification has no bearing on the voting decision. Voters must select among candidates from the same party. Candidates in an intraparty contest may also be difficult to distinguish in terms of ideological and policy differences (Stone, Rapoport, and Abramowitz 1992). Candidate qualities thus become an important factor in vote choice (Norrander 1989).

But where do perceptions of the candidates' viability or electability come from, and how do they affect voter support? We suggest these perceptions are obtained, in part, from awareness of early election results. This proposal is not novel—but the role Iowa specifically plays is not clear. Aldrich (1980) contends that a candidate's eventual success depends on a reciprocal relationship between resources (money, media attention, and popular support) and electoral outcomes (more specifically, exceeding or failing to meet prior expectations in a given contest). That is, the greater amount of resources spent by a campaign in a given state will lead to a greater likelihood that the candidate will exceed electoral expectations. Winners of the Iowa caucuses, or those exceeding expectations in early nominating events, can reap positive media coverage, given the media's tendency to focus on the horse-race aspect of the election and front-runners (Brady and Johnston 1987). Certainly, this role for the media is what we showed in chapter 7.

Bartels (1987) proposes that voters use information about candidate successes in early nominating events when choosing whom to vote for. He suggests that a conditional relationship exists between how favorably a voter sees a candidate and perceptions of the candidate's chance of winning the party's nomination. In 1984, support for Gary Hart was shown to be highest among people having low predispositions toward Walter Mondale and who also perceived that Hart could win the Democratic nomination. Abramson and colleagues (1992) also suggest that perceptions of candidate viability are important predictors of the vote in presidential nominations. They examined candidate choices in the 1988 presidential nomination contests by testing competing theories of rational (or sincere) voting and sophisticated (or strategic) voting. Although sincere voters may simply vote for the candidate they prefer the most, Abramson and colleagues contend that many voters used the information available to them (such as successes or losses in early nominating events) to make more strategic or sophisticated candidate choices. Voters used information about results from previous nomination contests to determine whether a candidate was viable, and then adjusted their initial candidate preferences accordingly.

Kenney and Rice (1994) examined the 1988 contest as well, and found that those who changed their candidate choice in favor of Vice President George H. W. Bush did so due to the excitement of Bush's early success in nomination contests, and because they felt it was impossible for Bush to lose the nomination. They also found that people who had no candidate preference before Super Tuesday changed their vote to Bush because they felt he had the best chance of winning the general election in November.

Abramowitz (1989) shows that the voter's forward-looking projections of whether a candidate is electable in the general election is an important factor structuring how primary and caucus voters make decisions. Using 1988 primary exit poll data from Georgia, he found that candidate evaluations and perceptions of electability had significant effects on candidate choice, although perceptions of how viable a candidate was in the nomination process did not. However, viability was found to have an indirect influence on candidate choice by affecting perceptions of electability.

Stone, Rapoport, and Abramowitz (1992) attempt to explain vote choice in Iowa itself, surveying Iowa caucusgoers in 1984, as well as delegates to the Iowa state convention. They show that the interaction of perceived candidate electability and candidate evaluations (how favorably a voter viewed a candidate) was the best predictor of candidate choice in Iowa. They also found that perceptions of electability predicted vote choice, while perceptions of viability in the nominating process did not. At the same time, our data from 2008 (as we reported in chapter 3) show that Iowans are more likely to vote sincerely, rather than strategically, choosing the candidate whom they prefer rather than focusing on electability. Taken together, the Stone, Rapoport, and Abramowitz (1992) and Abramowitz (1989) studies suggest voters' assessments of how well a candidate would do in the nominating process may be less relevant than concerns about electability in November, suggesting that results from Iowa or New Hampshire may play little role in affecting voter choices in subsequent primaries, except to the extent that they provide guidance about electability in November.

In sum, the literature on U.S. presidential nominations has identified the potential importance of momentum flowing from success at the Iowa caucuses and New Hampshire's primary. There is a general consensus that voter perceptions of whether a candidate can win the nomination (viability) or win the presidency (electability) can matter in structuring candidate choice. Yet few existing studies were designed to isolate the specific effects that information from Iowa (or New Hampshire) may have in shaping perceptions of the candidates among voters making choices in states that voted after Iowa and New Hampshire. No published studies have used survey questions that ask voters about the importance of Iowa and New Hampshire. As a result, we lack a clear understanding of the possible role that results from the early nominating events have in affecting results in other states.

Super Tuesday Survey Design

Nearly one month after the 2008 Iowa caucuses and the New Hampshire primary, twenty-four states conducted their primaries and caucuses on February 5, Super Tuesday. On this single day, 70% of elected convention delegates were awarded. Table 8.1 illustrates the sequence of primaries and caucuses that were held before February 5. Although both parties had already conducted contests in eight different states during January and the first days of February, many of these received scant attention compared to the events in Iowa and New Hampshire. Others, including the Florida and Michigan Republican primaries and the Nevada and South Carolina contests, attracted substantial media attention.

Despite the frontloaded schedule in 2008, by the time voters cast ballots on Super Tuesday, nearly a full month had passed since the New Hampshire primary. What effect, then, might awareness of results in the early states have on voters' choices after that much time has passed? If outcomes in early contests affect perceptions of viability and vote choice, we would expect that voters had become aware (or remained aware) of who won in Iowa and New Hampshire weeks after those contests were over. And, of course, there might be changes in these perceptions following Super Tuesday itself, so we are also interested in how perceptions of viability and electability may shift in the shorter term, in response to election results from the Super Tuesday states.

We assess how awareness of early election outcomes might affect voting later in the nomination sequence with a national telephone survey

TABLE 8.1. **2008 Presidential nomination calendar through February 2008**

January 3	Iowa caucus	D & R	Obama 38%	Huckabee 35%
January 5	Wyoming caucus	R		Romney 67%
January 8	New Hampshire primary	D & R	Clinton 39%	McCain 37%
January 15	Michigan primary	R*		Romney 39%
January 19	South Carolina primary	R		McCain 33%
	Nevada caucus	D & R	Clinton 51%	Romney 51%
January 26	South Carolina primary	D	Obama 55%	
January 29	Florida primary	R*		McCain 36%
February 2	Maine caucus	R		Romney 52%
February 5	Super Tuesday (25 states)	D & R		
February 9	Kansas caucus	R		Huckabee 60%
	Louisiana primary	D & R	Obama 57%	Huckabee 43%
	Nebraska caucus	D	Obama 68%	
	Washington caucus	D & R	Obama 68%	McCain 25%
February 10	Maine caucus	D	Obama 59%	

*Democratic National Committee rules at the time stated that results of these primaries would not be counted toward delegate allocation, and Democratic candidates did not campaign in these states.

conducted both before and after Super Tuesday. We designed the sample to include people residing in Super Tuesday states, as well as people living in states that would hold caucuses or primaries after Super Tuesday. Interviews in both sets of states were conducted from February 1 through February 4. After the February 5 contests, we went back into the field to continue interviews with people residing in states that had yet to vote. These interviews were conducted from February 7 through February 11. People who had voted before Super Tuesday (those in states such as Iowa, New Hampshire, and Florida) were excluded from the sample, which covered forty states.

This design allows us to conduct a general assessment of how much voters were aware of results from the earliest contests. Specifically, we can assess how a voter's longer-term perceptions about the candidates were affected by information about the winners of the earliest contests. It also allows us to test if voter assessments of candidate viability and electability shifted in the short term. Table 8.2 illustrates the design of our sample. Roughly one-half of the sample of respondents from states voting after February 5 were randomly assigned to be interviewed before the Super Tuesday results were known, and roughly one-half were assigned to be interviewed afterward.

There are additional advantages to our survey design in that it allows us to test for differences in perceptions of candidates that may be associated with exposure to a campaign. All respondents were asked for their

TABLE 8.2. **Super Tuesday survey sample design**

	Date of survey interview	
Respondent's state	Feb. 1–4	Feb. 7–11
Contest on Feb. 5	$n = 423$	No interviews
Contest after Feb. 5	$n = 352$	$n = 506$

perceptions of the candidates' chances of winning the nomination, and winning the general election in November. Since the sample of respondents interviewed before February 5 is divided into one group in which people were exposed to the Super Tuesday campaigns (states that voted on Super Tuesday), and another group not directly exposed to the campaigns (post–Super Tuesday states), we can assess how perceptions of candidates might be affected by the immediate context of the campaign.

Awareness of Results from Early Contests

Before unpacking the dynamics of how voters form their perceptions of candidate viability and electability, we need to establish if results from Iowa or New Hampshire resonate enough to be useful information to voters who make decisions weeks later in the Super Tuesday contests. Our survey respondents were asked open-ended questions about who won Iowa and New Hampshire; those planning to participate in Republican contests were asked who the Republican winners were, and those planning to vote in Democratic contests were asked who won the Democratic events. Table 8.3 illustrates a fairly high voter knowledge about the early results at the time of Super Tuesday on February 5. It is clear that voters were well focused on the 2008 contests, with over 70% saying they had "quite a lot" of interest in the election, and 84% saying they were following the news about the candidates "fairly closely" or "very closely." These high levels of interest correspond with relatively high awareness of the results from early January. Nearly 50% of respondents could correctly identify who won the January 3 Iowa caucuses, and 54% could name the New Hampshire winner. At the same time, when asked directly, relatively few respondents said that the Iowa or New Hampshire results played an important role in determining their candidate preference. But many did say the early results mattered at least somewhat: 25% of the people we surveyed in early February cited the Iowa results

TABLE 8.3. **Knowledge of Iowa and New Hampshire results nationally, February 2008**

Recall who won Iowa		
Correct	49.9%	628
Incorrect	21.9%	276
Don't know	28.1%	353
Recall who won New Hampshire		
Correct	53.9%	677
Incorrect	14.2%	178
Don't know	31.9%	400

as "very important" or "somewhat important" in affecting their decision about which candidate to support, and 25% said the same about the New Hampshire results.

As with chapter 7, we have relegated our statistical models to an appendix (appendix B). Here we will describe the results in what we hope is clear and easy-to-follow language. We begin by modeling who was able to correctly identify the Iowa and New Hampshire winners in February (table B.8.1), which reveals the usual suspects. Self-identified partisans (as opposed to independents), the better educated, those with higher income, those interested in politics, and those who regularly consume election news were all significantly more likely to know that Obama or Huckabee won in Iowa, and that Clinton or McCain had won New Hampshire. The model also demonstrates that people interviewed before February 5 were significantly more likely to know who won the first two contests than those interviewed later, as illustrated in figure 8.1. This difference could stem from the unique information environment associated with residing in a Super Tuesday state. Although we find no differences in levels of interest in the campaign associated with living in a Super Tuesday state, table 8.4 shows that voters in Super Tuesday states were slightly more knowledgeable about the Iowa and New Hampshire winners than those in other states interviewed at the same time. Super Tuesday state residents were notably more aware of the early winners than people interviewed after February 5 who lived in states that would vote later. All of this suggests that while there may be a slight decay over time in the resonance of information about the Iowa and New Hampshire winners, the information environment of active campaigns in Super Tuesday states may have countered the effects of such decay by bringing heightened attention to the candidates who won in earlier states. This may also suggest that voters in post–Super Tuesday states were more focused on the results of Super Tuesday itself and the information it pro-

TABLE 8.4. **Voter awareness of Iowa and New Hampshire winners, by time and place**

	Name Iowa winner	Name New Hampshire winner
Live in Super Tuesday state, interviewed before Feb. 5	54.6%	58.0%
Live in other state, interviewed before Feb. 5	50.0%	54.5%
Live in other state, interviewed after Feb. 5	46.2%	50.0%

Note: Cell values are the percentage who were correct in identifying the winner.

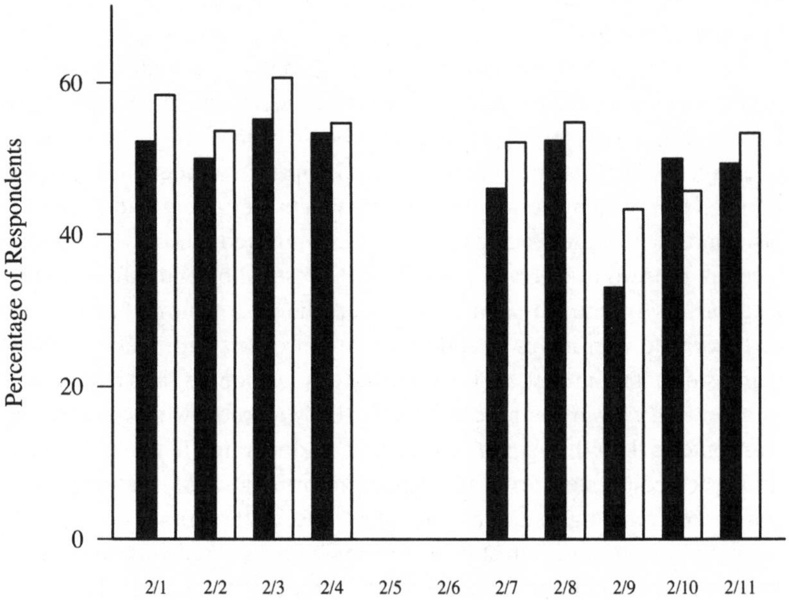

FIGURE 8.1. Percentage of respondents with knowledge of the Iowa and New Hampshire winner, by date of interview.

vided to them, and thus less likely to remain focused on Iowa and New Hampshire.

Perceptions of Candidate Viability

Our survey also included standard items designed to measure perceptions of each candidate's chances of winning his or her party's nomination, and of winning the general election. It is important to note that before February 2008, no clear front-runner had emerged in either party's contest. But immediately before we began our interviews, the candidate field did narrow. Former North Carolina senator John Edwards and former New York City mayor Rudy Giuliani both dropped out on January 30. Edwards had placed a distant third in the January 26 South Carolina primary, and then exited after receiving just 14% of the vote in Florida on January 29. Giuliani failed to break into double digits in any state until January 29, and he withdrew after receiving just 15% of the GOP vote in Florida.

Returning to table 8.1, we see that it illustrates the lack of any overwhelming front-runner in either party before Super Tuesday. By February 2, Illinois senator Barack Obama and New York senator Hillary Clinton each had victories in two contests. Clinton had led Obama in the national Gallup Poll through January, but her lead was down to 2 points by February 2. On the Republican side, Arizona senator John McCain led former Massachusetts governor Mitt Romney and former Arkansas governor Mike Huckabee (respectively) in national polls through January, but often with less than 30% support. By February 2, Romney had scored four victories to McCain's three (including his high-profile New Hampshire win). Despite having won Iowa, Huckabee's chances looked weak by February 2. He finished a poor third in New Hampshire and Michigan, lost narrowly to McCain in South Carolina, and then placed fourth in Florida behind Giuliani.

Table 8.5 displays how voters perceived candidate viability and electability around the time of the February 5 Super Tuesday contests. We measured perceptions of viability two ways. First, we used a 0–100 feeling thermometer score, "where 0 represents no chance for the candidate to win the nomination, 50 represents an even chance, and 100 represents certain victory." Second, we asked respondents to agree or disagree with a statement asserting that a candidate would win the nomination (viability), and with a statement that the candidate would be elected president if s/he won the nomination (electability). Voter perceptions reported in table 8.5 largely match the objective conditions in the contests at the time. On both measures, people participating in Democratic contests rated Clinton as having a greater chance than Obama of winning the Democratic nomination while making less distinction between the two in terms of their electability. Among Republicans, McCain was clearly perceived as more viable, and as being more electable than Romney or

TABLE 8.5. **Voter perceptions of candidate viability and electability in national sample, February 2008**

	Win nomination, 0–100 scale	
Clinton	61.4	
Obama	57.2	
McCain	73.5	
Romney	45.8	
Huckabee	24.6	

	Win nomination, 4-point scale	Elected president, 4-point scale
Clinton	2.84	2.97
Obama	2.68	2.92
McCain	3.15	2.76
Romney	2.26	2.35
Huckabee	1.89	2.02

Note: Respondents were asked if they strongly agreed, agreed, disagreed, or strongly disagreed with the statements "[Candidate] will win the nomination," and "If s/he does win the nomination s/he will be elected president." Higher scores (1- to 4-point scale) reflect greater agreement.

Huckabee. To understand the dynamics of momentum, however, we need to know how these perceptions are formed, and how they may change during the course of the nomination contest.

Shifting Perceptions of Candidates: Viability

Thus far, we have established that voters appear to pay attention to results from the earliest contests (or at least learn about these results at some point), and that some claim to use this information when deciding whom to vote for. We have also shown that perceptions of candidate viability fit fairly closely with how the candidates were actually doing. All of this is consistent with our view of the process that underlies voter choice: perceptions of viability are shaped, in part, by information about candidate performance in earlier states, and this can affect vote choice. However, we have not yet established how these pieces might fit together as a causal process. In other words, does knowledge of results from Iowa and New Hampshire explain something about how voters come to see candidates as being viable, and can we show that these perceptions shift in response to actual campaign results? There are a number of ways to address these questions. One way is to simply test if knowledge of the Iowa and New Hampshire winners predicts how voters rate each candidate's viability.

But we also expect that people update their perceptions of viability and electability in response to election results. Thus, people interviewed *after* February 5 may have changed their perceptions of a candidate's prospects in light of the Super Tuesday results. The 2008 Super Tuesday results were somewhat of a draw for the Democrats. Obama won thirteen states to Clinton's nine, with a near even split in total delegates won on February 5. However, these results may have solidified Obama's status as an equal to Clinton, and changed perceptions that he was the underdog in the contest for the Democratic nomination. In addition, some of our interviews were conducted after Obama ran off a string of victories beginning on February 9. If people updated their expectations about Obama's prospects in response to these events, we would expect to see those interviewed after Super Tuesday rating Obama's chances of winning as higher.

Super Tuesday produced a more decisive result for Republicans. McCain won nine states, including the four largest states with the greatest number of delegates. Huckabee won four southern states and West Virginia. Romney carried seven states on February 5, but many were sparsely populated and provided few delegates. Two days later Romney suspended his campaign, leaving McCain as the clear front-runner. Again, if voters shift their perceptions of viability in response to election results from states that had already voted, we should see McCain's prospects being rated higher among people surveyed after Super Tuesday.

Simple models estimating voter perceptions of a candidate's prospects of winning the nomination are reported in table B.8.2. Perceptions of viability are estimated with knowledge of who won Iowa and New Hampshire, and with a variable that identifies people interviewed after February 5. The results demonstrate that voter awareness of early victories appears to have shaped perceptions of viability, at least with some of the candidates. Democrats who were aware that Obama won Iowa were significantly more likely to believe he could win the nomination. Above and beyond that, we also see that Democrats interviewed after Super Tuesday gave Obama significantly higher marks in terms of his chances of winning the nomination. Obama may have benefited from the same process that built momentum for previous underdog candidates such as Jimmy Carter and Gary Hart: early success led people voting later to see him as being more viable. However, knowledge of the Iowa and New

Hampshire results had no clear effect on perceptions of Hillary Clinton's viability. The signs for the coefficients are in the expected direction but do not reach statistical significance: knowing that Obama won Iowa has an inverse relationship with Clinton's viability ratings, and knowledge that she won New Hampshire has a positive relationship with perceptions of Clinton's viability. The lack of a strong effect here may result from Clinton's beginning as a front-runner who was already perceived as being viable and electable. Early nominating events may do little to affect perceptions of viability for candidates who are already rated as highly viable.

Estimates of voter perceptions of the Republican candidates fit our model that voters form perceptions in response to past election results, and that they update those preferences over the course of the contest. Knowledge of McCain's victory in the New Hampshire primary appears to have increased the likelihood that people expected him to win the nomination while diminishing perceptions of Huckabee's chances. People who knew McCain won New Hampshire were marginally more optimistic about McCain's prospects and significantly more negative about Huckabee's. The Super Tuesday results further solidified the perception that McCain would win the nomination, and that Huckabee would not. Republicans interviewed after February 5 were significantly more likely than people contacted before Super Tuesday to agree that McCain would win the Republican nomination, and significantly less likely to agree that Huckabee would be nominated.

Shifting Perceptions of Candidates: Electability

Voters appear to have been adjusting their expectations about not only who they thought would win the 2008 nominations, but also who they thought could win the general election. When we predict how respondents rated the candidates' chances of winning the general election using models similar to those for viability, we find that Democrats who knew of Obama's win in Iowa were significantly more likely to expect he would be elected president if he were to win the nomination. Similarly, people interviewed after Super Tuesday were significantly more likely to agree that Obama (among Democrats) and McCain (among Republicans) would be elected. Republicans surveyed after February 5 were significantly less likely to think Huckabee would be elected president than people interviewed before the election. This suggests that the earliest results from Iowa (in the case of Obama) and results from Super Tuesday acted to define perceptions of a candidate's general election prospects. It remains to be seen how these perceptions of the candidates affected voter choices, but it is clear that perceptions of viability and electability were affected by earlier election results.

The relationship between the campaign, election results, and voter perceptions of a candidate's electoral prospects can be seen another way than what is presented in table B.8.2. One of our questions about viability and electability had response categories that ranged on a scale from 1 to 4, with 4 reflecting higher ratings. Using this scale, McCain was seen as being the most viable Republican going into Super Tuesday, with a mean rating of 3.01 among all voters surveyed before February 5. Romney rated 2.26, and Huckabee 1.94. Among Democrats, Clinton rated an average of 2.85 in the pre–Super Tuesday polling, compared with 2.64 for Obama. Table 8.6 reports similar viability and electability ratings for subgroups of voters in our sample. Again, these groups are differentiated by whether the respondents lived in a state voting on or after Super Tuesday, and whether they were interviewed before or after Super Tuesday. This allows us illustrate how evaluations of viability and electability changed after Super Tuesday, and to assess the potential effect of residing in a state that had a contest on Super Tuesday. We have already established that perceptions of viability shifted after February 5, as did perceptions of electability. This is further evident in table 8.6. Compared to people interviewed early, those interviewed after Super Tuesday living in states that had yet to vote were significantly more confident in McCain's and Obama's prospects, and significantly less confident in Huckabee's.

But one additional thing is noteworthy when we consider these subgroups of voters. It seems that people living in states that voted on Super Tuesday perceived the election as being more competitive than those interviewed at the same time but living in states that would vote later. Seeing the candidates competing in one's own state may have affected perceptions of viability. In addition to general information about candidate prospects available from national media, voters in Super Tuesday states were likely to have been exposed to campaign ads and local coverage of candidate appearances that gave the impression the candidate was alive and well in the contest. Voters in other states would not see candidate appearances or local coverage of candidates, and thus might discount some candidates' prospects more than people exposed to an active campaign. Thus, the gap in viability ratings between McCain and other Republi-

TABLE 8.6. **Average viability rating (candidate can win nomination) and electability scores (candidate can win presidency)**

	Republican candidates			Democratic candidates	
Viability	Huckabee win nom	McCain win nom	Romney win nom	Clinton win nom	Obama win nom
Live in Super Tuesday state, interviewed before Feb. 5	1.96*	2.98*	2.31	2.82	2.65
Live in other state, interviewed before Feb. 5	1.91	3.05*	2.21	2.90	2.63
Live in other state, interviewed after Feb. 5	1.83*	3.38*	n/a	2.81	2.75*
Total N	(547)	(549)	(321)	(612)	(607)
Electability	Huckabee win pres	McCain win pres	Romney win pres	Clinton win pres	Obama win pres
Live in Super Tuesday state, interviewed before Feb. 5	2.11*	2.74	2.35	2.97	2.90
Live in other state, interviewed before Feb. 5	2.08	2.66	2.35	2.96	2.84
Live in other state, interviewed after Feb. 5	1.90*	2.85*	n/a	2.96	2.98*
Total N	(532)	(494)	(321)	(632)	(634)

Note: Higher scores (1- to 4-point scale) reflect greater agreement, where 4 = "strongly agree." Question wording: "Candidate X will win his/her party's nomination." "Candidate X will win the presidency." Response options range from 1 (strongly disagree), 2 (disagree), 3 (agree), to 4 (strongly agree).
*p difference < 0 > .10

cans was slightly lower among voters in Super Tuesday states than people in other states. Before February 5, Romney and Huckabee were seen as being slightly more viable by people in states where the candidates were campaigning. The viability gap between Clinton and Obama before February 5 was also slightly lower in Super Tuesday states than elsewhere.

An Experiment on Voter Responsiveness to Early Results

Our Super Tuesday survey was designed to include one more test of the Iowa and New Hampshire results' potential to affect how voters perceived candidates' electoral fortunes in 2008. Recall that voters were asked to assess each candidate's prospects of winning a nomination, and they were also asked if they knew who won the Iowa caucus or the New Hampshire primary. People were not informed of who the actual winners were. We built a question-order experiment into the survey, so that half the respondents were randomly assigned to be asked the viability

TABLE 8.7. **The effect of prompting respondents to recall Iowa and New Hampshire winners**

	Thermometer ratings of chances to win nomination				
	McCain	Romney	Huckabee	Obama	Clinton
Prompted to recall who won Iowa and New Hampshire; then asked about candidate electoral prospects	75.0	44.7	26.0	56.9	61.4
Asked about candidate electoral prospects without being prompted to recall winners from Iowa and New Hampshire	71.8	47.0	23.3	57.4	61.4
$p <$ or > 0 (t-test)	.04	.17	.09	.41	.50
Degrees of freedom	561	342	554	660	665

questions before being prompted to recall the Iowa and New Hampshire results. The other half of respondents were randomly assigned to be asked those questions after being prompted to recall the winners of Iowa and New Hampshire. If the subtle prompt of being asked to recall the early winners had any effect on how people evaluated the candidates, we would expect that those who were asked the viability questions after the prompt would be more likely to discount the prospects of candidates with a recent defeat while rating candidates with a recent victory more highly.

Table 8.7 reports results of this experiment, which are somewhat mixed. We see that people asked to rate the prospects of Republican candidates after being prompted to recall who had won the early races were more likely to rate both McCain's and Huckabee's chances more highly than those who were not prompted. They were also more likely to discount Romney's prospects. On the other hand, there were no differences across the groups when it came to rating the prospects of Clinton and Obama. This lack of effect on the Democratic side likely reflects the fact that Clinton and Obama split the two earliest contests, which could neutralize the effect of the prompt. On the Republican side, however, we see evidence that a prompt even as subtle as being asked to recall who won New Hampshire may alter how voters assess the candidates' electoral prospects.

Perceptions of Viability and Candidate Choice

We have shown evidence on several levels that perceptions of a candidate's electoral prospects are grounded in awareness of results from states that have already voted. We even see some traces of this in the question-ordering experiment (table 8.7), and more concretely when we predict responses to viability and electability questions based on whether a voter was aware of who won in Iowa or New Hampshire (table B.8.2). We also see it clearly when tracking changes in evaluations of the candidates before and after Super Tuesday (table 8.6). Thus far, then, we have shown the first stages of the process we see as being the micro foundations of momentum in presidential nomination contests: voters draw from their interest in the campaign and their exposure to campaign news to become aware of results in early election contests. Awareness of these results in turn affects ratings of the candidates' chances of winning the nomination and the general election.

How, then, did these perceptions of viability and electability affect candidates in the 2008 nomination contests? Table B.8.3 reports predictors of vote choices for candidates, the final stage of the process forming the micro foundations of momentum. Here, perceptions of candidate viability and electability are used to predict candidate choice (among Democrats, voting for Obama or Clinton; among Republicans, voting for McCain or not). The models predicting candidate choice control for a host of other factors, including how favorably (or unfavorably) the voter rated the candidate on a 100-point feeling thermometer scale.[1] We include variables that control for the effect of the issue the respondent felt was most important in the election. We do this with dummy variables that reflect whether the respondent reported that the economy, the Iraq war, or health care was the most important issue. Voter assessment of relevant candidate characteristics was accounted for by including measures representing whether or not the respondent identified candidate "experience" or "stands up for their beliefs" as the more important candidate quality. Standard demographic factors, including the respondent's education, age, income, gender, and race/ethnicity are included. We also control for whether the respondent is a strong partisan or not.

The results in Table B.8.3 show that perceptions of viability and electability do predict candidate choice in 2008 after the early nominating events. Obama, Clinton, and McCain each received greater support from people who believed they were likely to win their party's nomination, with many other factors held constant. In February 2008, support for Clinton (among Democrats) and McCain (among Republicans) appears to have been greater among people who believed the candidate would win their respective party's nomination and also among people who thought these candidates would win the general election. Obama's support in early February, in contrast, does not appear to have been greater among people who thought he would be electable in November. However, his support was significantly greater (40% + increased probability, with other factors held constant) among people perceiving he was a viable contender for the nomination in February.

Momentum in 2008

All of this illustrates the dynamics of momentum in 2008, a year when neither of the eventual major party nominees began as a clear frontrunner. Knowledge of outcomes in Iowa, New Hampshire, and Super Tuesday was important in shaping perceptions about the viability and electability of some candidates seeking their party's nominations. Information about Obama's win in Iowa clearly made him appear more viable to Democrats voting after Iowa, and those perceptions of increased viability, in turn, made Democrats more likely to support Obama. Throughout December 2007, Clinton maintained a commanding 20-point lead over Obama in national polls, as relatively few voters saw Obama as being as viable or electable as Clinton. Clinton's national poll lead was cut in half after Iowa, when information about the Iowa results shifted perceptions of Obama's viability and electability. Likewise, the results of Super Tuesday did not alter perceptions of Clinton so much as they further solidified perceptions that Obama was also viable and electable.

A similar pattern appeared on the Republican side. In eighteen national polls taken the month before Iowa and New Hampshire voted in 2008, McCain's support averaged just 14%, usually trailing behind Rudy Giuliani, Mike Huckabee (at 19%), and Mitt Romney. Huckabee had a brief 6-point national lead immediately after his Iowa victory (at 25%), but McCain reversed that and led by 10 points after winning New Hampshire. Immediately after Super Tuesday, he led Huckabee by 20 points. Our analysis demonstrates that McCain's victory in New Hampshire, particularly his decisive win on February 5, made him appear more viable and electable to Republican voters. This, in turn, increased support for McCain among Republicans voting in the primaries.

In table B.8.4, we report three separate models predicting a vote choice for Obama for the three subgroups in our national survey (see table 8.2). For each subgroup, perceptions of Obama's viability were an important predictor of voting for him in the primaries. To show this more clearly, we estimate the substantive magnitude of perceptions of Obama's viability in predicting a vote for Obama, holding other variables in the model at their mean or modal values. Table 8.8 reports the results.[2] For respondents interviewed before February 5 and residing in a Super Tuesday state, viability was a very important factor in voting for Obama; holding all else constant, a respondent who believed Obama could win the nomination had a 46% increased probability of voting for him on Super Tuesday than a similar respondent who did not think Obama was a viable candidate. The effect of viability on candidate choice was at 22%, less than half the magnitude for those living in states voting after Super Tuesday, even though both groups were interviewed at the same time. This difference is only accounted for by the voting sequence. Those expecting to vote later (and thus not directly subjected to Super Tuesday campaigns) responded differently to perceptions of candidate viability.

For individuals in later voting states, viability peaked in the postelection survey, when it was now their turn to vote. For voters interviewed after Super Tuesday, believing Obama could win the nomination led to a 43-point increased probability of voting for him, compared with the 22-point increase for respondents from these same states interviewed pre-election. As the elections proceeded in sequence from Super Tuesday to later states, the importance of viability in predicting a vote for Obama grew as well. Before Super Tuesday, viability had limited effects for post–Super Tuesday voters; after Super Tuesday, viability mat-

TABLE 8.8. **Change in predicted probability of voting for Obama by perceptions of viability**

	Obama can win the nomination	Obama cannot win the nomination	Difference in probability (Obama vote)
Super Tuesday contest state	.53	.07	+.46
(Feb. 1–4 interview)	(.09)	(.04)	
Other state	.32	.10	+.22
(Feb. 1–4 interview)	(.11)	(.07)	
Other state	.54	.11	+.43
(Feb. 7–11 interview)	(.10)	(.07)	

Source: Estimated with Clarify from models in appendix B, table B.8.4.
Note: Explanatory variables set at mean/modal values. Standard errors in parentheses.

tered much more in these later states. This is clear evidence that winning earlier contests resulted in a real sense of momentum for Obama, visible in the increased importance of viability over time.

Summary

The aggregate analysis in chapter 7 and our analysis of public opinion data in this chapter illustrate that election results from states holding the earliest contests affect the outcomes in states that vote later by changing voter perceptions about the viability and electability of the candidates. At the same time, our 2008 Super Tuesday survey was not designed to allow us to test whether early election results of some particular magnitude are required to generate momentum. Indeed, while our questions focused on knowledge of who had won in Iowa and New Hampshire, there is no reason to expect that a candidate actually has to *win* in one of these early states in order to start the process of building momentum. All that is required is that an early election result changes how voters perceive a candidate's electoral prospects. For this to occur, some voters must learn of the results from the early contests, and adjust their perceptions accordingly. The conditions for this to occur simply require media attention to the early contests, and voters who pay attention to the media. And there is no doubt that the media focus like a laser on Iowa and New Hampshire. Moreover, our data show that many voters pay attention and incorporate this information into their decision making.

It is now well established that, for some candidates, results from Iowa and New Hampshire have played a key role in building the momentum that propelled their campaigns further than they might have otherwise reached. This chapter expands on our understanding of how this process works. Since 1972, it has also been the case that Iowa and New Hampshire hold the early contests that start this process. What does it mean for the nominating process, then, to have the same state vote first every four years? Results from Iowa "matter" in that they can play a fundamental role in shaping public perceptions of the viability or electability of candidates—either by providing media the ability to interpret the meaning of Iowa's results, or by providing voters direct information about the results. Either way, the Iowa results are critical in that they are one of the earliest forces that can affect the trajectory of momentum in a nomination campaign.

CHAPTER NINE

Participation and Engagement in 2008 Caucuses and Primaries

With William W. Franko

I left the "star-sighting" Mecca of downtown Manhattan, but a recent lunch at a local hamburger joint was a-flash with cameras and news crews because Mitt Romney wanted a burger, too, and my afternoon coffee break yesterday was an opportunity to chat with John Edwards while reporters pushed in to listen to his last-minute pitch for my vote. — Christine Whelan, University of Iowa http://www.huffingtonpost.com/christine-whelan

A s we have seen in the last two chapters, the sequential nominating process has consequences for candidate choice as well as the winners and losers in the nomination contest. But what about the voters? Does the fact that presidential nominations are decided through sequential elections influence whether and to what degree voters participate in those contests? We certainly know that competition matters—voter turnout is substantially lower in noncompetitive elections and in states that end up holding primaries or caucuses after the party nominees have been decided (Atkeson and Maestas 2009). But participation is far more than simply turnout, and the extended 2008 Democratic nomination contest gives us a good opportunity to look into the question of voter mobilization and participation in a competitive environment. The 2008 nominations also ushered in a new era of widespread online campaigning and mobilization. What are the consequences of digital politics for participation in nominating events and the composition of primary and caucus electorates?

Since Iowa starts the process, we will start this chapter by taking another look at participation in the Iowa caucuses. The question of participation in Iowa is rich with irony. For a year or more before voting kicks off, the Iowa caucuses are the epicenter for presidential candidates, campaigns, and the national media (Hull 2007). Yet as we described in chapter 6, they are at the same time derided as "low-turnout" affairs leading to an unrepresentative electorate with far too much power (Winebrenner 1998; Wang 2007; Stone, Abramowitz, and Rapoport 1989; Squire 1989; Stone, Atkeson, and Rapoport 1992). Concern about Iowa's first-in-the-nation status in the presidential nomination naturally follows. Caucuses are portrayed in the media and by scholars as overly complex and burdensome compared to voting in primary elections, yet Iowans have long been praised as being highly engaged in the caucus process (Squire 1989). Caucuses in general have been criticized for lower voter turnout compared with primaries, yet historic turnout in 2008 nomination contests, including the Iowa caucuses, shattered all previous records.

While we do not belittle the importance of turnout as a measure of democratic health, participation in primaries and caucuses cannot be measured by voting alone. There are multiple dimensions of participation beyond turnout, including both online and offline direct political participation (contributing financially to campaigns, attending rallies, working for a candidate, visiting a candidate's Web site, and so on) and political engagement, including interest in the nomination and following campaign news. While some might argue that all these kinds of participation are meaningless if they do not lead to casting a ballot, simply voting without much involvement or giving much thought to the election is not participation capable of sustaining a strong democratic polity (Barber 1984).

We are particularly interested in comparing participation in Iowa with later primaries and caucuses and looking at the extent to which the sequential nature of the nomination season affects participation. We have a unique opportunity to do so because of the competitive nature of the 2008 Democratic campaign, which remained unsettled through its final primaries. We also have a unique opportunity to examine the nature of participation in both traditional "real-world" activities, such as attending campaign events, and the new e-politics of the Internet, which became more important than ever in 2008. It may be that the rise of the Internet provides new opportunities for participation among a wider range of citizens (see Hull's [2007] discussion of e-mentum). We explore these questions using our sequential survey data conducted before key caucuses and primaries in 2008. Three of our telephone surveys are used in these analyses, including one of Iowa registered voters, a nationwide survey of registered voters before and immediately after Super Tuesday, and a final survey of registered Democratic voters in Pennsylvania just before that state's primary in April.

Elections and Participation

To the extent that research exists on the effects of electoral competition on voter participation in the United States, it focuses almost exclusively on competition in general election campaigns, using presidential battleground or swing states, state-level races, or competitive congressional races to draw conclusions (for example, see Cox and Munger [1989]). But, of course, the nominating process comes first, and needs its own focus, although few scholars have directly examined the effects of competition in primaries and caucuses (see Moran and Fenster [1982]; Norrander [1986b] for exceptions). So we ask if citizens are in fact engaged and mobilized by competitive primaries and caucuses; especially those citizens who often do not participate, such as the young and the less educated. We also ask if citizens are mobilized to do more than simply show up on caucus night or at their polling place on election day. We have a laboratory of sorts to test this, given that the 2008 nominating process was among the most competitive ever. If nothing else, the amount of money raised by the candidates for the presidential nomination—$296 million for Barack Obama, $238 million for Hillary Clinton, and $122 million for John McCain just through May 2008—broke all previous records (Mann 2009).

We explore whether such a highly competitive presidential nomination contest increased mobilization and engagement among all voters and especially among traditionally disadvantaged groups. In doing so, we consider both online and offline political participation, comparing the two modes across the sequence of early and late primaries and caucuses. We also explore *who* is mobilized in presidential primaries. Frequent Internet use has been found to increase both online and offline political participation, with larger boosts occurring among young voters (Mossberger, Tolbert, and McNeal 2008; see also Tolbert and McNeal [2003]; Bimber [2003]). Krueger (2002, 2006) argues that the Internet engages some individuals who otherwise would not be involved in politics, showing that this pattern is most evident among younger individuals. In contrast to traditional modes of participation, in this chapter we look at how online mobilization in presidential nomination contests increases participation by otherwise underparticipating groups.

Using these two conceptual lenses—competition and online politics—we attempt to make sense of participation in primaries and caucuses across the American states. We want to know whether and to what degree Iowa is unique—or whether later states share in a participation bounty beyond voter turnout when the nomination remains competitive over a long period of time. Our data show that contrary to the prevailing understanding based on turnout statistics alone, political participation was generally higher in the Iowa caucuses than nationally, yet political interest in and direct attention to the campaign may be higher in states voting later in a competitive nomination campaign. What appears to operate as a transfer of information from early to later states may be a unique advantage to sequential elections.

While overall Iowans are more engaged both online and offline than voters in later states, there are differential effects, with the young significantly more engaged online and the less educated relatively more engaged offline (likely due to retail politics) than nationally. One of the knocks pundits and scholars give to Iowa (and often nomination contests in general) is that with low turnout comes significant bias in the electorate. Nomination contests may represent mostly partisan extremes, as those who care the most—strong partisans of either party and those of higher socioeconomic status—may be the most likely to become engaged in a campaign and to vote in the election (Squire 1989). But as we saw in chapter 6 with Iowa in 2008, something different may happen in highly competitive nominations where interest and awareness are high and where alternate means of participation are likely—such as well-developed Internet-based campaigns. Highly competitive primary elections and caucuses, combined with a new era of digital democracy, may reduce the bias of the electorate (see Gimpel, Kaufmann, and Pearson-Merkowitz [2007] on the benefits of electoral competition generally).

Record Turnout in 2008 Caucuses and Primaries

Criticism of the Iowa caucuses for low (and potentially biased) turnout has been a consistent feature of caucus commentary. While voter turnout in the 2008 Iowa caucuses set a record on both sides of the aisle with 236,000 Democrats and 120,000 Republicans attending, this record is not terribly impressive, since as we've seen by any measure—whether our 37% of the state's Democrats and 20% of its Republicans from chapter 6, or McDonald's (2008b) claim of 16% of the voting eligible population (VEP)—far less than a majority of Iowans actually turned out. Most presidential primaries do not fare much better, especially once the nomination is wrapped up, which in most years occurs only a few weeks after it all begins.

But unlike most years, the 2008 presidential nomination contests were competitive over the full primary schedule, as the Democrats battled into June with high turnout in primaries and caucuses across the nation. And even though John McCain became the presumptive Republican nominee when he garnered a majority of delegates in early March, the Republican race was also hotly contested to that point. Turnout, of course, is one of the easiest ways to get a sense of the competitive nature of an election. At the same time, there are varying ways to measure turnout percentages in primaries and caucuses. Some measure turnout as a percentage of a state's total VEP, others measure it as a percentage of the total registered voter population, and still others compare the turnout with a baseline turnout in the general election (Norrander 1986b; see also Norrander [1989] on the debate concerning how to measure primary turnout). Others measure turnout as votes cast, divided by the percentage of either registered Democrats or registered Republicans, since caucuses are closed party events and primaries in many states are as well; that is, independents cannot participate.[1] Figure 9.1 graphs turnout in 2008 primaries as a percentage of the VEP using estimates by McDonald (2008b), which means that noncitizens and disenfranchised felons are excluded from the state population estimates (McDonald and Popkin 2001).

In typical years, turnout at presidential primaries slowly decreases over time as the field of candidates is winnowed and a clear winner emerges (Atkeson and Maestas 2009; Stone, Rapoport, and Atkeson 1995). Figure 9.1 shows a very different trajectory, with turnout in primaries high and increasing through late May of 2008. Compared with 30% in 2004, turnout in the 2008 New Hampshire primary was over 50% of the eligible voter age population, a 20-point increase. Because Michigan's delegates were stripped by the Democratic Party for violating party rules and cut by half by the Republicans, turnout in that state (voting January 15) was abnormally low (20%t), as it was in Louisiana, where there was little campaigning. With these exceptions, turnout in state pri-

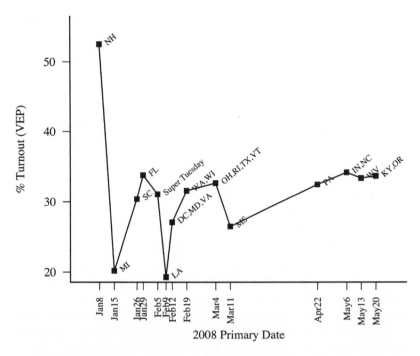

FIGURE 9.1. Voter turnout in the 2008 presidential primaries. For dates with multiple state primaries, average turnout was used. The West Virginia primary on May 13 was only for the Democratic Party.

maries from January through May was well over one-third of the VEP across the nation. From an average of 30% turnout among Super Tuesday voting states (February 5), turnout grew to over 30% in later primaries, including first Ohio (March 4), then Pennsylvania (April 22), and finally North Carolina and Oregon (May 20). Figure 9.1 shows evidence of a highly competitive presidential nomination contest throughout the primary season, driven after Super Tuesday primarily by the battle between Barack Obama and Hillary Clinton.

It is clear that turnout in 2008 benefited from a spike in voter interest from two highly competitive races, get-out-the-vote mobilization efforts that emphasized person-to-person contact and the young, and extensive online campaigning. Research has found that competitive races at the national or state level generally boost turnout (Moran and Fenster 1982; Norrander 1986b; Rothenberg and Brody 1988), especially at Democratic primaries (Geer 1988; Norrander 1992). Record campaign fund-raising in 2008 also appears to be indicative of the extraordinarily high level of public interest in the election and diverse candidate choices for both parties (Mann 2009). And in particular, most serious candidates spent the previous year (and in some cases longer) building impressive organizations in Iowa and nationally that were particularly effective in mobilizing turnout.

A unique feature of 2008 was the apparent mobilization of young voters, particularly at the Iowa caucuses. McDonald (2008b) argues, "Unlike previous efforts to mobilize young voters by concerts and celebrities, young voters are particularly energized when encouraged to vote by their peers. Obama's campaign specifically tailored mobilization efforts to young voters. It clearly worked, as the youth were a larger share of caucus attendees than they were four years ago." By one account, the turnout of younger voters in Iowa tripled in 2008 compared with 2004 and 2000.[2] According to exit polls, voters under the age of thirty made up 22% of the Democrats and 11% of the Republicans in 2008. While Republicans did not have competitive caucuses in 2004, so no comparison is possible, the same source estimates that 17% of Democratic caucusgoers in 2004 were under age thirty. In 2000, across both parties, younger voters represented only 9% of all caucusgoers. So 2008 represented a substantial increase in youth turnout in Iowa. Mobilizing the youth to attend the Iowa caucuses may have had a significant impact on the nomination beyond Iowa, because young voters were a larger share of the electorate there than in primary states such as New Hampshire (McDonald 2008b), and as we show in chapter 7, Iowa's influence reaches well beyond just New Hampshire.

In addition, candidates in 2008 capitalized on the continuing development of the Internet as a tool to mobilize participation. This is a communication forum particularly effective with young voters (Bimber 2003; Mossberger, Tolbert, and McNeal 2008). As Hull (2007) has argued, the Iowa caucuses and the presidential nominating process in general are now "wired and wild" affairs. Barack Obama, for example, raised huge amounts of money online from small donations. While not unprecedented—after all, former Vermont governor Howard Dean made significant use of the Internet in 2004—presidential candidates built new, comprehensive Internet strategies that did more than just duplicate offline campaigning efforts. Candidates used Web sites, social networking tools, and e-mail lists to teach voters about the caucuses and the voting process, perhaps helping to demystify things for those who were most likely to have never attended a caucus before. The three Democratic front-runners—Obama, Clinton, and former North Carolina senator John Edwards—each had information on their Web site educating voters on how to navigate a caucus. Obama's and Edwards's campaigns initially focused exclusively on the Iowa caucus. Obama's site included The Caucus Center, featuring video, descriptions of the caucus process, and the opportunity to sign up for rides to the caucus and child care while there. It also offered an online tutorial that broke down the caucus process into simple steps. Edwards's site included video that used comic-strip sequences to explain the caucus process and describe what happens in a Democratic caucus, with a particular focus on the realignment process (see chapter 3). Republican Web sites, on the other hand, did not need to get so detailed. The Republican nominating process is much simpler, as there is no realignment process and caucus attendees simply cast a straw ballot.

Do Competitive Elections Reduce the Bias of Primary Electorates?

Given the increased level of voter mobilization and turnout in 2008, one could easily support the notion that highly competitive caucuses and primaries lead to a more democratic nominating process. But it is possible that even with higher turnout, bias might still remain, as those with greater resources—time, money, knowledge, and the like—participate, while those without do not (for example, Wolfinger and Rosenstone [1980]). On the other hand, highly competitive elections may stimulate political interest and provide opportunities for increased participation by individuals traditionally less likely to vote, such as the young, the less educated, and the financially less well off.

A number of studies have identified the positive effects on turnout of electoral competition, in U.S. midterm and general presidential elections (Patterson and Caldeira 1983; Cox and Munger 1989; Copeland 1983; Jackson 1996, 1997, 2002; Franklin 2004) and cross-nationally (Blais and Dobrzynska 1998). But few scholars have studied *who* is mobilized by exposure to contested elections and active campaigns. One of the few studies to do so focuses on the effects of presidential battleground states on political engagement of the poor (Geer, Kaufmann, and Pearson-Merkowitz 2007), while Holbrook and McClurg (2005) find presidential campaign activity affects the aggregate partisan composition of an electorate and Pacheco (2008) finds that in competitive campaigns youth turnout increases, although other groups of individuals may be less likely to vote, including the less educated.

Why might competitive elections mobilize turnout of at least some voters traditionally less likely to vote? One answer comes from Bowler and Donovan (2007), who argue that electoral competition may have a more pronounced mobilization effect among individuals with low interest in politics. They propose that there is a pool of citizens who are not regular voters and who have low levels of either interest in politics or political information. Absent active presidential campaigns that increase interest, these voters are not very likely to participate, while citizens who are interested in politics may choose to participate even without competitive races and media coverage. Although presidential contests may have the greatest effects on mobilization, close congressional races may also stimulate turnout (Cox and Munger 1989) or political knowledge and awareness of U.S. Senate candidates (Kahn and Kenney 1999). When the stimulating effects of presidential races are absent, other campaigns can have mobilizing effects. Gubernatorial and U.S. Senate races have larger effects on turnout in midterms than in presidential years (Jackson 1996, 1997, 2002; Patterson and Caldeira 1983). When initiatives and referenda appear on statewide ballots, they can also generate additional information and spark media campaigns, leading to increased turnout (Smith 2001; Lacey 2005; Tolbert, Grummel and Smith 2001; Smith and Tolbert 2004). Citizens exposed to spending in initiative campaigns, as well as higher spending in federal candidate races, are more likely to vote; the effects are the greatest for those with low education (Tolbert, Bowen, and Donovan 2009). Ballot measures may even mobilize nonpartisans relative to partisans, especially in off-year elections (Donovan, Tolbert, and Smith 2009). By stimulating interest among people who are less engaged with politics, electoral competition may have a greater propensity to mobilize the young, those with less formal education, and even nonpartisans.

To sum up the research, campaigns are about information, and competitive campaigns are more likely to provide potential voters with the information they need to become involved and interested in politics. Previous research has been conducted exclusively on simultaneous elections, taking place all on one day. We extend this research here to presidential nomination contests. As we argued earlier, voting is just one

piece of participation. Competitive elections may be a process that reduces the existing bias in who votes in America, but they may also equal-
ize the playing field in other ways by differentially engaging the young or
the less educated.

Does Online Participation Reduce the Bias of Primary Electorates?

Beyond winning the Iowa Democratic caucus, Obama's eventual success
in 2008 has been attributed at least in part to Internet fund-raising and
online mobilization and networking, practices first honed by 2004 Democratic presidential candidate Howard Dean. The Internet has increasingly become an integral part of society, and with its growth it offers new
opportunities for information and communication, potentially influencing political participation (Mossberger, Tolbert, and McNeal 2008).
Communication and mobilization over the Internet means that organizing begins before major media outlets release a story or traditional leaders endorse a candidate. The Internet provides a venue for its users to
react to information by engaging in discussion online or using the communication aspects of the technology to mobilize others. It is the interactive character of the Internet that sets this new medium apart from
broadcast and print media. As mobilization tools, e-mail and newer social networking sites such as Twitter and Facebook enable users to reach
a large audience quickly. Donations can be made online, networks established, and offline political events organized.

A growing body of research demonstrates that the information capacity of the Internet can increase offline participation—for example, those
who read online news or are engaged in online political activities are
more likely to vote (Tolbert and McNeal 2003), contribute to political
campaigns (Bimber 2001, 2003; Kenski and Stroud 2006), attend campaign meetings or volunteer for a campaign (Kenski and Stroud 2006),
and engage in community activities (Shah et al. 2005). Using e-mail, chat
rooms, and online news for political purposes all increase the probability of voting and participation more generally, holding other factors constant (Mossberger, Tolbert, and McNeal 2008). It is worth noting, though,
that not everyone agrees with this rosy view of the Internet and politics.
One British study concluded that more than half of those who were ac-

tive online were not involved offline (di Gennaro and Dutton 2006), and Putnam (2000) warned that online participation is no substitute for face-to-face interaction, necessary for building social capital.

Does the Internet bring in new participants who otherwise would not be involved in politics? If so, and particularly if so during nomination contests, perhaps any bias in who participates might be reduced. This question is at the heart of debates about the utility of the Internet for politics. Political participation traditionally increases with age (Campbell et al. 1960; Wolfinger and Rosenstone 1980), but young people are consistently more likely to participate online in a range of political activities (Bimber 2003; Mossberger, Tolbert, and McNeal 2008; Muhlberger 2003; Gibson, Lusoli, and Ward 2005; di Gennaro and Dutton 2006; Best and Krueger 2005). Drawing on recent Pew Research Center survey data, Mossberger, Tolbert, and McNeal (2008) find that frequent Internet use is associated with increased political participation online, and that for young and middle-aged respondents, Internet use is a significant factor in online participation, even for those who have low levels of political interest. Offline political participation is often influenced by participation online. Internet use appears to have the ability to engage new participants, especially but not solely among the young.

How does the Internet expand participation? Mossberger, Tolbert, and McNeal (2008) argue that it may expand political participation for five reasons: (1) mobilization via e-mail, (2) lowered costs in time and effort, (3) increased benefits of participation, (4) reduced resources needed for participation, and (5) heightened exposure to political stimuli and information online through accidental mobilization. Online participation may engage those who have only a modest interest in politics, including the young and even those with less formal education, although those with greater interest may find it possible to participate at even higher levels using the tools of the Internet.

This growing research on the Internet and political participation has been conducted almost exclusively in the context of general elections. But the sequential nature of presidential nomination contests provides an opportunity to study participation online (and offline) in different states over time, as campaigns ebb and flow and as voters in later states learn about what happens in the earlier ones. In particular, we can look especially closely at the potential of the Internet to mobilize the young over the course of the primaries, since younger citizens are historically much less likely to participate. We have the chance to examine how the

Internet might differentially mobilize disadvantaged groups, such as the young or the less educated.

The 2008 Nomination Contest as a Laboratory

To answer questions of *who* is engaged in the presidential nominating process, we draw on three of our pre-election University of Iowa Hawkeye Polls conducted during the 2008 nomination campaigns with virtually identical question wording, but conducted in different states voting at different times. For the present analyses we use our October 2007 Iowa registered voter survey (742 respondents), our February 2008 national survey of registered voters in forty states (1,285 respondents; respondents from states that had already voted were omitted, as were Alaska and Hawaii) conducted immediately before and after Super Tuesday, and our April 2008 Pennsylvania Democratic primary survey (205 respondents).[3] All were conducted before the caucuses or primaries in the states surveyed. In each of the registered voter samples, a respondent had to self-select into a battery of questions asking if they planned to participate in the Republican or Democratic primaries or caucuses. Independents were included if they said they planned to vote in one or the other party's contest, but those who would not select a party were omitted from the sample. That had the effect of making all the samples slightly more likely voter samples. These three surveys cover a lengthy period of time, from the run-up to the caucuses, the high point of simultaneous primaries, and a Democratic contest that stood alone near the end of the campaign.[4] We pool responses to these three surveys to compare differences in participation and engagement among respondents voting early, middle, and late in the presidential nomination.

Descriptive Patterns

Our goal here is to compare participation in Iowa with what happened in later states in the sequential nominating process. Respondents in all three surveys were asked a battery of questions about their online participation in politics. Figure 9.2 shows the percentage of respondents from each sample who engaged in varying political activities online. The figure shows relatively higher online engagement in politics for Iowa voters compared with voters nationally. At the time of the survey, 50% of the Iowa caucus sample had visited a candidate's Web site, compared with roughly one-quarter of registered voters nationally or in Pennsylvania. Similarly, almost half of Iowa voters had sent or received political e-mail, compared with one-third of the national sample. However, roughly the same proportion of Iowans and Americans from other states read political news online (50%), or gave money to a candidate online (6%–7%). Unfortunately, the Iowa survey did not ask questions about watching a campaign video on YouTube or signing up online to support a candidate, but nationwide and in Pennsylvania, roughly 14% had done the former and 10% the latter. Figure 9.2 paints a picture of growing online participation in the 2008 presidential nominating process and shows higher engagement at the Iowa caucuses in a couple key areas. Despite lower turnout at caucuses than at primaries, Iowans were very engaged politically online.

Figure 9.3 reports the percentage of respondents in the three samples who engaged in traditional grassroots political activities, such as at-

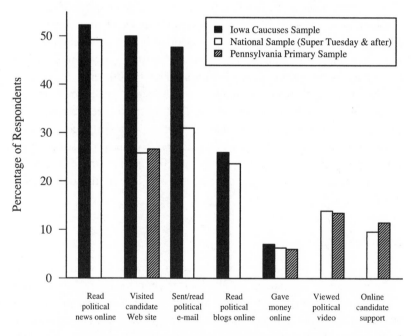

FIGURE 9.2. Percentage of respondents politically active online in presidential primaries and caucuses, comparing early-, middle-, and late-voting states.

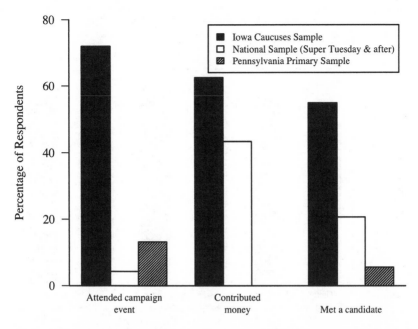

Percentage of Respondents

- Iowa Caucuses Sample
- National Sample (Super Tuesday & after)
- Pennsylvania Primary Sample

Attended campaign event

Contributed money

Met a candidate

FIGURE 9.3. Percentage of respondents politically active offline in presidential primaries and caucuses: comparing early-, middle-, and late-voting states.

tending a campaign event, contributing money to a candidate or party, or meeting a candidate for elected office. In each case we see much higher offline political participation among Iowa caucusgoers and registered voters than registered voters nationwide or in Pennsylvania. In the Iowa sample, almost three-quarters (72%) had attended a campaign event, compared with only 4% nationally and 13% of Pennsylvania registered voters. This reflects retail politics in Iowa and the attention lavished on the state by presidential candidates and the national media. In other words, Iowans have the *opportunity* to participate if they wish to do so, and they appear to take that opportunity. Again, almost 63% of Iowans had contributed money to a candidate (offline), compared with 40% nationally, a 23-point difference. Most shockingly, more than half the Iowa sample voters had actually met a presidential candidate, compared with 21% nationally. This is consistent with Hull's (2007) account of the Iowa caucuses in the 2004 presidential nomination as a place where "grassroots politics rule." Despite lower turnout in caucuses compared with primaries, there is clearly high political participation in the Iowa caucuses.

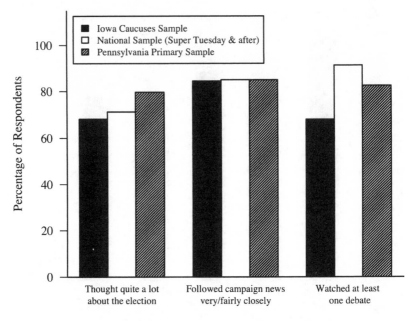

FIGURE 9.4. Percentage of respondents interested in presidential primaries and caucuses: comparing early-, middle-, and late-voting states.

Figure 9.4 displays measures of civic engagement across the three samples, and here we see a reverse of the earlier trends. Registered voters nationally and in Pennsylvania were more likely than Iowans to report they were very interested in the campaign ("had thought quite a lot about the election") or had watched at least one debate among the political candidates, possibly due to their longer exposure to the campaign. Among those voting late in the primary season (Pennsylvania primary), nearly 80% of respondents had thought a lot about the election and 82% had watched a political debate, compared with 68% of Iowans. This result may also reflect that the Iowa survey was conducted nine weeks before the caucuses, and the other surveys taken almost immediately before their events. However, candidates had been active in Iowa for over a year at that point, so few Iowans would have been unaware that they had a caucus coming up. Surprisingly, nearly identical percentages of respondents from all three samples (85%) said they followed campaign news very or fairly closely. Figure 9.4 shows increased interest and very high engagement in the 2008 presidential nominations overall, but also evidence that residents of late primary states benefit from increased information generated by earlier nomination contests, supporting our aggregate findings in chapter 7 (see also Battaglini, Morton, and Palfrey [2007]).

Figure 9.5 pools respondents from the Iowa and national samples to explore the frequency of online political participation for varying age groups. Online activities include whether the respondent had (1) read political news online; (2) visited a candidate Web site; (3) sent or received political e-mail; (4) read a political blog online; and/or (5) donated money to a candidate online. There is strong evidence that the young (18 to 29 years old) were significantly more likely than the middle-aged and older respondents to be engaged in presidential electoral activities online. Of young respondents, 22% were highly engaged in the presidential nomination online (reporting engaging in 4–5 activities), another 43% were moderately active online (2–3 activities), and only 35% were either not engaged in the nomination online or had only low engagement (1 activity). Thus, 65% of young people in our samples of registered

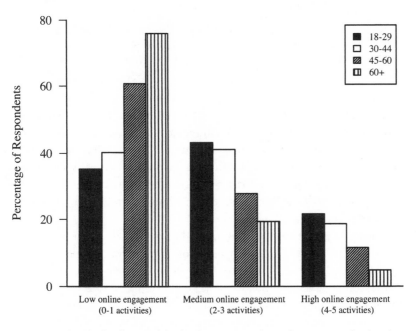

FIGURE 9.5. Level of online participation by age group in 2008 caucuses and primaries. Online activities include whether the respondent had (1) read political news online, (2) visited a candidate Web site, (3) sent or received political e-mail, (4) read a political blog online, and/or (5) donated money to a candidate online.

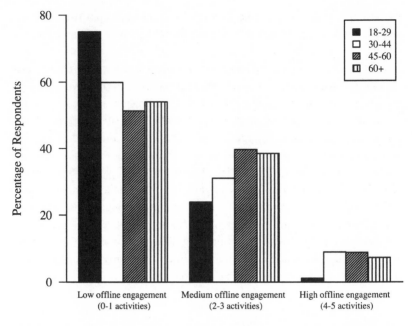

FIGURE 9.6. Level of offline participation by age group in 2008 caucuses and primaries. Offline activities include whether the respondent had (1) attended a campaign event, (2) contacted an elected official, (3) contributed money to a candidate, (4) met a presidential candidate, and/or (5) worked on a campaign as a volunteer.

voters were active (moderate or high level) in the presidential nomination online. In comparison, of those in the oldest age group (60+), only 5% were very active online, another 19% were moderately active online, and most (76%) were either not involved politically online or only slightly so (1 activity). Figure 9.5 provides strong evidence that the young may benefit the most from campaigning and mobilization online in presidential nomination contests.

Figure 9.6 graphs levels of traditional or grassroots political participation by the four age groups, again pooling the Iowa and national survey samples. These offline activities include whether the respondent had (1) attended a campaign event; (2) contacted an elected official; (3) contributed money to a candidate; (4) met a presidential candidate; and (5) worked on a campaign as a volunteer. Here we see the opposite trend, with the middle-aged or older group being the most engaged in traditional offline politics. Of those 45 to 60 years old, 9% were highly engaged in the presidential nomination offline and 40% were moderately active. Combined, almost 50% of the middle aged were engaged politically in the 2008 presidential nomination. Of the young (18 to 29 years old), only 1% were highly engaged offline and another 24% were moderately engaged. Traditional political participation in Iowa and nationally remains a domain where increased age leads to higher engagement. These patterns mirror the existing research on online participation in general elections.

Figures 9.7 and 9.8 examine activities by levels of education and show that those with the most education (college degree or postgraduate education) were the most likely to be engaged both online and offline in 2008. Of those with a college degree, over half were moderately or very engaged in politics online, compared with those with a high school education or less, only 23% of whom were engaged at this level. This pattern of increased education correlating with online political activity is consistent with work on the digital divide (Mossberger, Tolbert, and Stansbury 2003). Education is considered the single most important predictor of political engagement and turnout (Wolfinger and Rosenstone 1980),

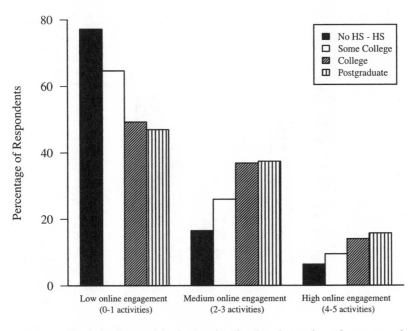

FIGURE 9.7. Level of online participation by educational attainment in 2008 caucuses and primaries. Online activities include whether the respondent had (1) read political news online, (2) visited a candidate Web site, (3) sent or received political e-mail, (4) read a political blog online, and/or (5) donated money to a candidate online.

and our data from presidential nomination contests demonstrate that
those with more education are more engaged in politics both online and
offline.

Recent research argues that "digital citizens," or those who are online daily, are much more likely to use the Internet for politics as well as
at work and for economic activities. Frequency of Internet use leads to
the migration of many daily tasks online (Mossberger, Tolbert, and Mc-
Neal 2008). Figure 9.9 shows strong evidence of this during the 2008 caucuses and primaries. Of respondents who are online hourly, 28% were
very active in politics on the Web, while another 49% were moderately
active during that period. Combined, 77% of respondents who are online virtually all the time reported active use of the Internet for political
engagement in the 2008 presidential nomination campaigns. Similarly,
56% of respondents who are online daily reported moderate to high online engagement in politics. But when we look at those who use the Internet more sporadically—about once a week—we find only 31% politically

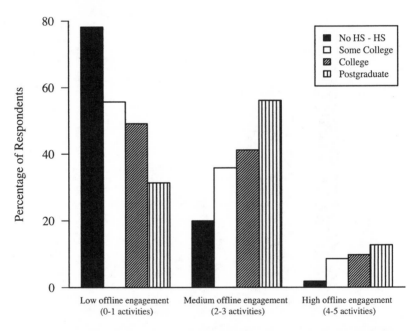

FIGURE 9.8. Level of offline participation by educational attainment in 2008 caucuses and
primaries. Offline activities include whether the respondent had (1) attended a campaign
event, (2) contacted an elected official, (3) contributed money to a candidate, (4) met a
presidential candidate, and/or (5) worked on a campaign as a volunteer.

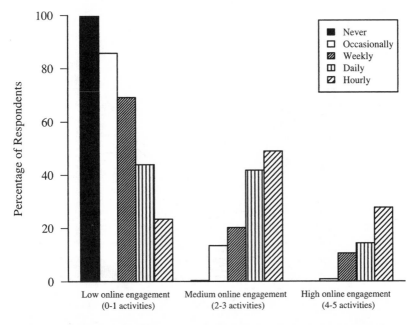

FIGURE 9.9. Level of online participation by Internet use in 2008 caucuses and primaries. Online activities include whether the respondent had (1) read political news online, (2) visited a candidate Web site, (3) sent or received political e-mail, (4) read a political blog online, and/or (5) donated money to a candidate online.

active online. Figure 9.10 shows the same pattern for offline participation in caucuses and primaries, although not quite as strong. Respondents who are online nearly all the time also have the highest level of offline engagement in the presidential nominating process.

In addition to the other patterns, an unmistakable general pattern is higher participation among Iowans compared with the national sample. Respondents residing in states voting early in the presidential nominating process, such as Iowa, clearly benefit from increased online and offline participation, although there is some evidence that respondents in late-voting states may have increased interest in the election and exposure to political information.

Multivariate Analysis: Who Participates in Caucuses and Primaries?

The descriptive analysis clearly suggests that participation rates differ among voters in early and late states, and that offline and online partic-

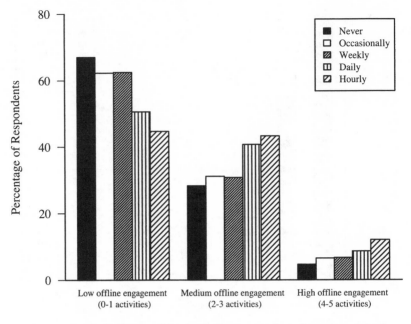

FIGURE 9.10. Level of offline participation by Internet use in 2008 caucuses and primaries. Offline activities include whether the respondent had (1) attended a campaign event,
(2) contacted an elected official, (3) contributed money to a candidate, (4) met a presidential candidate, and/or (5) worked on a campaign as a volunteer.

ipation are different things. But do these results hold when the impact
of other demographic and attitudinal factors are taken into account, or
when overlapping factors such as age, education, and income are measured together? To answer this question, we turn to multivariate regression analysis to predict who was engaged and politically active in caucuses and primaries nationwide. Assessing the influence of multiple
factors also allows us to understand, with a level of statistical certainty,
the size of the effect a given factor has on participation.

We develop several multivariate models, with the details presented in
appendix C. Here we will describe the results of those models. The Iowa
caucus sample and the national sample are first analyzed separately, as
they were conducted at two different points in the nominating process.
The Pennsylvania primary sample is not individually analyzed due to its
relatively low number of respondents. We then analyze a pooled sample
consisting of the Iowa caucus and national samples, followed by an examination of all three samples combined. The results from the pooled

samples, using dummy variables to account for the various time periods, provide insight into participation and engagement over the span of the sequential election process.

We examine four dependent variables—two of which are related to political participation, and two to civic engagement: (1) *online partici-pation*, (2) *offline participation*, (3) *political interest*, and (4) *following campaign news*. *Online participation*, discussed above, is simply a mea-sure of the total number of online political activities in which the respon-dent reported taking part. *Offline participation* is a similar construct measuring the total number of traditional or grassroots political activi-ties in which the respondent took part. When analyzing the Iowa caucus sample, the national sample, or the combination of the two, the *online and offline participation indices* measures range from 0 to 5 activities.[5]

The remaining two dependent variables capture a sense of civic en-gagement during the nominating process. *Political interest* in the pres-idential nomination is measured by the question, "How much thought have you given to the coming 2008 presidential election?" with higher values measuring increased interest in the election.[6] *Following cam-paign news* is based on the question, "How closely have you followed news about the candidates for president?" again with higher values mea-suring closely following election news.[7] These two questions were in-cluded on all the survey instruments used for this analysis. Since all the dependent variables examined are categorical with three or more cat-egories, ordered logistic regression was employed to estimate all the models.[8]

The models include a number of control variables. The models pre-dicting political participation control for political interest[9] and fre-quency of Internet use.[10] We also measure a number of socioeconomic/ demographic variables that are commonly found to be associated with political participation, including educational attainment (categor-ical, 1–7), family income (categorical, 1–9), age (measured in years), gen-der (binary, 1 = male), marital status (binary, 1 = married), and strong partisanship (Democrat or Republican = 1 and nonpartisans coded 0). Individuals who identify as strong partisans are often found to be more active and interested in politics and more likely to participate. We also measure frequency of attendance at religious services, given reported links to political participation (Putnam 2000) and individual political efficacy.[11] Those who are efficacious are thought to be more likely to par-ticipate in political activities and be more politically engaged.

Iowa Caucus Results

Table C.9.1 presents the first set of political participation (columns 1 and 2) and civic engagement (columns 3 and 4) results using the Iowa caucus sample. As expected, Iowans who are interested in the election are more likely to participate in the presidential nominating process, both online and offline. Higher Internet use increases political participation and civic engagement generally, but at the same time Internet use does not increase the likelihood of following campaign news specifically. This may be because much campaign news is still presented through traditional media, such as television or newspapers. Frequency of church attendance is associated with higher traditional political participation, but not online participation. As expected, respondents with higher political efficacy are more likely to participate in the caucuses, be interested in the election, and follow campaign news. There is nothing terribly surprising in any of these results. But the patterns indicate measurement and construct validity.

Increased education leads to higher political participation and following news online, as expected, but not to political interest per se. Those with low and high education were statistically the same in terms of interest in the caucuses. Interest in the Iowa caucuses among the less educated may have been spiked by the intensive campaign. Additionally, retail politics in Iowa may cause respondents of all education groups, even the less educated, to be more likely to be interested in the election.

While wealthier individuals are more likely to participate in the caucuses, as predicted by the literature, poorer individuals are statistically more interested in the Iowa caucuses. This suggests that highly competitive races and retail politics, which characterize the Iowa caucuses, may increase political interest among the poor (Gimpel, Kaufmann, and Pearson-Merkowitz 2007). Participation of the poor and less educated in the Iowa caucuses is unique (Stone, Abramowitz, and Rapoport 1989), as few scholars have found mechanisms that reduce the class bias of the electorate (Schattschneider 1960; Verba, Schlozman, and Brady 1995).

Older respondents are more likely to participate in offline activities, be interested in the caucuses, and follow campaign news, as expected. At the same time, the negative coefficient for age and online participation suggests that the young may be more likely to be active online, although this finding does not quite reach statistical significance.[12] Strong Democrats are significantly more likely to participate in traditional po-

litical activities (offline), and be more engaged (political interest and follow campaign news) than weak partisans or independents, but they are
not more likely to be active online. This suggests that online engagement
in the caucuses may have mobilized weak partisans and independents.
Many of the control variables are statistically significant, suggesting a
good fit of these data to the model.

Overall we see evidence that the higher turnout in 2008 at the caucuses and online politics may have led to less bias in political participation and engagement beyond turnout, specifically among the less educated, less affluent, weak partisans or independents, and the young.
These findings reinforce the results of the analysis of Iowa turnout presented in chapter 6, where we find relatively few differences between
Iowa caucus attendees and the registered voter population.

National Sample Results

Table C.9.2 in reports results using an identical set of explanatory and
outcome variables as table C.9.1, but for the national Super Tuesday
(and later) sample from forty states. One additional variable, *minority*,
is added, which is a binary variable indicating whether the respondent
is nonwhite (Latino, black, or Asian American).[13] While frequency of
Internet use and formal education are statistically significant predictors
of higher political participation generally and following campaign news,
higher family income is associated with traditional political participation and political interest in the national sample, unlike the Iowa sample.
Older respondents are more likely to participate in traditional nomination activities and the two measures of civic engagement, but less likely
to participate online, while younger voters are more likely to be engaged
online. Minority respondents are less likely to be interested in the presidential nomination or follow campaign news, but no less likely to be active politically. Strong partisans are significantly more likely to participate and be engaged (all four variables), unlike in Iowa, where strong
Democrats are not more likely to be politically active online. Political efficacy is positively associated with all four of the dependent variables.

While there are similarities between factors predicting participation
and engagement in the Iowa caucuses and nationally in other primaries
and caucuses, there are also significant departures. The highly competitive Iowa caucuses appear to have engaged peripheral voters, such as the
poor, the less educated, and even nonpartisans and weak partisans, more

than nominating events in later states. We also see evidence in both analyses of mobilization and engagement of the young online.

Pooling the Iowa and National Samples

Table C.9.3 allows us to make comparisons between the Iowa caucus sample and the national sample by pooling the two. The models in table C.9.3 were estimated using the same set of predictor variables as the previous two tables, but with the addition of a dummy variable for Iowa respondents. The regression coefficient for the Iowa variable for political participation is positive and statistically significant. Iowa respondents are more likely to participate in both online and offline activities when compared with those interviewed in states that voted on Super Tuesday or later, holding other factors constant. When looking at civic engagement, however, Iowa voters are less likely to have thought extensively about the election or followed news about the campaigns. Table C.9.4 adds in the Pennsylvania primary survey to the pooled sample. The estimation of the models in table C.9.4 is similar to the models discussed above, with a few minor exceptions and more limited dependent variables due to question wording.[14] The results are consistent with those reported in table C.9.3. Individuals from the national and Pennsylvania samples are significantly less likely to be politically active than those from the Iowa sample, and more likely to be politically engaged (interested and follow campaign news).

One way to interpret these results is that the first-in-the-nation role of the Iowa caucuses, along with extensive grassroots campaigning and a highly competitive election, increased participation in Iowa compared with primaries and caucuses nationally. The extended and competitive race between Obama and Clinton was able to create greater levels of public attention to the process than normal, but did not increase participation to the level of the Iowa caucuses.

Clarifying the Results: Different Effects in Different Nomination Contests

However, since it is difficult to interpret the magnitude of these effects from the regression coefficients alone, we turn to predicted probability graphs to understand the substantive meaning of the ordered logistic regression coefficients reported in table C.9.4. In figure 9.11, we graph the probability of being politically engaged online in 2008 presidential

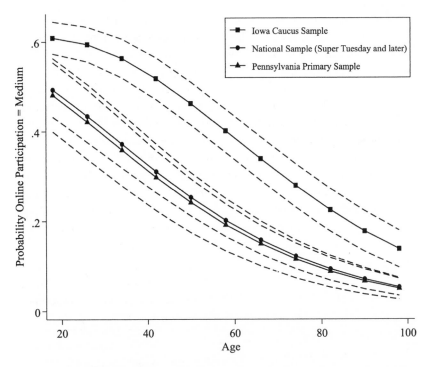

FIGURE 9.11. Predicted probability of online participation (medium level) by age, pooled samples. Predicted probabilities are based on the *Online Participation* model from table C.9.4. The variable *Age* was set to vary over all possible values. All other variables were set to their mean or modal value depending on their level of measurement. The dashed lines represent the 95% confidence intervals of the predicted probabilities.

nomination contests, comparing respondents from Iowa, nationally, and from Pennsylvania based on the coefficients in table C.9.4, column 1. Along the horizontal axis is the respondent's age. The dashed lines represent the 95% confidence interval around the predicted values. Across all three samples we see not only that the young have a much higher probability of engagement in politics online than the middle aged or older, but that Iowans have a higher probability of using the Internet for political involvement than respondents nationally or in Pennsylvania. Holding all other factors constant (such as a respondent's education, income, gender, partisanship, and so on), a thirty-year-old from Iowa has a 60% probability of being moderately engaged online, compared with a thirty-year-old in other states, who has only a 45% probability of moderate online engagement—a difference of 15 points based on state residence alone. In comparison, a sixty-year-old from Iowa has a 40% probability of moderate engagement in the caucuses online, compared with a sixty-year-old nationally, who has only a 20% probability of this same level of online engagement—a 20-point difference. The figure provides evidence of a differential mobilization of the young from politics online surrounding the 2008 presidential nomination, both in Iowa and nationally, but the effects are most pronounced in Iowa. Again, we have an indication of the unique intensity of the Iowa campaigns.

Figure 9.12 plots a similar estimate for the probability of traditional or offline political engagement in caucuses and primaries based on table C.9.4, column 2. There is a stark contrast, with Iowans having a much higher probability of offline political participation than registered voters nationally and in Pennsylvania, but this time we see no differences by

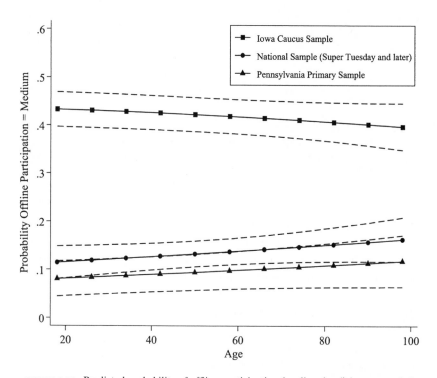

FIGURE 9.12. Predicted probability of offline participation (medium level) by age, pooled samples. Predicted probabilities are based on the *Offline Participation* model from table C.9.4. The variable *Age* was set to vary over all possible values. All other variables were set to their mean or modal value depending on their level of measurement. The dashed lines represent the 95% confidence intervals of the predicted probabilities.

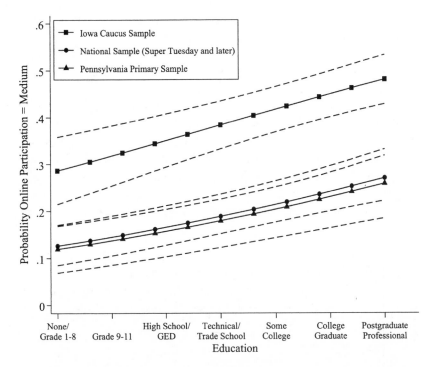

FIGURE 9.13. Predicted probability of online participation (medium level) by educational attainment, pooled samples. Predicted probabilities are based on the *Online Participation* model from table C.9.4. The variable *Education* was set to vary over all possible values. All other variables were set to their mean or modal value depending on their level of measurement. The dashed lines represent the 95% confidence intervals of the predicted probabilities.

age. The young, middle aged, and older respondents all have roughly the same probability of a moderate level of offline political participation. However, traditional engagement in the Iowa caucuses is almost 30 points higher than nationally; respondents from Iowa have a 45% probability of being moderately engaged in the caucuses (1 of 2 activities), while nationally the probability of engagement is just over 10%. In sum, only online participation provides a distinctive advantage for the young. While turnout is relatively low at caucuses compared with primaries, varying forms of active political participation beyond voting, using the Internet, and traditional politics were higher in Iowa than nationally in 2008.

Figure 9.13 graphs the probability of a moderate level of online political participation by an individual's education level. Consistent with the descriptive graph (fig. 9.7), increased education leads to a higher probability of being politically active online at caucuses and in primaries nationwide. We see that engagement in the Iowa caucuses (top line) is 20 percentage points higher than nationally for all education levels, consistent with the previous graphs.

Retail politics in Iowa, however, provides an opportunity for intensive campaign exposure without needing skills to use a computer or access the Internet. Figure 9.14 graphs the probability of offline or grassroots political participation, comparing the Iowa caucuses, primaries and caucuses nationwide, and the Pennsylvania primary. While again traditional political participation is much higher at the Iowa caucuses than nationwide, the less educated are not disadvantaged, and in fact those

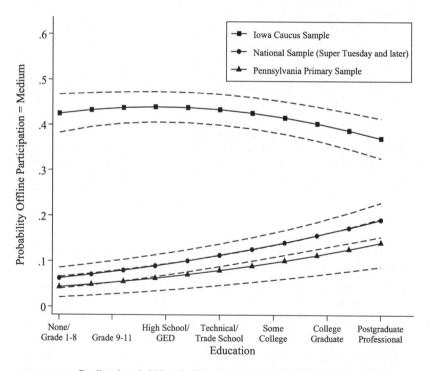

FIGURE 9.14. Predicted probability of offline participation (medium level) by educational attainment, pooled samples. Predicted probabilities are based on the *Offline Participation* model from table C.9.4. The variable *Education* was set to vary over all possible values. All other variables were set to their mean or modal value depending on their level of measurement. The dashed lines represent the 95% confidence intervals of the predicted probabilities.

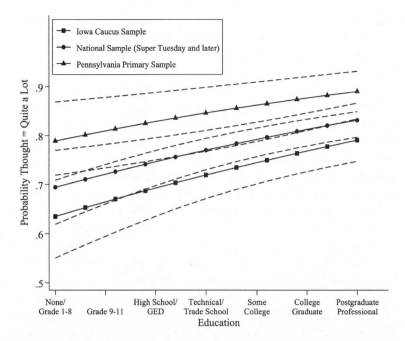

FIGURE 9.15. Predicted probability of high political interest by educational attainment, pooled samples. Predicted probabilities are based on the *Thought Given to Elections* model from table C.9.4. The variable *Education* was set to vary over all possible values. All other variables were set to their mean or modal value depending on their level of measurement. The dashed lines represent the 95% percent confidence intervals of the predicted probabilities.

with only a high school diploma or an associate's degree tend to have a slightly higher probability of participation than a respondent with a college or postgraduate degree, all else being equal. On the other hand, the slope of the curves for the national sample and the Pennsylvania sample follows the expected pattern, with increased education leading to a higher probability of traditional political engagement. There is evidence of a differential mobilization effect for the less educated, who are relatively more engaged offline in the Iowa caucuses (likely due to retail politics) than nationally. Consistent with some previous research, highly competitive elections, like the Iowa caucuses, may mobilize turnout of the young and less educated (Donovan and Tolbert 2007). This may be the most important result reported in this chapter.

Figure 9.15 shows the predicted probability of expressing interest in 2008 primaries and caucuses. Here we see evidence of early nominating events generating information used by voters in later states, consistent with previous research based on experiments in laboratory settings (Battaglini, Morton, and Palfrey 2007) and with our argument in chapter 7. While political interest increases with education across the three samples, we see the probability of being very interested in the nomination is the highest in Pennsylvania (80% probability) compared with 70%–80% nationally, and is the lowest among Iowa caucusgoers. Again, this may reflect the timing of the Iowa caucus survey, which was conducted nine weeks before the caucuses. Nevertheless, late nominating events appear to benefit from widespread civic engagement among the population and extensive media information, if not higher political participation per se.

Lastly, there is some evidence that daily Internet use matters, in that it shapes participation in politics both online and offline and in sequential presidential nominations. In Iowa and nationally, respondents who never use the Internet or only occasionally use the medium are predicted to not be active politically online. This is expected. Yet, moving from weekly use to daily use and hourly use, we see a steady and steep increase in the probability of being moderately active online (3 of 5 political activities). This evidence supports Hull's (2007) "wired and wild" impact of the Iowa caucuses, as online participation increases with frequency of Internet use faster in Iowa than nationally. Overall, more frequent use of the Internet is associated with increased engagement in 2008 primaries and caucuses, controlling for other demographic factors.

Conclusion: Iowa as the Most Contested Election

By many accounts—media coverage, the field of candidates, candidate visits—the Iowa caucuses are the most "competitive" contest in the presidential nomination, as the winnowing process has yet to begin. The media campaign and competition among so many presidential hopefuls experienced by Iowa citizens may be comparable to key swing states in recent general presidential elections, such as Ohio and Pennsylvania in 2008, Ohio in 2004, or Florida in 2000. One measurable and institutionalized effect of the Iowa caucuses is money from candidate campaigns, media coverage, and voter mobilization drives. These three ingredients, however, are associated not only with the Iowa caucuses or competitive nomination contests in other states, but with competitive presidential, congressional, and state-level races, and salient ballot measure elections held in the United States and cross-nationally (Tolbert, Bowen, and Donovan 2009; Blais and Dobrzynska 1998). If competitive elections are defined as having these beneficial spillover effects, we may have confidence that the same participatory dynamics found in Iowa would occur in other states if they lead in the process.

The 2008 presidential primaries and caucuses may be an ideal test case of the effects of electoral competition on participation and the composition of state electorates. While Iowans are more engaged both online and offline than those in later voting states, we see differential effects by both age and education. Young voters are significantly more engaged online in primaries and caucuses nationwide, while the less educated are relatively more engaged offline in the Iowa caucuses than nationally. This is consistent with scholars who argue that competitive elections may improve democracy (Donovan and Hunsaker 2009; McDonald and Samples 2006), but also with those who contend that Iowa's grassroots politics is key (Hull 2007). There is also evidence that the poor are more interested in the Iowa caucuses, paralleling higher engagement by the poor in battleground states during the general election (Gimpel, Kaufmann, and Pearson-Merkowitz 2007), but this finding is not evident in our national data. We also find that those voting later in the process may be more interested in the nomination and following election news more closely. This shows the benefits of the sequential nominating process, where earlier voters create information used by later voters (Morton and Williams 2001).

Conventional wisdom holds that participation is high at early nominating events and then falls steadily throughout the nominating process. The anomaly of the highly competitive 2008 Democratic nomination and record turnout across primaries and caucuses is a good indication that competition fosters mobilization, participation, and turnout in states beyond Iowa. Competitive nominating events and online politics may reduce the bias of primary electorates by mobilizing the young, the less educated, and the less affluent, and even nonpartisans. A take-home lesson from 2008 may be that competitive presidential nominations make the process work better, leading to more representative electorates and reducing bias in participation.

This research also has implications for theory building. The evidence presented here is from a nomination campaign, not a general presidential or midterm election, which is the basis for previous research. Thus, we extend the literature on the effects of electoral competition, politics online, and the composition of electorates to a primary/caucus environment. This suggests that theories of competition and online mobilization based on simultaneous elections do apply to sequential elections, but the effects are attenuated in states voting early in the process, not late. In sum, while turnout is relatively low in caucuses compared with primaries, there are multiple facets of participation beyond turnout, and we find a differential mobilization of disadvantaged groups through retail politics in Iowa and online politics in Iowa and nationally. If electoral activity mobilizes disadvantaged voters (young, less educated, poor) more than others, then competitive elections may have consequences not only for increasing turnout, but also for altering the composition of the electorate in nominations as well as general elections.

Political scientists have long been concerned about the bias of the electorate (Schattschneider 1960), as an electorate with an upper-class bias can lead to public policy favoring the preferences of voters rather than nonvoters (Lijphart 1997; Griffin and Newman 2005; Bartels 2008). An advantage of highly competitive elections and campaigning online may be to lessen the *bias* of state primary and caucus electorates. These benefits are most pronounced in early nominating events, such as the Iowa caucuses, but there is some evidence for it nationally, specifically in the online mobilization of young voters.

PART IV
Changing the Rules

CHAPTER TEN

Reforming the Presidential Nominating Process

With Daniel C. Bowen

If we had an opportunity to design from scratch a way to pick a president, it is inconceivable that we would arrive at our present system. — Thomas E. Mann, "Is This Any Way to Pick a President?" (2009)

One thing that should be apparent from the previous chapters is that the rules of the game, and of the Iowa caucuses in particular, structure presidential nomination contests and affect outcomes. These rules govern which states vote early and which vote later in the sequential process, and why some states use caucuses and others primary elections. But we also know from a growing literature on election reform and political institutions that rules governing politics can and do change (Cain, Donovan, and Tolbert 2008; Smith and Springer 2009; Kamarck 2009). In fact the rules of the presidential nominating process, although appearing quite stable since the early 1970s reforms, have in fact had many changes over the years. Some of these changes were efforts by candidates to structure the process to their own benefit, while others have been about the parties' efforts to increase transparency and representation (Kamarck 2009). And change is often debated following the completion of the nomination season, usually most vociferously by the party that loses the general election.

Many argue that despite the changes over the past thirty years—or perhaps because of those changes—the way we nominate our presidential candidates today is unfair. The citizens in states that hold their nomination contests early in the process get smothered with attention from candidates and media, while citizens in states that vote later barely get noticed. Frequently, the contest is over almost before it starts, leaving many citizens (sometimes the majority of Americans) with no role in selecting their party's nominee. Turnout in these later states naturally plummets. The 2008 contests were the exception that proves the rule. Even though we all remember that the Democrats went down to the wire, the Republican nomination was decided by the beginning of March, excluding Republicans voting in later states from the process of determining their nominee. Critics of the current system argue that the selection of presidential candidates, one of the most important decisions that American voters make, should not be determined by a haphazard sequencing of state nomination contests. So in this chapter we focus on alternative rules that might be used to structure American presidential nominations, namely holding a national primary or rotating the order of state primaries and caucuses. We use public opinion data to examine reactions to proposals for reforming existing nomination system rules, testing whether individual support for reform is shaped by self-interest as defined by state population, state sequence, and perceptions of state influence in selecting presidential nominees. In the next and final chapter, we offer our own views about what might be done to improve the nominating process.

The Chaotic Race to the Front in 2008

As discussed briefly in chapter 2, the 2008 presidential nomination was marked by the most aggressive state frontloading in recent history. Frontloading occurs when states schedule their primaries and caucuses near the beginning of the delegate selection calendar in order to have a greater voice in the process (Mayer and Busch 2004). In response to increased frontloading over the years, both the Democratic and the Republican National Committees revised their schedules and rules for 2008. The Democrats allowed two states (Nevada and South Carolina) to join Iowa and New Hampshire in violating the official February 5 start date. Nevada and South Carolina were selected because of their racial diversity— Hispanic in the former case, African American in the latter case—in order to compensate for the racially unrepresentative character of Iowa and New Hampshire. The Republicans also set a February 5 start date for their nomination contest window.[1] Although the Republican rules called for states going too early to lose half their delegate vote, the Democrats implemented a "death penalty," threatening such states with the loss of all their delegates. The *New York Times* called these changes "the biggest shift in the way Democrats have nominated their presidential candidates in 30 years."[2] Yet these changes did little to lessen frontloading or modify the course of events in 2008; 70% of all delegates were chosen by the beginning of March.

Despite the threat of lost delegates, two large states (Michigan and Florida) defied both national parties and moved the dates of their primaries to before the official February 5 start. Initially, these large-population states were sanctioned by both political parties in accordance with the rules, and were stripped of their delegates.[3] However, because the Republicans only took away half their delegates, Republican candidates ran active campaigns in both states, with former Massachusetts governor Mitt Romney winning Michigan and Arizona senator John McCain winning Florida. The Democrats, on the other hand, pledged not to campaign in either state, so as not to anger voters in Iowa and New Hampshire. While all candidates remained on the ballot in Florida, election law in Michigan allowed them to withdraw, and all but New York senator Hillary Clinton and Connecticut senator Christopher Dodd did so.

The Republican rules meant that Florida and Michigan still "mattered" before February 5, and the result was that while Romney won Michigan, he gained no momentum from it after losing Iowa and New Hampshire. Moreover, his victory was in keeping with expectations, since Romney had Michigan ties, including that his father had been governor there. McCain went on to win South Carolina, cementing his front-runner status, which he all but sealed in Florida one week before the official start date of February 5. Following Super Tuesday, McCain wrapped up the nomination quite quickly, finally acquiring an absolute majority of delegates by March 5. Here Republican rules mattered greatly. Many Republican contests were winner-take-all. McCain only needed a plurality of votes in many states to take all the delegates, allowing him to quickly build an insurmountable lead.

Things went quite differently for the Democrats. Although several candidates dropped out immediately after Iowa, and former North Carolina senator John Edwards withdrew just before Super Tuesday, Clinton and Illinois senator Barack Obama battled for six months before Obama emerged with a majority of the elected and unelected (super) delegates after the final primaries on June 3. It seems possible that the outcome could have been different had Michigan and Florida not been sanctioned and had the candidates campaigned there. Clinton, who won both states, might have gained momentum if Michigan's 157 delegates and Florida's 211 delegates had been counted in full early on in the primary season. This momentum may have resulted in more positive media attention and campaign donations for Clinton. Thus, the Democratic Party's choice of a presidential candidate might have hinged in part on the frontloading decisions of Michigan and Florida and the sanctions levied by the national party.

The chaos associated with the rush to the front is exacerbated by what is known as the "invisible primary," that is, the period before the first nominating event, when candidates engage in extensive fund-raising (Cohen et al. 2008; Aldrich 2009). As candidates increasingly opt out of public financing of their campaigns for both the primaries and the general election, early money may matter even more than it has in the past. One concern with a highly frontloaded nomination schedule is that only those candidates with the most money, name recognition, and media attention early on can win their party's nomination.

Events in 2008 and in previous years encouraged continued discussion among policy makers, elected officials, the media, scholars, and the general public about the perceived failures of the current nominating process and the need for reform (Tolbert and Squire 2009; see also Mayer [2009]; Mayer and Busch [2004]; Cook [2003]; Donovan and Bowler [2004]; Smith and Springer [2009]). But even as consensus develops every four years that reform is needed, there is much less agreement on the type of reform. In most discussions, however, some version of a national primary or rotating state primaries are the most salient proposals for restoring order to the way presidential nominees are selected.

In the rest of this chapter, we briefly explore the history of political reforms that resulted in the current nominating process. We then summarize two of the most salient reform proposals and examine what the public thinks about the process. We surveyed Iowa caucus voters, registered voters nationally, and Pennsylvania registered Democrats to explore the factors shaping public support for reforming the United States' method of selecting presidential candidates. What we find is that support for reform is conditioned on a certain kind of self-interest. Voters who reside in states that have a great deal of influence in the current system (electoral winners) are far less supportive of reform than those living in states that have less influence under the current rules (electoral losers). Thus, support for reform, while fairly broad among American voters, is also conditional, suggesting that any reform that creates different winners and losers will be supported by different groups of voters.

Unintended Consequences of Presidential Nomination Reform (1824–2008)

The framers of the U.S. Constitution were silent on the issue of presidential nominations, for they did not anticipate the rise of political parties. The Electoral College process was designed to make it difficult for any one candidate to get a majority, with the Electoral College acting as a sort of nominating group that would forward only the top candidates to the U.S. House of Representatives for election. Once parties began nominating candidates, rules were needed to determine the nominees. What developed was a hodgepodge of rules and processes guided largely by the self-interest of individual state legislatures, secretaries of state, or state political parties who determined the timing of caucuses or primary elections and whether independents could participate in these party events. Institutionally, the presidential nominating process was never rationally designed. Instead, a number of reform efforts were made, each determined to make the nominating process more democratic. What existed as of 2008 was largely structured by three historical reform movements and rules changes that took place over the course of nearly two hundred years.

The presidential candidacy of Andrew Jackson in 1824 and his election in 1828 marked the first mass political movement and popular vote contest in the United States. The first national convention was held in 1832 to choose a new running mate for Jackson, nominating Martin Van Buren for vice president, and endorsing the reelection of Jackson. By 1832 the two-major-party system was in place, and some rank-and-file partisans participated indirectly in candidate nominations via local, state, and national conventions that chose party candidates.

The Progressive Era (1896–1920) marked a second period of reforms that affected the nominating process. A number of electoral procedures were adopted during this period that challenged the autonomy of party organizations, including off-year local elections, nonpartisan elections, the government-printed secret (Australian) ballot, direct election of U.S. senators, and direct democracy (Hofstadter 1955; Burnham 1970). The origins of direct primaries predated the Progressive Era somewhat. In the latter part of the nineteenth century, state and local party organizations adopted direct primary rules, at least in part because party elites found them a better means for institutionalizing control than the old, informal convention/caucus systems (Ware 2009). By 1916, twenty states had adopted primaries, allowing members of a party to vote directly for their presidential nominees. Through most of the twentieth century, however, the majority of delegates sent to national nominating conventions were selected by state and local party officials.

A third major set of reforms was precipitated by proposals that emerged in response to the disastrous 1968 Democratic convention. The Democrats' McGovern-Fraser Commission report changed many aspects of the party's delegate selection process, and triggered state law changes that also affected the Republican process in the 1970s (Polsby 1983; Kamarck 2009). These rules changed how delegates to the nominating conventions were selected, opening up the process much further than the primaries adopted during the Progressive Era. After 1972, most delegates were directly elected by voters in primary elections or public caucuses rather than being hand-picked by state party leaders and elected officials. More states held primaries as a result, from 16 choosing 38% of the delegates in 1968 to 30 state primaries choosing 73% in 1976. In 2008, 37 states plus the District of Columbia (and, for the Democrats, Guam and Puerto Rico) held some form of primary, and the remaining states used caucuses and conventions to select their delegates, or some combination of both (for example, Texas). (See Kamarck [2009] for a detailed discussion of how the rules changed over the 1970s and 1980s.)

As direct primaries proliferated, participation in presidential nominating events increased significantly. Estimated turnout grew from 12 million in 1968 to 22 million in 1972 to over 35 million in 1988 (Altschuler 2008). These turnout numbers were shattered by 2008 nomination contests, in which over 55 million votes were cast in primary elections alone (not counting caucuses) (McDonald 2008b).[4] The Democrats set turnout records in 23 states while the Republicans set records in 10 states. Turnout was higher in most states in 2008 than in 2004 (McDonald 2008a).

Table 10.1 shows turnout estimates over time. It is abundantly clear that 2008 set records for both parties; no previous primary season comes close. The reforms of the early 1970s—led particularly by the McGovern-Fraser Commission of the Democratic Party—appear to have had at least one desired impact: increasing participation when nominations are highly competitive.

TABLE 10.1. **Primary turnout from 1972 through 2008: Total votes cast by party (in millions)**

Election	Number of primaries	Dem.	GOP	Total	Major candidates Democrats	Major candidates Republicans
1972	21	16.0	6.2	22.2	McGovern, Humphrey, Wallace	Nixon*
1976	27	16.1	10.4	26.4	Carter, Brown, Wallace	Ford*, Reagan
1980	36	18.7	12.7	31.4	Carter*, Kennedy	Reagan, G. H. W. Bush, Anderson
1984	30	18.0	6.6	24.6	Mondale, Hart, Jackson	Reagan*
1988	37	23.0	12.2	35.1	Dukakis, Jackson, Gore	Bush, Dole, Robertson
1992	39	20.2	12.7	32.9	Clinton, Brown, Tsongas	Bush*, Buchanan
1996	42	10.9	14.0	24.9	Clinton*	Dole, Buchanan, Forbes
2000	43	14.0	17.2	31.2	Gore, Bradley	G. W. Bush, McCain
2004	38	16.2	7.9	24.1	Kerry, Edwards	G. W. Bush*
2008	38	35.2^	19.8^	55^	Obama, Clinton, Edwards	McCain, Romney

Source: Larry Sabato's Crystal Ball Web site (http://www.centerforpolitics.org/crystalball) and CQ Press (2005, 2007). Figures for 2008 (^) are estimates derived from Michael McDonald's Web site (http://elections.gmu.edu/voter_turnout.htm).
*Incumbent president.

At the same time, there were clearly many unintended consequences. As we discussed in chapter 3, the 1970s also mark the era when Iowa became important in the process, due largely to decisions by the state's parties and legislature (Squire 1989). In 1972 Iowa Democrats moved their caucus to late January to accommodate rules changes that required at least thirty days between official party events in order to foster participation. The end of January was the latest the precinct caucuses could be held given the new thirty-day rule, because electing delegates in Iowa requires four steps—caucuses, county conventions, district conventions, and finally the state convention. The rules were not adopted so that Iowa could be the first nominating event, ahead of even the New Hampshire primary, but that is exactly what happened (Squire 1989, 2). While the McGovern campaign noted the new potential of Iowa, it was Jimmy Carter's successful drive to be the 1976 Democratic nominee that made the Iowa caucuses important. Carter emerged as the winner of the Iowa Democratic caucuses (defying expectations, though technically he lost to "uncommitted") and went on to win the White House, making the Iowa caucuses significant to future campaigns and the mass media.

As it became clear that early states received the most candidate and media attention, more states decided to hold nominating events earlier rather than later. One result was the development of Super Tuesday, a single date when a large number of states hold nominating events (Norrander 1992). A group of southern states decided in 1988 to create a regional primary, and Super Tuesday was born. By 2008 it had reached a zenith, approaching a national primary, with primaries or caucuses held in twenty-four states on the first officially sanctioned primary date, February 5. This dramatically frontloaded 2008 nomination schedule gave many states—including large ones like California, Florida, New York, and Illinois—an unprecedented opportunity to vote in the early weeks of the primary season.

As Mayer (2009, 2) points out, reformers did not want to want to "lengthen the presidential nomination campaign, create a highly frontloaded primary and caucus calendar, or turn national conventions into meaningless formalities put on largely for the benefit of television." But each party's delegate selection rules had, in fact, created such changes well before 2008 (Mayer and Hagen 2000). This largely unregulated, if not wild and wooly, nominating process is the result of unintended consequences from reforms layered on one another over time.

Calls for Reform

One major criticism of the current presidential nomination schedule is that it gives undue weight to the states holding early primaries or caucuses, as those states are thought to build momentum for leading candidates (Winebrenner 1998). Iowa, South Dakota, and Montana are three small, relatively homogeneous states, and yet the choices faced by their voters in nomination elections were vastly different in 2008. The field of presidential candidates (both Republican and Democrat) was reduced from sixteen at the beginning of the Iowa caucuses to just two viable Democratic candidates by the nation's last primaries in South Dakota and Montana (June 3). The Republican nomination was decided soon after Super Tuesday (February 5), leaving Republicans voting in later states to chose between the known nominee, John McCain, and the "losers," Texas representative Ron Paul or former Arkansas governor Mike Huckabee.

Although a large number of proposals have been advanced for reforming the presidential nominating process (Mayer and Busch 2004;

Donovan and Bowler 2004; Norrander 1992), two of the most widely discussed are (1) rotating which states vote first while maintaining sequential contests, and (2) holding a national primary. The first of these is championed by The Center for Voting and Democracy. Their "American Plan," or graduated random presidential primary system, begins with contests in small-population states where candidates do not need extensive financial resources to compete (http://fixtheprimaries.com/solutions/americanplan/). A lesser-known candidate's surprise successes in the early rounds may attract campaign donations from many small contributors, for the candidate to spend in later rounds of primaries. Under this proposal, ten election dates would be scheduled, spaced two weeks apart, during which *randomly* selected states would hold their primaries. Early contests would be held in small states, while larger states would have to wait until later. Every four years the order in which the states vote would change, potentially giving every American a chance for a meaningful vote in selecting presidential candidates. Proponents argue that rotation would preserve retail or grassroots politics by beginning the process in small-population states, bring order to the system, and be fair. Opponents argue that changing the sequence every four years might be confusing, and that large-population states would be prevented from having a real voice in the outcome, as they must vote in later rounds (Altschuler 2008). In addition, a major change to the existing primary schedule would be the elimination of the Super Tuesday tradition. Such a reform might face resistance from small states that currently have privileged positions, but also large states that would be required to vote in later rounds, especially those currently voting on Super Tuesday.

Another proposal is for a single national primary in which all states vote on the same day, similar to simultaneous elections for midterm and presidential elections. This would eliminate the existing sequential system in favor of a single primary election. While representing a dramatic change from the current system, a national primary has long been popular with Americans, as voters from all states would cast a meaningful vote for the presidential nominees. As early as 1912, Theodore Roosevelt offered to use a national primary in the Republican nomination contest, but the incumbent, President William Howard Taft, declined (Altschuler 2008). Despite many years of polls indicating overwhelming support for a national primary, it has never been seriously considered by the parties. Proponents argue that a national primary would eliminate many of the serious flaws of the current system, including frontloading, and might increase turnout and representation (Altschuler 2008): there is some evidence of higher turnout with the onset of Super Tuesday, and a national primary would be simple to conduct and would make all votes equally meaningful. Opponents argue that a national primary would restrict the nominees to candidates who were already well known or well financed (Mayer and Busch 2004), may eliminate the possibility of dark-horse candidates building momentum on early successes in small states, and could increase the influence of money needed to purchase campaign advertisements in the mass media.

Public Attitudes toward the Nominating Process

Before we examine how people assess these two proposals, we consider how the public viewed the nominating process in 2008. Reform of the presidential nomination system is an inside game, as candidates, state political leaders, and party insiders jockey for position in an effort to tilt the system to their benefit. But during some nomination contests, questions about the existing system spill out into the public domain, as pundits openly question the rationality of frontloading, low turnout, and the privileged position of Iowa and New Hampshire. The result is that the American public seems to have some interest in revamping the nomination system (see Smith and Springer [2009]; Tolbert and Squire [2009]).

We surveyed a random sample of nearly 1,300 registered voters in the forty states voting on Super Tuesday or later. The results shed some light on how people view the current process, and suggest some level of ambivalence—at least with regard to the role of Iowa. Adapting a Pew Research Center survey question, respondents were asked, "How much influence do you think voters of Iowa and New Hampshire have?" in selecting presidential candidates. Of Americans voting on Super Tuesday or later, only 31% said "too much," while 53% said "just about right" and 16% said "too little." Respondents were less sanguine about the role of "the average voter." Fifty-four percent said the average voter played "too little" of a role, with another 40% responding it was "just about right." When asked about the role of "party leaders," 48% said their influence was "just about right" and 42% said it was "too much."

One major target of public frustration is the media. When asked, "How much influence do news organizations have?" 77% said "too much." A 1999 Pew poll asking the same question found 64% of the respondents saying the news media had too much influence. Much of this probably reflects growing public discontent with the media generally; Pew documented that "believability" of the media hit an all-time low in August 2008. We might expect that some respondents saying that the "media has too much influence" were responding to the disproportionate attention granted to Iowa and New Hampshire. But only one in three Americans say that Iowa and New Hampshire have too much influence.

Winning, Losing, and Public Opinion on Nomination Reform

How might we expect Americans to respond to calls for reforming presidential nominations? At the time of our survey, the nominating process was based on a sequence of state elections. We suspect the state a person resides in plays a large role in how proposals for reform are evaluated. Living in a state that can be perceived as a loser in the sequential nominating process may condition whether or not someone supports or opposes proposals to change the primary schedule.

Cross-national opinion research suggests a relationship between winning and losing under various election rules and people's attitudes toward political institutions (Anderson et al. 2005). Studies of public opinion find that citizens who are electoral losers under a current set of institutional rules may be more likely to support overhauling those procedures (Anderson et al. 2005; Anderson and LoTempio 2002; Bowler and Donovan 2007; Donovan and Bowler 2004). We are interested in whether citizens who are losers under the rules used to nominate presidential candidates are more likely to support changing the nominating process. We define citizens who vote late in the process, or who are from small-population states other than those that went early in 2008, as potential losers in the process. We assume that people from such states had the least influence in determining the nominee (and thus are losers in some sense), and may be least attached to the status-quo rules. The irony is that in 2008, late states determined who the Democratic Party nominee was, but at the time the national survey was in the field (Super Tuesday) no one expected the Democratic nomination to extend until June.

We take as our starting point the assumption that individuals base some of their attitudes about potential reforms in rational self-interest. In other words, *ceteris paribus*: individuals prefer reforms that maximize their own influence in determining the major party nominees. Voter self-interest during the primary process is bound up in state self-interest. Voters residing in states with "influence," as determined by several factors such as the relative timing of the primary compared to other states, proportion of total party delegates to be assigned to a state, and the importance of the state to the party's ability to win in the general election, we predict, should be less likely to support changing the process than those residing in states with little influence.

Two potentially contradictory intervening factors reduce the role of self-interest in supporting presidential nominating process reforms: perceptions of fairness and support for political tradition. We suggest Americans do care about the perceived fairness of a system, particularly when it comes to the "one person, one vote" democratic ideal (Mansbridge 1986). Even if one state benefits extraordinarily from existing rules (for example, Iowa and New Hampshire in the current system), not all respondents from that state would necessarily support the existing system, since it may be perceived as being unfair to voters from other states. We expect fairness to play a moderating role on state self-interest. Tradition also certainly plays a role. As noted above, we found most Americans were generally satisfied with the role Iowa and New Hampshire played in 2008. Some respondents may support status-quo processes, even when doing so reduces their state's role in determining nominees vis-à-vis other states.

The above two caveats notwithstanding, we hypothesize that self-interest affects attitudes toward reforms. Three criteria determine our assessments of a state's influence—and hence whether a person is seen as winning or losing under the status-quo nomination rules: (1) the timing of the primary or caucus relative to other states, (2) the population size of the state (which largely determines the number of delegates to be pledged), and (3) individuals' perceptions of the importance of their state, separate from actual importance. These three factors provide the opportunity to test our theory that support for electoral reforms is motivated largely by self-interest, as determined by state importance in the nominating process.

Data and Methods

To answer the question of who supports reforming the presidential nominating process, we draw on three of our University of Iowa Hawkeye Polls conducted during the 2008 nominations and containing identical survey question wording: the survey of Iowa caucus attendees, the forty-state survey of registered voters around Super Tuesday, and the survey of registered Pennsylvania Democrats (more details about these surveys are given in chapter 9). Each telephone survey provides a snapshot of attitudes of respondents residing in states voting at different times in the sequential process. The data analysis draws largely on the national survey, using the Iowa and Pennsylvania data for contextual leverage. We also rely on the 2008 Cooperative Campaign Analysis Panel (CCAP), conducted by Polimetrix.[5] This nationally representative Internet survey sampled almost twenty thousand respondents in six panel waves (December 2007; January, March, September, October, and postelection in November 2008) during the 2008 presidential campaign with an extensive battery of questions. Questions on support for a national primary and rotating state primaries ran on the October and November waves of the survey and were administered to roughly one thousand respondents. Identical question wording was used for the Hawkeye Polls and the CCAP, allowing us to compare the results.

Respondents in all four surveys were asked if they supported rotating the order of primaries: "There are proposals to change the presidential nomination process. One would rotate states so a different state goes first each time. Would you strongly favor, favor, oppose or strongly oppose such a plan?"[6] The next question specifically prompted respondents about the role of Iowa and New Hampshire: "How about if such a plan eliminated Iowa and New Hampshire's traditional first in the nation status?" Respondents in three of the four surveys were also asked about support for a national primary: "Other have proposed a national primary, similar to Super Tuesday, where every state would hold their caucuses or primaries on the same day. Would you strongly favor, favor, oppose or strongly oppose such a plan?" Taken together, these opinion data provide a unique window into presidential nomination reform across very different states and at different times of the nominating process, and give us an opportunity to test the principle of state-based self-interest.

Findings: Who Supports Reforming the Nominating Process?

Table 10.2 and figure 10.1 display support for electoral reform among the three Hawkeye Poll sample populations: Iowans, the national/forty-state sample, and Pennsylvania Democrats. Strikingly, over 70% of

Americans support a national primary (see column 2 of table 10.2). Reforming the presidential nominating process appears to have wide support across the United States. These numbers mirror the 2008 CCAP national opinion survey, in which 68.5% of Americans said they favored a national primary. These numbers track closely with results from earlier surveys regarding widespread support for a national primary (Altschuler 2008; Smith and Springer 2009). In the CCAP survey, when proposals for a national primary are framed in terms of risk (respondents are prompted that "if a national primary is adopted small population states may lose influence"), a majority of Americans continue to support a national primary, but support drops to about 51% (see Bowler and Donovan 2007).

The Super Tuesday Hawkeye poll found that 72% of Americans favor rotation of presidential primaries or caucuses. However, in the CCAP survey, a bare majority (51%) reported they strongly favored or favored this reform, a 20-percentage-point difference. This may be because respondents from all fifty states are included in the CCAP survey (including those voting early in the process), while the Hawkeye Poll sampled respondents from only forty states (those voting on Super Tuesday or later). We would expect support for reform to be higher among citizens residing in states voting later in the process, than among individuals living in early-voting states. It may also have something to do with timing, since the CCAP survey was conducted in the midst of the general election, whereas all the others were during the nomination contest. When half the CCAP sample was randomly assigned the same question wording, but including this additional phrase—"This could mean that states that held their primaries and caucuses early will have less influence than they would have under the existing system"—support for rotating primaries remained constant at 51% of Americans. While considerably fewer Americans favor rotating state primaries than those who favor a national primary, these data reveal that most Americans are not very concerned that states holding early primaries or caucuses would lose influence in such a rotation. It is notable that a national primary is the most preferred option, compared with rotating state primaries and caucuses.

Interestingly, however, there appears to be some evidence that Americans have come to view the role of Iowa and New Hampshire as at least partly legitimate, given the drop in support for rotating primary order when Iowa and New Hampshire lose their first-in-the-nation status (see table 10.2). Over 8% fewer respondents nationally (Hawkeye Poll) and

TABLE 10.2. **Percentage supporting reforming the presidential nominating process: Comparing Iowa, national sample, and Pennsylvania**

	Iowa		National (vote on or after Super Tuesday)		Diff. between national and Iowa		Pennsylvania	
Rotate primary state order								
Strongly agree	3.59	25.95	22.12	71.64	18.53	45.68	18.63	67.08
Agree	22.36		49.51		27.15		48.45	
Disagree	42.41	74.05	21.44	28.36	−20.97	−45.7	21.74	32.92
Strongly disagree	31.65		6.92		−24.73		11.18	
	(N = 474)		(N = 1026)				(N = 161)	
Rotate order (no IA or NH first)								
Strongly agree	1.69	15.82	15.76	63.56	14.07	47.73	15.03	61.44
Agree	14.14		47.8		33.66		46.41	
Disagree	50.63	84.18	29.68	36.44	−20.95	−47.73	29.41	38.56
Strongly disagree	33.54		6.76		−26.78		9.15	
	(N = 474)		(N = 977)				(N = 153)	
National primary								
Strongly agree	n.a.		39.31	73.42	n.a.		35.96	71.35
Agree	n.a.		34.11		n.a.		35.39	
Disagree	n.a.		19.57	26.58	n.a.		17.42	28.66
Strongly disagree	n.a.		7.01		n.a.		11.24	
			(N = 1155)				(N = 178)	

5.5% fewer Pennsylvania Democrats are willing to support rotation if Iowa and New Hampshire lose their traditional position. A question on support for rotating primary order if Iowa and New Hampshire lose their status was, unfortunately, not asked on the CCAP survey.

The third column of Table 10.2 shows that Iowans recognize their own self-interest. Support for rotating the primary order is approximately 50 percentage points lower among Iowans than voters nationally. Only one in four Iowans we interviewed favored rotating primary order if Iowa and New Hampshire didn't vote first. Iowa caucusgoers know that their unique position is of value to the state, and their political attitudes appear to be shaped by state self-interest.

Figure 10.1 graphs the percentage of each sample that answered either "strongly favor" or "favor" for rotating state primaries or holding a national primary. As noted above, Iowans clearly do not want to rotate primary order (only 26% favored this reform), compared with 72% nationally and 67% of Pennsylvania-registered Democratic voters. While a question on support for a national primary was unfortunately not asked of Iowa voters, close to three-quarters of respondents nationally and

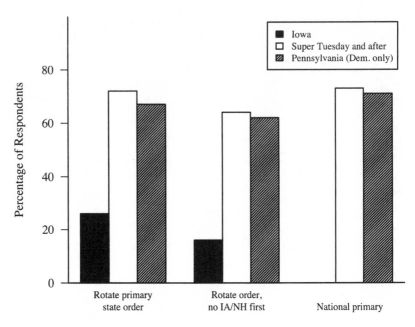

FIGURE 10.1. Support for presidential nomination reforms: comparing Iowa, national, and Pennsylvania samples (Hawkeye Polls).

from Pennsylvania support a national primary. These survey data suggest that opinions about presidential nomination reform are colored by individual self-interest about one's state.

The percentage of respondents in the national Hawkeye Polls either strongly favoring or favoring the reforms, split into small and large states, is presented in figure 10.2.[7] There is little difference between support for rotating primary order among respondents from small-population states and large states. Support for rotating primary order drops among both small states and large states when the question specifically mentions that Iowa and New Hampshire will lose their first-in-the-nation status, although the drop is greater for voters in large states. In fact, respondents from small states are actually *more* likely than respondents from large states to favor rotation when Iowa and New Hampshire lose their position. This suggests that other small-state respondents might prefer Iowa and New Hampshire not going first. There is little difference between respondents from small states and those from large states regarding support for a national primary.

The last two columns of figure 10.2 show support for a national primary by small and large states *and* by whether the state's election was held on or after Super Tuesday. As hypothesized, the effect of population size is conditional on timing. Small Super Tuesday states, clearly "losers" since they are easily overshadowed by large Super Tuesday states, want reform. Three-quarters of respondents from small Super Tuesday states express support for it. Respondents from large Super Tuesday states, on the other hand, are over 5 points less likely to support a national primary (only 69% favor it). The inverse of this relationship can be found among respondents from states holding their nomination contests after Super Tuesday: those from large states have over a 4-point greater probability of supporting a national primary than those from small states.

Figure 10.3 displays support for reform in the national Hawkeye Polls by individuals' perceptions of their own state's influence in choosing the presidential nominees. Respondents were asked, "I'd like to ask you to think about the role that *your* state plays in determining who the presidential candidates will be." Eighty percent of respondents who think

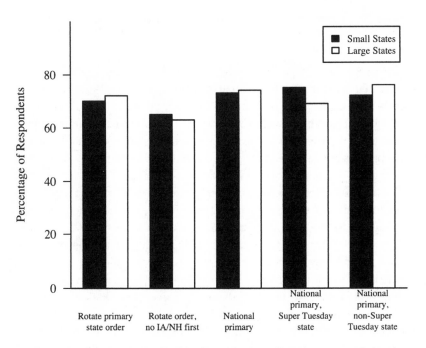

FIGURE 10.2. Support for various presidential nomination reforms by state population size and Super Tuesday–voting state or later.

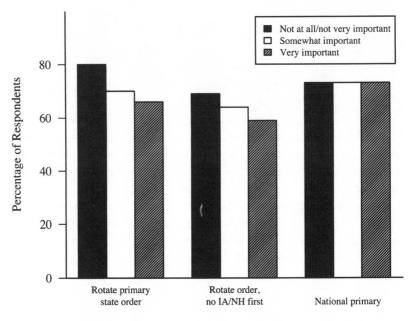

FIGURE 10.3. Support for reforming the presidential nominating process by electoral losers (individual perceptions of state importance in selecting candidates—"My state is . . .").

their state is not important in the nominating process support rotating which states go first. This compares with 70% among those who think their state is somewhat important in the process and only 66% who want reform if they think their state is very influential in the nominating process. Stated differently, those who think their state has no influence in the process are 14 percentage points more likely to favor rotation in state primaries.

This result stands in stark contrast to the levels of support for the national primary, where assessments of state influence make no difference in support for the reform. Almost identical percentages (73%) of respondents from states that think their state is not important, somewhat important, and very important in the process favor a national primary. We believe this result is capturing perceptions of fairness. A national primary would certainly decrease the role of some states that are privileged under the current system, but may do so in a way that is perceived as fair, compared to rotation of primaries. Two separate surveys conducted in 2008 found that Americans prefer a national primary over rotation of state primaries and caucuses.

Results Controlling for Overlapping Factors: Multivariate Analysis

Descriptive statistics are suggestive of the relationship between state context and support for election reform, but do these results remain when the impact of other demographic and attitudinal factors are taken into account? To answer this question, we turn to multivariate logistic regression analysis of support for a national primary, drawing on both the 2008 national Hawkeye Poll and the CCAP survey.[8] Use of two separate surveys conducted in 2008 provides validity. The outcome variable in both surveys is coded 1 if the respondent favors a national primary ("strongly favors" or "favors") and 0 for opposition ("oppose" or "strongly oppose") to the reform proposal.

To test the hypotheses presented earlier, three primary explanatory variables are used. We hold constant other potential explanations of support for a national primary to try to isolate the independent effect of state population size on public opinion. To measure the impact of population size, we use the log of the respondents' state population to capture diminishing effects in states with very large populations.[9] In the Hawkeye Poll, sequence is measured with a dichotomous variable, where respondents are coded 1 if their state's primary or caucus was held on Super Tuesday and 0 if their primary came after Super Tuesday (this is because the sample only included respondents from states voting on Super Tuesday or later). In the CCAP survey, which included respondents from all fifty states, sequence is measured with a dichotomous variable, where respondents are coded 1 if they are from Iowa, New Hampshire, Nevada, or South Carolina (four early-voting states in 2008) and 0 if they vote on February 5 or later. Perceptions of the importance of the respondent's state are measured by the variable *state influence*, which is coded 1 if the respondent thought his or her state was "very important" or "somewhat important" in the nominating process and 0 if not important.

Several political and demographic variables are included in the models as control variables. The percentage of the respondent's state population that has a high school education or higher is included in the model to control for differences in state socioeconomic conditions. Individual-level education, income, gender, race, and age are all taken into account.[10] Party identification is measured with binary variables for Republicans and Democrats, with independents as the reference category.[11] Finally, we control for external efficacy in the models.[12] We expect that those who do not feel they can influence government will support

changing the nomination system, while those who feel they can influence government will be less likely to support the various reforms. In the
CCAP analysis, similar demographic and partisan control variables are
used, but vary slightly, given data availability. Since both individual-level
and state-level effects are considered, we cluster the model coefficients'
standard errors by state to account for spatial autocorrelation.[13] We first
discuss the Hawkeye Poll results and then the CCAP results. As with
earlier chapters, we have relegated the detailed models to an appendix to
facilitate discussion of the results here.

SUPPORT FOR A NATIONAL PRIMARY: HAWKEYE POLL.   Table D.10.1 in
appendix D presents the results for support for a national primary using
our Hawkeye Poll data. Consistent with the descriptive statistics, none of
the three key explanatory variables (state population, primary sequence,
or perceptions of state influence) are significant in the base model presented in column 1. Two interaction terms are included in the models.
The first tests if the effect of population varies depending on whether respondents think their state is important or not by including an interaction term of the log of population multiplied by perceptions of state influence. The second tests whether the effect of population is conditional
on timing by multiplying state population by an indicator of whether the
state voted on Super Tuesday. In column 2, interacting state population
and perceptions of state importance, the interaction term is significant
and positive, while the constituent terms of population (log) and state
influence are also statistically significant but negative. In column 3, the
coefficient for the interaction term (population size multiplied by Super
Tuesday state) is significant and negative. The use of interaction terms
makes it difficult to understand the substantive meaning from the logistic regression coefficients alone. Predicted probabilities from the logit
coefficients, holding other explanatory variables at their mean or modal
values, aids in interpretation.

Figure 10.4 shows that the effect of state population size on support
for a national primary is found among residents from Super Tuesday
states only. Among individuals from states voting after Super Tuesday
(late in the process), roughly the same 80% favor a national primary,
and this does not vary by the population size of their state. However, respondents from large states voting on Super Tuesday have lower support
for a national primary. Ten percent fewer residents of large states voting
on Super Tuesday want a national primary, compared with those from

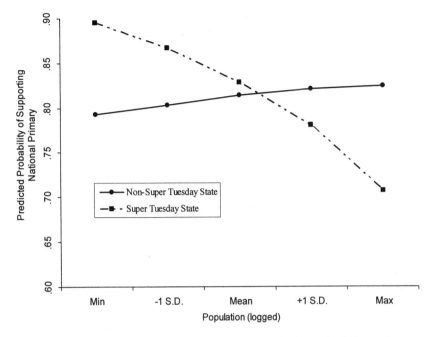

FIGURE 10.4. Predicted probability of supporting national primary by timing and state population size (log).

large states voting after Super Tuesday. Residents of early-voting large-population states have a privileged position and thus are less likely to favor reforming the process.

Figure 10.5 shows the effect of population size on support for a national primary among those respondents who believe their state has influence in the process compared with those who do not. There is virtually no effect of population size on the probability of supporting a national primary among those who feel their state has influence in selecting presidential nominees. Among those who feel their state does not play an important role in the process, however, those from small states are much more likely to support a national primary than are those from the largest of states. Population (logged) accounts for over a 20-percentage-point increase in the probability of supporting the reform, going from the largest states to the smallest among those who feel left out. While conventional wisdom holds that large-population states would benefit from a national primary, and in general this may be true, analysis reported here finds residents of small-population states voting on Super Tuesday or

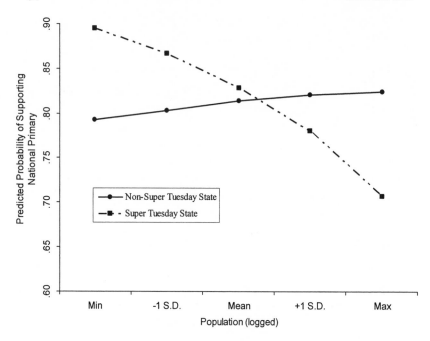

FIGURE 10.5. Predicted probability of supporting national primary by assessments of state importance and state population size (log).

later, or who believe their state has little say under current rules are the most in favor of a national primary. When Iowa, New Hampshire, and other early-voting states are excluded, citizens of small-population states favor reform. Also, 80% of citizens residing in large-population states voting late in the process (after Super Tuesday) also favor a national primary. However, it should be noted that majorities of citizens from early and late voting states, and from large- and small-population states prefer this reform of the nominating process.

The control variables in our models actually tell an interesting story as well. Partisan losers are more likely to support a national primary. Both dummy variables for Republicans and Democrats are negative and reach statistical significance in two out of the three models, indicating that independents are more likely than partisans to support a national primary.[14] Depending on its rules, a national primary could allow independents to play a larger role in the process than a series of state primaries and caucuses, whether rotated or not, since many states used closed primaries, which exclude independents. Political efficacy also significantly influences support for a national primary, and does so in the expected direction: the more respondents feel that people like them can influence government, the less likely they are to support a national primary. Interestingly, education has no impact on attitudes about a national primary. Gender is important, as men are less likely to support a national primary than are women. This latter finding fits nicely with previous research finding men to be particularly aware of procedural fairness in terms of election reform (Tolbert, Smith, and Green 2009; Karp 2007). Additionally, when we include a control variable for whether the respondent resides in a state using a caucus system versus a primary (results not shown), there is no statistical difference in support for either a national primary or rotating primaries. Surprisingly, individuals from caucus states are slightly more likely to favor a national primary (77%) compared with those from primary states (73%), but the difference is not statistically significant.

SUPPORT FOR A NATIONAL PRIMARY: CCAP SURVEY. We replicate our analysis using the 2008 CCAP survey, which includes respondents from all fifty states. In table D.10.2, we display two simple logistic regression models predicting support for a national primary. Holding other factors constant overall, respondents from large-population states are *more* likely to favor a national primary (see column 1). When the conditional relationships between population size and perceptions of state influence are omitted, as reported in table D.10.1, it is residents of large-population states that are most in favor of reform. This make sense, as presumably they would have more influence than under the current system, where small-population states such as Iowa and New Hampshire (joined by Nevada and South Carolina in 2008) have disproportionate influence. Similarly, older respondents favor a national primary, as do those who are white and non-Hispanic. Perceptions of state influence are not statistically significant.

    In column 2 the state influence variable is omitted, and instead a binary variable is included for residents of the four early nominating event states. Individuals from early-voting states are significantly less likely to favor a national primary, as expected, and consistent with the graphs presented earlier. That is, individuals residing in Iowa, New Hampshire, Nevada, and South Carolina are more likely to oppose a national primary compared with those from the forty-six other states, consistent with our expectations about state self-interest. Again, older respondents and non-minorities favor reform.

From the statistical analysis of the 2008 CCAP data, two conclusions are apparent: individuals who vote early in the current process are likely to oppose reform, and those from states voting later are likely to favor it. Residents from large-population states may be favorably disposed toward a national primary in general, although the Hawkeye Poll analysis suggests that individuals from large-population states voting early (on Super Tuesday) may have slightly lower support for reform. Nevertheless, large majorities of Americans favor a national primary.

SUPPORT FOR ROTATION OF STATE PRIMARIES (HAWKEYE POLL). Table D.10.3 displays the results from the multivariate logistic regression predicting support for rotating which states vote first, using the Hawkeye Poll and the same modeling as table D.10.1. Again, model 1 is the baseline and includes no interactions. Model 2 adds to the base model the interaction term of state population multiplied by perceptions of state influence in the nominating process, and model 3 adds to the base model the interaction term of state population size and whether the respondent lives in a Super Tuesday voting state. Model 1 supports what was found in the descriptive analyses: no direct effect for population or timing/sequence on support for rotating primaries, while individual perceptions of state influence are very important (remember, the survey includes only individuals voting on Super Tuesday or later). The coefficient for state influence is negative and statistically significant at the $p < .01$ level. Respondents who think their state is very or somewhat important in the nominating process (electoral winners) are significantly less likely to favor rotating the order of state primaries, as expected.

State population size does have a significant effect on the probability of supporting rotation of primary state order; the effect is simply conditioned on perceptions of state influence in the nominating process and the timing of the primary. In model 2 the interaction term between population and state influence is marginally significant (90% confidence interval) and positive, while the constituent term for perceptions is also significant and negative. In model 3, the constituent term for population (log) is marginally significant and positive.

To understand the substantive effects, figure 10.6 displays the predicted probability of favoring primary rotation (based on model 2) while

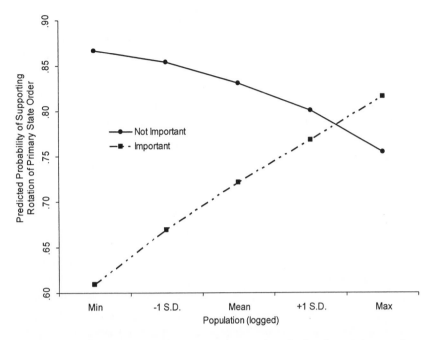

FIGURE 10.6. Predicted probability of supporting rotation of primaries, varying population and state role.

varying population (log) from the smallest to largest values and perceptions of state influence, holding the other explanatory variables at their mean or modal values. Respondents from the smallest of states who feel their state is unimportant have almost a 90% chance of supporting rotation, while respondents from the largest states that feel their state is unimportant have a 75% probability of supporting the reform—a 15-point difference based on population size alone (solid line). Whereas support for reform is high across the board for respondents who think their state lacks influence in the process (as expected), this support varies by state population size. Respondents from small states who perceive that their state lacks influence have the highest support for reform.

The reverse relationship exists among those who feel their state is influential (dotted line): the larger the population size of the state, the more likely the respondent is to support a reform to rotate primary order. These individuals may believe their state is important because it is large and economically powerful, has many delegates, and/or is a swing state in the presidential election, but not because they vote early in the nominating process. The word *important* may have different meaning in large versus small states. Respondents from states that have a population (logged) that is one standard deviation above the mean value (that is, large states) are 10 points more likely to support the reform than are respondents from states with a population (logged) one standard deviation below the mean (small states). This again suggests that individuals from large states may feel their role in the nominating process is marginalized.

These results shed some light on support for rotating primaries and largely confirm our hypotheses. The highest support comes from respondents who feel that their state has little say in selecting presidential nominees and reside in small-population states. Rotating which state goes first would give voters in more states a chance to play a role similar to Iowa and New Hampshire, in which the attention of the candidates and media would be focused solely on their state for a time. Support for reform is also high among large states voting later in the process (after Super Tuesday) (see model 3 of table D.10.3). Such states can be considered losers in the current system, since they have no guarantee that their primary or caucus will be of any importance to the nominations.

Two factors are consistent across the models predicting support for a national primary or rotating state primary order. Respondents who believe their state is unimportant in the process (perceived loser) and reside in a small-population state are the most likely to favor both reforms of the presidential nominating process. Similarly, large states voting late in the schedule (after Super Tuesday) are significantly more likely to favor reform. These two dimensions appear to highlight the true "losers" in the current nominating process.

Supporting Reform

Most of the discussion of nomination reform proceeds from pundits and politicians and even political scientists with little systematic empirical analysis of public support for change. We draw on our sequential state and national opinion surveys to show that support for reforming presidential nominations has a lot to do with where people live. We find empirical evidence that large proportions of Americans favor changing the rules governing presidential nominations; the overall high level of support for reform is noteworthy. While Iowans oppose changing the process, three in four Americans nationally support reform. Using two national surveys conducted independently in 2008, we found more consistent support for a national primary than for rotating state primary order.

There is, however, significant variation in support for reform based on an individual's state context and whether that person's state wins or loses under current rules. Overall, individuals from large-population states are more likely to favor a national primary than those from smaller states. At the same time, residents of states voting early in the process (with a favored position) are more likely to oppose reform. Individuals from large states voting late in the nominating process are highly supportive of reform, while citizens from large states voting relatively early in the process (Super Tuesday) are somewhat less likely to favor reform, because they already have a privileged position. Individuals residing in small states who believe their state does not have influence in the current system almost universally support reform of the process. We provide empirical evidence that winning and losing under different reform proposals shape public opinion about reform of presidential nominations.

These opinion data can be best understood by viewing voters as seeking to improve their chances of having some influence in selecting presidential candidates. Their influence is tied to the role their state plays in the process, thus defining their interest by the interest of their state. Population, order of primaries and caucuses relative to other states, and individual perceptions of state importance all play important roles in determining support for reforms of the presidential nominating process. Electoral losers in terms of timing are more likely to support reforming the nominating process, and this effect is seen among residents of large- and small-population states alike. The data presented here show Americans are willing to adopt a different nominating process, but reformers should be cautious. We find evidence that the American public is indeed motivated by self-interest, and will be less likely to support changing the system if it entails a reduction in influence for their state. Of course, since change inevitably would create new winners and losers, change may be less likely than it would appear from the raw public opinion data. These data suggest that reasoning about institutional change by the mass public is more sophisticated than previously understood. Not only can the mass public reason strategically about election rules, but they understand how their state matters in the process.

CHAPTER ELEVEN

Why Iowa?

Continuity and Change in Presidential Nominations

Perhaps the most interesting thing about standing in the middle of the bedlam that is an Iowa caucus is ordinary people with ordinary day jobs try to express what they like about their candidates without the aid of spinmeisters or pollsters. — Luiza Ch. Savage, writing in *Maclean's Magazine*, January 4, 2008

On January 3, 2008, hundreds of thousands of Iowans came out to caucus at local schools, community centers, churches, and the like, launching the long process of electing the next president of the United States. Large crowds formed at precincts all over the state, and parking was at a premium. Many people walked through the snow, only to find long lines to sign in to their caucus. It was the culmination of months and even years of campaign speeches, living room events, large-scale rallies, phone calls, television ads, and mailers. Our surveys show that Iowans generally enjoyed the experience.

On the Democratic side, expectations were high for Barack Obama, Hillary Clinton, and John Edwards. People supporting other Democratic candidates who were more of a long shot had the luxury of sticking by those choices in the first round of voting, knowing they could change to a more viable candidate in the second round. Crowds were so large that it was difficult for supporters of front-runners to have discussions with people supporting candidates who did not make it past the first round of voting, but attempts were made. Lines for the Republican precinct caucuses were a bit shorter, but the excitement was just as palpable. Their contest for first place was between Mike Huckabee and Mitt Romney, although several other candidates hoped to meet or beat expectations with a strong third-place showing. Republicans cast a single secret ballot, and were generally able to finish their business before the Democrats.

This book has chronicled how the 2008 Iowa caucus—and early nomination contests generally—play a significant role in the larger presidential nominating process. As was the case in 2000 (and in 2004), the Iowa winner was the Democrats' nominee. In 2008, the momentum from Obama's Iowa victory led to his becoming the forty-fourth president of the United States. For the Republicans, Iowa played spoiler. Although vastly outspent, Huckabee beat expectations by defeating Romney convincingly. This weakened Romney's chance at building early momentum, and opened the way for John McCain to eventually win the nomination. In both cases, Iowa helped determine the nominees. Why Iowa? Why might such a small state play a potentially decisive role? As answers, we have demonstrated that the sequential rules of the game matter—they set conditions that structure campaigns, media attention, voter information, voters' perceptions of candidates, and, ultimately, the choices voters have in front of them as the process unfolds. That Iowa comes first matters. That Iowa holds a caucus and not a primary matters. And that the media pay disproportionate attention to Iowa matters—in doing so, the media magnify the importance of Iowa's election rules. As we have noted earlier, these rules (caucuses, sequential voting) are the wheels that start the process and propel a candidate toward the nomination, while media attention to the Iowa caucuses is like the grease that lubricates the sequential election process.

Different Rules, Different Outcomes

Imagine the American presidential nominating process without any sequential component. What would it be like? Given contemporary attitudes about participation and public cynicism about political parties (Dalton 2004; Norris 1999), any return to the pre-1976 party convention method of nominations is highly unlikely as an alternative. And in any case, that old system, we should recall, also included a dose of sequential preconvention contests that provided party leaders with information about candidate electability (Polsby 1983).

One of the more widely discussed alternatives to the process is a national primary, as we described in chapter 10. It is also one of the most popular suggestions, with about three-quarters of Americans supporting it. Our survey shows that most people think a national primary is the fairest nomination system. Like any major change in electoral rules, this reform would likely produce a different set of winners and losers. Simultaneous state elections, as would be the case with a national primary, have the advantage of eliminating temporal inequity among the states, and might result in a more even distribution of electoral competition across the nation—at least in well-populated areas. Logic suggests that a national primary contest would drive campaigns toward larger-population states, and increase turnout overall (Knight and Shiff 2007; Atekson and Maestas 2009). As the previous chapters have shown, Super Tuesday voters generally have higher levels of turnout in normal nomination years, greater political knowledge (compared with those voting later), and greater political interest and attention to media. We can think of Super Tuesday voters as a proxy for how voters might respond to a national primary if it brought campaigns and attention to them in a way the current system might not. Increased turnout in nominating events is generally desirable and may produce more representative candidates. It may be that the presidential nominating process would be seen as more legitimate if a national primary increased voter participation—but this assumes that legitimacy is based only on maximizing public participation.

It is important to remember that the point of the nominating process is for political parties—as private organizations—to select their standard-bearers. By this criterion the scope of public participation in the process may be less relevant. Moreover, as much as Polsby (1983) and others viewed caucuses and primaries as a threat to the autonomy of parties, a single-day national primary that produces a decisive, majoritarian outcome may produce uncertainty about the influence of party elites. We also expect that a national primary would further propel the front-runner candidates who start with the most name recognition and financial resources—although in the current system, candidates with the most money the year before Iowa caucuses often have huge advantages to begin with (Mayer 1996; Aldrich 2009; Cohen et al. 2008). A national contest would be fought largely through the electronic mass media rather than in the coffee shops and living rooms of a few small states. Had a single-day national primary been used in the past, it could have produced a different set of nominees, and different presidents. In 2008, the leading candidates in national polls before the Iowa caucuses were

Hillary Clinton and former New York City mayor Rudy Giuliani. Both might have won an initial plurality in a national primary on name recognition alone early in 2008. Jimmy Carter probably would have fared poorly in any national primary held before Iowa in 1976. Only some type of ranked voting system with preference transfers (Instant Runoff Voting, or IRV) could have produced a clear winner from the crowded 1988 Democratic and Republican fields, the 1996 Republican or 2004 Democratic contests, and both parties' contests in 2008.

Retail politics, whether in Iowa, New Hampshire, or other small states, provides for identifiable advantages over a national primary. A select group of voters see the parties' candidates up close and candidates have opportunities to learn about "real" people, escaping at least briefly the bubble that envelops them as the campaign progresses. Retail politics combined with a sequential process provides additional advantages. A crowded field of candidates is reduced. Underdogs have a chance to win by gaining momentum from early nominating events. But even when they don't win—which is most of the time—they have an influence on the campaign, and the ideas and issues they discuss often find their way into leading candidates' rhetoric and party platforms.[1] Sequential elections allow for learning from one state to the next, as election outcomes from early state contests create information used by voters in later states to shape their decisions. Of course, that information may be biased by where it is generated from, but it is useful information nonetheless. Early wins in these small states change the landscape of momentum for the candidates, and readjust the odds.

The Virtues of Caucusing: Iowa's Burden?

This book has focused mainly on demonstrating why Iowa matters in the larger scheme of presidential nomination politics. This begs the question, however, of why Iowa should retain its privileged first-in-the-nation position, and how any reforms to the nominating process should affect Iowa's status. It is tempting to conclude that there is something particularly special about Iowa, and Iowans. After all, decades of going first have institutionalized a wonderful and unique form of retail politics. The authors of this book, by virtue of spending years or even a few days in Iowa, have had multiple opportunities to have pizza, beer, coffee, a

slice of pie, and conversations with several high-profile presidential candidates and their spouses. And such opportunities are not limited to a
few college professors or other elites.

Caucuses require candidates to engage in grassroots or retail
politics—old-fashioned face-to-face campaigning on the part of candidates and voters. In 2008, Edwards visited all 99 Iowa counties at least
once and visited nearly half of them more than once. Obama made it to
90 counties, and Clinton visited 65. Candidates written off by the media, like Connecticut senator Chris Dodd, New Mexico governor Bill
Richardson, and Delaware senator Joe Biden, made personal visits to
most Iowa counties in 2008. The Republican campaigns were different—
particularly in terms of evidencing much less door-to-door campaigning—
but the candidates themselves still spent a great deal of personal time on
the ground in Iowa, visiting communities large and small throughout the
state. For many Iowans, this is a common experience that unfolds every
four years. Over time, they have come to expect it, and they are ready
and willing to ask candidates serious questions. One of our Iowa colleagues (with tongue only halfway in cheek) suggested that the process
can grow quite tiresome, and that Iowans should be commended for car-
rying on this burden of hypercitizenship as their duty to voters in other
states. Our polls show that the majority of Iowans prefer the burden
of their caucus when offered the more pedestrian option of a primary.

Our assessment of voter learning in the sequential nominating process demonstrates that there is something to this idea that Iowans are
doing other voters a favor. We find that information originating at the
start of the sequential nominating process does provide useful cues to
other voters. The quality of these cues, in a normative sense, depends
on Iowans (or citizens in any state that goes first) doing the hard work
of evaluating candidates. This means that these early voters may bear
greater participation costs (Battaglini, Morton, and Palfrey 2007). Our
findings reported here, and our observations of retail politics in Iowa,
lead us to conclude that Iowans are up to this task. But this still begs
the question: why Iowa? We could defend Iowa's peculiar status on the
grounds that only Iowans are up to the task, or that no other state would
have enough time to "teach" its voters how to play the role of going first.
Such logic, however, runs dangerously parallel to Kipling's (1899) "White
Man's Burden" homage to imperialism. Regardless of what we can re-
solve about the issue of Iowa's first-in-the-nation status, this book dem-

onstrates the virtues of engaging retail politics at caucuses early on in a sequential nominating process.

Many proposed reforms of the nomination system focus on eliminating Iowa's first-in-the-nation status. In addition to the national primary, there are several variants of proposed reforms that would retain the sequential nature of the nominating process, but alter the order of the sequence. There is some chance that rotating the sequence could lead to confusion—both for the media in terms of deciding which states are most important to cover, and for voters looking to assess which early events provide meaningful cues about candidate viability or electability. The process of mixing things up every four years could further weaken whatever ties are left between candidates and their personal campaigns, and parties and their activists. One reason parties are strong in Iowa is because they know they must gear up on a regular basis to run the Iowa caucus, the quintessential party activity. Candidates know where they must campaign first, and they bring the party into that process—even in nomination fights—by providing support to party organizations and legislative candidates in the years before the next presidential election. Journalists know where the stakes are highest, and know that the game of handicapping events in Iowa is more meaningful than reporting on caucuses in Idaho, Montana, or Washington.

We suggest that grassroots politics allows voters to better check candidate quality than a campaign run by television and radio commercials alone, where there is no feedback loop or interactive communication. Perhaps the greatest strength of the Iowa caucus is that it is possible for candidates to meet and shake the hands of a large percentage of those who will actually be supporting them at the caucus. But this presents some intriguing questions for social scientists. If candidates and the media knew four years in advance that the first caucus in 2012 was to be held in, say, Maine, rather than Iowa, and that Iowa would vote in June, would Maine experience the same onslaught of retail campaign activity that Iowans have grown accustomed to? If so, would studies of Maine voters in 2012 produce the same sort of results as our study of Iowans in 2008? We expect that there is nothing particularly distinctive about Iowans as deliberative citizens and caucusgoers, other than the fact that they have been blessed for decades with the certainty that their state goes first and thus understand the importance of the role they play.

It is important to remember that Iowa uses a caucus, and this makes all the difference. Our chapters on caucus rules illustrate advantages of caucuses, at least in the case of Iowa, over primaries. Such advantages would be lost with a national primary, or even a system that started with state primaries, but could be retained in a process that had caucuses at the beginning of some sequence of contests. Some caucus rules in practice as of 2008 may have also encouraged sincere (over strategic) voting. The Iowa Democratic Party rules provide for a second round of voting, which encourages sincere expression preferences in the first round. At the same time, Iowa Republicans also evidenced more sincere voting as well, even with their secret-ballot straw poll. Of course, voting in any primary could be altered to allow ranking of choices and preference transfers, which could also encourage sincere expression of preferences.

Reform Goals

Almost 75% of Americans are dissatisfied with the current presidential nomination system and desire change. The political parties are faced with enduring calls to "fix" the nomination system. They faced additional pressure to adjust their rules in response to state parties attempting to hold their contests closer to, or earlier than, Iowa's. In 2008, both parties found it impossible to craft rules that prevented states from moving their primaries earlier in the schedule. The Democrats came perilously close to a crisis in which their 2008 nominee could have been determined by whether or not delegates from Florida and Michigan, states that violated national party rules by going early, would be seated at the national convention. By eventually seating these delegates, the Democrats sent signals to other states that penalties for ignoring the calendar rules could be minimal. What, then, should be done? Proposals to reform the nominating process are never in short supply. But the specific goals of reform are often unclear. We suggest four goals to help structure any evaluation of nomination reform proposals.

Any presidential nominating process should provide *opportunities* for a broad range of candidates, and not simply anoint the best known or the best financed. We are in no position to determine if the old convention system, the post-1972 system, or some future system would produce better-quality candidates. Whatever the rules, party nominees should be representative of their party, and be able to win in the general election. A sequential process with early caucus events may expand the range of quality candidates in the mix by leveling the playing field, at least somewhat. As we have demonstrated, campaigning in small-state environments, such as Iowa or New Hampshire, fosters retail politics. As costly as campaigning in early states has become, it is less expensive than conducting a full-blown national campaign, because there are opportunities to contact voters beyond reliance on broadcast media. Engaging retail politics early on in the nominating process can expand the range of candidates for a party's voters to consider.

Second, any process in which voters pick their party's nominee should provide voters with *information* about a candidate's electoral prospects. John Kennedy contested the West Virginia primary in 1960 to send signals about his electability to Democratic Party elites who held sway over the convention delegates who selected the nominee. Likewise, a sequential election system can allow party voters in early nomination contests to send similar cues to voters in later states. A sequential process can accumulate information in a manner that is not possible in a one-off, simultaneous voting environment.

Third, a nomination system should encourage increased *participation* so that the electorate participating in each party's process is more representative of the wide range of people who identify, respectively, with each party. That is, the nominating process should be designed to engage voters and thus result in increased voter turnout.

Finally, the nomination system should strive for some measure of *equality* (or fairness) among the fifty states in terms of allowing many Americans to cast a meaningful vote. The current system gives disproportionate influence to voters from Iowa and New Hampshire. Many citizens from large states that vote later in the process often have little influence in the selection of nominees. Many candidates who started before Iowa withdraw soon after—often as a result of the outcome in Iowa. Voter choices in subsequent states are advantaged by information voters receive from early states, but their choices are also constrained by effects of the Iowa caucuses and by other states that vote early.

Many state legislatures, secretaries of state, and state party leaders have an interest in holding their state's nominating event early in the process. Iowa has a law that requires moving the caucuses to an earlier date if other states threaten Iowa's first-in-the-nation status. But other states hope to emulate Iowa by going as early as possible. Indeed, states have many real incentives for holding their nominating events as early as possible—chief among them, more visits by candidates, increased media attention, an invigorated state economy, and affecting how the field of candidates is defined for later states. By this standard, Michigan and Florida acted rationally by breaking party rules (despite the prospect of losing national convention delegates) to hold early nominating events in 2008. If left to their own self-interest, states may continue to move their primaries and caucuses earlier and earlier to trump or match Iowa. In the 2008 cycle, these frontloading pressures almost forced Iowa to move its January 3, 2008, caucus to November or early December 2007. New Year's, Christmas, and Thanksgiving holidays constrain Iowa's ability to remain first without going several weeks earlier than January 3.

Reforming the Sequence: A Proposal for a Caucus Window and a National Primary

A number of reform proposals call for the national party committees to retain, but modify, the sequential nature of the nominating process. Some of these proposals divide the states by region or by population size. One proposal is for state contests to be clustered, with four separate regional primaries conducted in different weeks or months. Another proposal would have sets of states holding simultaneous contests in a sequence in which the ten smallest states vote on one day, followed by the ten next-smallest states on some later day, and so on, with large states voting last (see chapter 10). Many find flaws in the regional primary, suggesting that a regional primary could winnow the field such that a leading candidate with a solid base in just one region could win. Such a process could produce nominees who are not representative of their entire party.

Sequencing by state population could make it easier to determine who goes first, but this would institutionalize a process that forces the most-populous states to always vote last; in contrast, the current system enables some large states, such as California, to vote relatively early on Super Tuesday. An obvious practical problem with this proposal is that it would require party officials from the largest states to abandon attempts at persuading their national committees to let them hold early contests. A single-day national primary, on the other hand, would reduce some of the complexity of negotiating interstate agreements by eliminating sequence. But we show here that an early caucus can play an important role in helping voters evaluate candidates by providing voters in later states with important cues about the candidates. A single-day primary would swamp the beneficial effects of early grassroots campaigning that we have documented in this book.

We propose to take the benefits of existing nomination rules seriously, and suggest dividing states not by region or population size, but by whether they use a caucus or a primary. We believe that any reforms to the nominating process should preserve some aspects of early caucusing and sequence. This would help meet the goal of permitting a wide range of candidates to have a chance, and advance the goal of generating useful information about the candidates. At the same time, we suggest that new rules should encourage increased participation so a party's nominees reflect the broadest range of people who affiliate with it.

This could be accomplished if the national parties adopted some variant of a system that allowed a caucus state (or a number of caucus states) to vote first, followed by a national primary. The "caucus window" could run for several weeks. The major point here is that the benefits of early caucuses would be preserved. Any state that elects to have a caucus could hold their contest in this window. As with the existing system, small states that go first in the months-long, multitier caucus process are not particularly relevant as a means for collecting convention delegates. These nominating events, however, are a way to expose candidates to retail politics and media scrutiny. After this window, and after information is generated about the candidates from caucus states, voters in all fifty states—including those who have already caucused—would be given the opportunity to participate in their party's national primary, held on one day. This would likely result in significantly higher turnout for presidential nominations than the current process and give voters nationwide a chance for meaningful participation in the process. Here we take public opinion seriously, and acknowledge that widespread support for a national primary may not be misguided.

The national parties would determine how to translate votes from a national primary into convention delegates. A national primary with three or more candidates allocating delegates according to the proportional rules used by the Democrats could easily fragment the delegate count and deny any candidate a majority at the national convention. If a party wanted to renew the role of party elites at conventions, this could be a means to that end. If, however, a party sought an absolute outcome via a national primary, winner-take-all rules, majoritarian ranked-choice voting systems, a two-round contest with a runoff election, or, most efficiently, instant runoff voting would facilitate decisiveness. Regardless of how primary votes are translated into delegates, the caucus window would winnow the candidate field, allowing the national primary to produce a decisive result.

This proposal is not all that radical. In fact, the contest in 2008 was, de facto, something similar to what we suggest here, with twenty-four states holding primaries or caucuses on Super Tuesday (February 5). As they did in 2008, the national parties could let their state parties decide if they want to allocate all delegates based on caucus results, or via the primary, or some combination of both. The point is to build a process that tests candidates early, that disseminates information from those tests to the widest set of voters possible, and then allows those voters an opportunity to cast a vote that may play a meaningful role in selecting their party's nominee.

A "caucus window/national primary" concept leaves unresolved the question of who goes first. We suggest that the national parties could opt for a process in which any number of states could hold caucuses on the first voting day of the sequence. Another alternative would have the parties retaining a sequence in which Iowa, or some other relatively small state, is granted first-in-the-nation priority. Whatever the decision may be about who goes first, we see the value in engaging retail politics at the front end of the sequence.

Improving the Caucuses

Iowans have a strong attachment to the caucuses, although, as figure 11.1 shows, that attachment is stronger among those who are repeat caucusgoers. While just over 30% of those experienced in caucuses say they would support changing Iowa to a primary-election system, more than half of first timers said they would support such a change. Given that we asked this question in our postcaucus telephone poll, this result suggests that even after caucusing, those with less attachment to the process

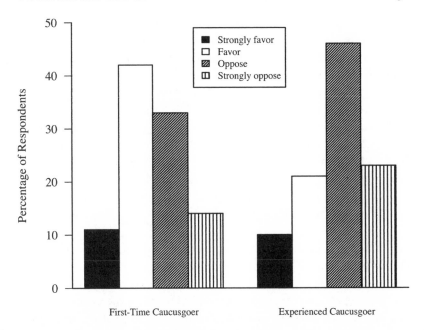

FIGURE 11.1. Support for switching from caucus to primary voting method among Iowa caucus attendees. 196 respondents categorized themselves as first-time caucusgoers, while 240 respondents had previously attended at least one other Iowa caucus.

are less supportive of it as well. Of course, such a change would not only completely change the character of campaigns in Iowa, but would almost certainly mean losing Iowa's first-in-the-nation status. Thus, there has been no serious talk of changing to a primary since Iowa tried it briefly in the early twentieth century (see chapter 3).

Regardless of whether Iowa retains its privileged position, we suggest that there are some changes that could improve the role that Iowa—or any early caucus state—plays in the nominating process. First, the state parties using caucuses to select their convention delegates should provide accurate information about the distribution of support for candidates. Democratic caucuses have a long-running practice of only reporting how many delegates a candidate wins in the precincts, rather than reporting the actual number of votes cast for each candidate. This has the potential to distort how the media reports the results of caucus events, and thus distort information about candidate viability. Delegate totals are calculated after the second-round votes are counted, and fail to reflect the actual distribution of voter support for candidates. Only reporting delegate totals amplifies the discretion that reporters, editors, and pundits have in interpreting what really happened in Iowa. Thus, we believe that the Democrats should report their turnout and vote counts for both rounds of voting, thereby improving transparency.

A second recommendation is that parties work to increase participation at their caucuses. Participation might increase, if only modestly, if the national parties adopt rules that compel states to let people register to vote (and participate) at the caucuses. Several caucus states—including Iowa—already do this, in part as a vehicle for building their local parties. All states should do this. State parties that opt for caucuses should also expand their public education campaigns about how the events work, so people are not intimidated by what might seem to be an idiosyncratic process.

Some have suggested that caucuses should allow absentee ballots, and should be scheduled when more people might be available, such as on weekends. The latter makes sense, and perhaps scheduling on a Saturday evening as Yepsen (2008b) suggests might allow the greatest participation. Absentee ballots are more problematic, at least on the Democratic side, given the practice of debate and discussion before the second round of voting. If caucuses are about developing parties from the grass roots up, absentee ballots might undermine this basic purpose. In the end, while there are ways in which the caucuses could be improved, our assessment is that they add value to the nomination system even as they stand.

Although we believe our proposals are reasonable, the chances of reform are complicated by American federalism. National political parties, state political parties, and state governments vie for control of the nominating process. States, state parties, and national parties often seek different goals. The national parties seek a rational schedule for nominating events, with adequate spacing between state elections. Individual states have the incentive to push for holding their primaries and caucuses earlier in the election season. The national political parties are private entities with control over internal party rules, organization, and management. As such, they would need to be the primary agents of change. Their legal standing places them in the best position to incite changes, and to create the sanctions and incentives that facilitate state compliance.

But we have no illusions. The national parties have deferred to Iowa for decades, and as of this writing appear to be doing so again for 2012.

Their rules essentially stipulate that Iowa leads, followed by New Hampshire. So while reforms will continue to be proposed, from our vantage point it seems likely that Iowa will continue to be first in a sequential nominating process—even if this requires it to hold its caucuses right after Thanksgiving! If this is the case, the findings in this book illustrate a process that is likely to continue through the foreseeable future.

Rules Matter

This book is structured around the idea that the rules governing presidential nominations matter, specifically the sequence of voting *and* the method of voting (caucuses versus primaries). We have argued that the caucus process and the sequential nature of the process are both important and shape outcomes in presidential nominations. Mass-media attention to the Iowa caucuses moves what happens in Iowa to the national stage, affecting contests in later voting states. Although the presidential nominating process might be improved if these rules were altered, the current system has its benefits, which is why we call for marginal changes rather than wholesale revision.

Moreover, this book is not just about Iowa. If rules were changed such that some other small caucus state was granted tremendous attention by virtue of holding the first contest, we suspect that much of what we have learned from Iowa could apply there as well. Iowa has played an important role in the existing sequential process simply because it votes first. If Iowa were not first, the odds are very high that it would gain little attention. But Iowa is first, and we show that it does influence candidate strategies during the nominating process and voter decision making in later states. Given that, we have explored rules that make the Iowa caucuses unique, including how variation in party rules produced differences in the grassroots politics practiced by candidates contesting a caucus.

While we are convinced that we can generalize beyond Iowa, and beyond 2008, it is important to note that aspects of 2008 were singular. Accelerated frontloading of the caucus and primary schedule for that year may have increased the importance of Iowa and New Hampshire. Twenty-four states held contests on February 5. By limiting the amount of time between the early contest and Super Tuesday, outcomes in the early events may have been more immediately salient to a broader set of voters than in previous years. Ironically, this may have been the opposite of what states moving earlier wanted (particularly some of the states holding contests on February 5). At the same time, the unusually competitive 2008 Democratic primary meant that a number of later states had more importance in the process than in previous years.

A Postscript for the 2008 General Election

On November 4, 2008, Barack Obama easily won Iowa over John Mc-Cain. Given results of previous general elections, all early expectations saw Iowa as one of a handful of battleground states in which the general election would be fought. After all, in 2000 Democrat Al Gore had won the state by only 4,000 votes out of 1.3 million cast. In 2004, Republican George W. Bush won the state back, by only 10,000 votes out of 1.5 million. But by August 2008, polling was telling a different story. A University of Iowa Hawkeye Poll that month gave Obama a 7-point lead over McCain in the general election. Other polls over the next two months showed the lead as anywhere from 5 to 13 points. In the end, Obama's margin was more than 140,000 votes, and his nearly 820,000 votes were the most ever won by any presidential candidate in Iowa. What happened?

Although many factors played a role in Obama's win in Iowa—particularly an economic crisis that made him competitive even in states that were usually solidly Republican, along with his financial advantage over McCain—one additional advantage was his organization in Iowa during the caucus campaign. Obama became well known in the state, and his general election campaign operation built on the lessons learned there and in other caucus states—lessons about organizing "on the ground," opening offices, knocking on doors, and all the rest of what makes up grassroots campaigning. John McCain, on the other hand, did not make much more than a token effort in Iowa during the caucus campaign, ceding it (he thought) to Mitt Romney. The result was that once the general election campaign rolled along, McCain had already been out-organized in Iowa months before. Moreover, Obama did not forget the lessons learned in Iowa; he brought them to the other states that did become battlegrounds, particularly Ohio and Pennsylvania. Granted, Obama had money: he outspent his competitors in the Iowa caucus by a factor of two, but by late October the Obama campaign was so confident about Iowa that they shifted their ad spending to "red" states and did not bother to match McCain's spending in Iowa.[2] Obama did buy television and radio advertising—but he also spent significant amounts of money on grassroots mobilization through telephone contacts, mailings, and what seemed like armies of young people knocking on doors. This mobilization was learned and honed in the long run-up to the Iowa caucus, and in the end added to Obama's competitive edge over his general election foe.

Why Iowa? Because the lessons learned there—or in any early grassroots state—can be powerfully applied throughout both the nomination and the general election contests. Candidates learn from Iowa, and the smart ones—and the successful ones—know this. As we opened this book with Barack Obama's homage to Iowa in his October 30, 2008, speech in Des Moines, so we close it with an earlier statement by John Edwards's campaign spokesman, Dan Leistikow, at the time when the state of Michigan was moving its primary to an earlier date to gain some of the glory:

> In Iowa, regular people can look candidates in the eyes, size them up, and ask tough questions. Changing the schedule to favor larger states where TV commercials matter more than face to face contact with voters might be good for the front runner, but it isn't good for our democracy. (Eby 2007)

Although we may imagine a different system, Leistikow's comment about "face to face contact with voters" may be as clear a reason for "Why Iowa?" as any other we could find.

Multivariate Tables for Chapter 7

TABLE A.7.1. **Predictors of media attention to Iowa candidates, 1976–2008**

Predictor variables	b (s.e.)
Pre-Iowa national poll standing percentage (Gallup)	.54
	(.08)
Fund-raising (millions of dollars)	.21
	(.08)
Time spent in Iowa (share of visits)	.32
	(.05)
Incumbent	31.3
	(9.5)
Home state IA (Harkin)	45.0
	(10.4)
Constant	−4.0
	(3.0)
R^2	.77
Adjusted R^2	.73
N	91

Note: Dependent variable = percentage of all precaucus references to candidate. Unstandardized OLS coefficients; b is the unstandardized coefficient, and p is the p-value. Standard errors in parentheses. All models estimated with binary variables for 1976, 1980, 1984, 1988, 1992, 1996, 2000, and 2008 (coefficients not reported).

TABLE A.7.2. **Predictors of Iowa caucus results, 1976–2008**

Predictor variables	Vote percentage				Place (1st = 1)[a]	
	b (s.e.)	b (s.e.)	b (s.e.)	b (s.e.)	b (s.e.)	b (s.e.)
Pre-IA media attention	—	.65 (.11)	.79 (.06)	—	—	-.09 (.02)
Predicted pre-IA attention (instrument from table A.7.1)[b]	—	—	—	.87 (.09)	—	—
Pre IA National Poll Percent (Gallup)	.45 (.09)	.11 (.10)	—	—	-.04 (.02)	.01 (.02)
Fund-raising (millions of dollars)	.16 (.09)	.02 (.07)	—	—	-.03 (.015)	-.01 (.01)
Time spent in Iowa (share of visits)	.33 (.07)	.13 (.08)			-.05 (.02)	-2.2 (1.2)
Home state IA	51.7 (12.1)	22.6 (11.3)	22.5 (9.7)	16.8 (12.3)	.45 (2.0)	4.6 (2.0)
Incumbent president	34.6 (11.1)	14.4 (9.9)	9.2 (9.0)	5.4 (11.1)	-2.6 (1.9)	.33 (1.8)
Constant	-1.6 (3.5)	1.0 (2.9)	1.4 (1.8)	1.7 (12.8)	6.4 (.59)	6.0 (.53)
R^2	.69	.78	.77	.69	.48	.60
Adjusted R^2	.64	.75	.75	.64	.39	.52
N	91	91	91	91	91	91

Note: Unstandardized OLS estimates; b is the unstandardized coefficient. Standard errors in parentheses. All models estimated with binary variables for 1976, 1980, 1984, 1988, 1992, 1996, 2000, and 2008 (coefficients not reported).
[a]Instrument generated from table A.7.1, without binary variables for year.
[b]Same substantive results with ordered probit.

TABLE A.7.3. **Predictors of New Hampshire primary results, 1976–2008**

Predictor variables	Vote share		Win NH?[a]	Place in NH[b] (1 = 1st)
	B (s.e.)	b (s.e.)	b (s.e.)	b (s.e.)
Iowa vote percentage	.37 (.08)	.40 (.09)	.032 (.022)	−.063 (.014)
Change media attention (percentage) (pre-IA to post-IA)	—	.25 (.12)	.23 (.33)	−.52 (.21)
Pre-Iowa national poll standing percentage (Gallup)	.39 (.10)	.40 (.09)	.039 (.025)	−.035 (.017)
Fund-raising (millions of dollars)	.06 (.09)	.06 (.09)	.005 (.024)	−.012 (.015)
From nearby state	11.3 (3.8)	9.9 (3.8)	1.6 (1.0)	−1.2 (0.7)
Constant	0.8 (3.4)	0.6 (3.3)	−4.1 (1.3)	5.9 (.60)
R^2	.63	.65		.52
Adjusted R^2	.58	.59		.44
Pseudo R^2			.23	
N	91	91	91	91

Note: Unstandardized OLS estimates unless noted otherwise; b is the unstandardized coefficient. Standard errors in parentheses. All models estimated with binary variables for 1976, 1980, 1984, 1988, 1992, 1996, 2000, and 2004 (not reported).
[a]Logit estimates.
[b]Same substantive results via ordered probit.

TABLE A.7.4. **Predictors of aggregate primary vote and nomination outcomes**

	Vote share			Won nomination?[a]
Predictor variables	b (s.e.)	b (s.e.)	b (s.e.)	b (s.e.)
Pre-Iowa national poll standing (Gallup percentage)	.61 (.11)	.71 (.10)	.68 (.11)	.08 (.04)
Fund-raising (millions of dollars)	−.01 (.17)	.06 (.15)	.05 (.15)	.02 (.05)
Iowa vote percentage	.11 (.10)	.20 (.08)	.17 (.09)	.03 (.05)
Percent change in media attention post-Iowa	.29 (.15)	.42 (.12)	.39 (.13)	.05 (.06)
New Hampshire vote percentage	.51 (.13)	—	.11 (.15)	.06 (.05)
Won New Hampshire?	—	21.5 (3.5)	19.5 (4.5)	—
Percent change in media attention post-New Hampshire	.35 (.14)	.25 (.13)	.25 (.13)	.01 (.04)
Constant	−1.0 (4.1)	−0.6 (3.6)	−0.9 (3.6)	−6.0 (1.6)
R^2	.79	.84	.84	
Adjusted R^2	.75	.81	.81	
Pseudo R^2				.60
N	76	76	76	76

Note: Unstandardized OLS estimates unless noted otherwise; b is the unstandardized coefficient. Standard errors in parentheses. All models estimated with binary variables for 1976, 1980, 1984, 1988, 1992, 1996, and 2000 (not reported).
[a]Logit estimates.

Multivariate Tables for Chapter 8

TABLE B.8.1. **Who has knowledge of winners of the 2008 Iowa caucuses and New Hampshire primary?**

	Iowa caucus				New Hampshire primary			
	Super Tuesday state		Pre-/post-Super Tuesday		Super Tuesday state		Pre-/post-Super Tuesday	
Predictor variables	b (s.e.)	p	b (s.e.)	p	b (s.e.)	p	b (s.e.)	p
Democrat	.526 (.184)	.004	.529 (.185)	.004	.362 (.177)	.041	.354 (.177)	.045
Republican	−.652 (.184)	.000	−.668 (.185)	.000	−.328 (.180)	.068	−.327 (.180)	.069
Strong conservative	.440 (.187)	.019	.416 (.186)	.026	−.089 (.184)	.628	−.123 (.184)	.505
Strong liberal	−.019 (.248)	.940	−.038 (.250)	.880	.218 (.238)	.359	.209 (.238)	.379
Age	−.007 (.004)	.102	−.006 (.004)	.107	.007 (.004)	.082	.008 (.004)	.063
Income	.103 (.036)	.005	.105 (.036)	.004	.114 (.036)	.001	.117 (.036)	.001
Education	.149 (.048)	.002	.153 (.048)	.001	.126 (.046)	.006	.128 (.046)	.006
Male	.525 (.136)	.000	.550 (.136)	.000	.448 (.130)	.001	.473 (.131)	.000
Following campaign	.882 (.106)	.000	.877 (.106)	.000	.564 (.100)	.000	.559 (.100)	.000
Political interest	.279 (.095)	.003	.288 (.094)	.002	.240 (.087)	.006	.248 (.087)	.004
Ethnic/racial Minority	.075 (.214)	.726	.092 (.215)	.667	−.062 (.204)	.759	−.041 (.204)	.840
Voted on Super Tuesday	.285 (.140)	.042	—		.253 (.135)	.060	—	

(*Continued*)

Predictor variables	Iowa caucus				New Hampshire primary			
	Super Tuesday state		Pre-/post-Super Tuesday		Super Tuesday state		Pre-/post-Super Tuesday	
	b (s.e.)	p	b (s.e.)	p	b (s.e.)	p	b (s.e.)	p
Interviewed pre-election/ Feb. 5	—		.389 (.136)	.004	—		.365 (.131)	.005
Constant	−5.132 (.522)	.000	−5.333 (.529)	.000	−4.410 (.505)	.000	−4.612 (.514)	.000
Pseudo R^2	.15		.16		.10		.10	
Log likelihood	−676.97		−675.75		−714.68		−714.52	
N	1,153		1,156		1,153		1,156	

Note: Dependent variables: respondents were asked, "As best as you can recall, who won the Iowa Caucuses?" Democrats were coded 1 if they said Obama and 0 for other or don't know. Republicans were coded 1 if they said Huckabee and 0 for other or don't know. Respondents were asked, "As best as you can recall, who won the New Hampshire primary?" Democrats were coded 1 if they said Clinton and 0 for other or don't know. Republicans were coded 1 if they said McCain and 0 for other or don't know. Unstandardized logistic regression coefficients; .b is the unstandardized coefficient, and p is the p-value. Robust standard errors in parentheses. Probabilities based on two-tailed tests.

TABLE B.8.2. **Predictors of viability nationally—candidate will win their party's nomination (2008)**

Predictor variables	Perception candidate can win the nomination (viability)									
	Obama		Clinton		Huckabee		McCain		Romney	
	b (s.e.)	p	b (s.e.)	p	b (s.e.)	p	b (s.e.)	p	b (s.e.)	p
Knowledge of IA Winner	.357 (.193)	.065	−.253 (.207)	.221	−.265 (.285)	.354	−.112 (.291)	.700	.294 (.265)	.267
Knowledge of NH Winner	.046 (.194)	.812	.262 (.206)	.205	−.665 (.276)	.016	.389 (.298)	.191	−.272 (.264)	.303
Interviewed after Super Tuesday	.312 (.172)	.069	−.133 (.179)	.459	−.649 (.287)	.024	1.248 (.346)	.000	—	
Constant	−1.47 (.94)	.118	1.57 (.99)	.116	1.97 (1.5)	.203	−4.71 (1.8)	.010	−.815 (.183)	.000
Log likelihood	−401.11		−371.64		−209.8		−190.65		−196.23	
N	606		611		545		547		320	

Note: Dependent variable: respondents were asked, "Candidate X will win the nomination," with strongly agree and agree coded 1, and disagree and strongly disagree coded 0. For example, "Obama will win the nomination," "McCain will win the nomination," etc. Unstandardized logistic regression coefficients; .b is the unstandardized coefficient, and p is the p-value. Robust standard errors in parentheses. Probabilities based on two-tailed tests.

TABLE B.8.3. **Predictors of candidate preference/vote choice**

Predictor variables	Obama vote b (s.e.)	p	Clinton vote b (s.e.)	p	McCain vote b (s.e.)	p
Candidate favorability rating (feeling thermometer)	.052 (.008)	.000	.040 (.007)	.000	1.440 (.186)	.000
Candidate viable ("can win the nomination")	1.991 (.328)	.000	2.224 (.366)	.000	1.645 (.578)	.004
Candidate electable ("can win the presidency")	.237 (.359)	.510	1.015 (.338)	.003	.519 (.278)	.062
Education	.137 (.094)	.147	−.188 (.092)	.039	−.001 (.091)	.993
Age	−.024 (.008)	.003	−.005 (.009)	.530	.002 (.007)	.778
Income	−.024 (.067)	.717	−.109 (.065)	.096	.121 (.073)	.095
Male	.310 (.273)	.256	−.050 (.253)	.844	.304 (.238)	.202
Minority	.423 (.389)	.278	−1.121 (.367)	.002	−.121 (.609)	.843
Issues						
Iraq most important	.196 (.399)	.623	−.024 (.363)	.946	−.453 (.422)	.283
Economy most important	−.428 (.337)	.205	.164 (.326)	.616	−.179 (.264)	.498
Health care most important	−.591 (.381)	.121	.606 (.372)	.103	.698 (.514)	.174
Candidate characteristics						
Experience more important	−4.132 (1.031)	.000	1.811 (.460)	.000	.140 (.399)	.726
Stands up for beliefs	.376 (.363)	.301	−.273 (.383)	.476	−.007 (.310)	.981
Strong liberal	−.250 (.362)	.489	−.221 (.349)	.528	−.059 (.264)	.823
Born again/ evangelical Christian	.034 (.332)	.918	.644 (.321)	.045	−.073 (.248)	.767
Constant	−4.758 (.857)	.000	−3.984 (.923)	.000	−3.610 (.951)	.000
Pseudo R^2	.45		.43		.27	
Log likelihood	−196.21		−208.18		−218.24	
N	527		526		433	

Note: Dependent variables: respondents who state they will participate in Democratic primary/caucus for column 1, a vote for Obama coded 1, for all others coded 0. In column 2, a vote for Clinton coded 1, for all others coded 0. Respondents who state they will participate in Republican primary/caucus for column 2, a vote for McCain coded 1, for all others coded 0. Undstandardized logistic regression coefficients; b is the unstandardized coefficient, and p is the p-value. Robust standard errors in parentheses. Probabilities based on two-tailed tests.

TABLE B.8.4. **Predictors of Democratic candidate preference/vote choice (Obama)**

Predictor variables	Super Tuesday contest state (Feb. 1–4 interview)		Noncontest state (Feb. 1–4 interview)		Noncontest state (Feb. 7–11 interview)	
	b (s.e.)	p	b (s.e.)	p	b (s.e.)	p
Obama favorability rating	.049	.000	.084	.000	.062	.000
(feeling thermometer)	(.013)		(.020)		(.013)	
Obama more viable	2.877	.000	1.620	.061	2.482	.000
(can win nomination)	(.661)		(.866)		(.631)	
Obama electable (can	1.401	.054	1.111	.201	−.641	.341
win the presidency)	(.728)		(.869)		(.673)	
Education	.126	.380	.564	.021	.034	.834
	(.143)		(.244)		(.164)	
Age	−.006	.628	−.065	.007	−.023	.049
	(.012)		(.024)		(.012)	
Income	−.215	.053	.041	.786	.036	.713
	(.112)		(.152)		(.098)	
Male	.550	.188	.353	.544	−.169	.692
	(.418)		(.582)		(.427)	
Minority	.515	.322	1.683	.081	.236	.642
	(.520)		(.965)		(.509)	
Issues						
Iraq most important	.888	.152	.218	.758	−.044	.950
	(.620)		(.710)		(.711)	
Economy most						
important	.282	.569	−.532	.526	−.792	.146
	(.495)		(.841)		(.544)	
Health care most						
important	.296	.687	.223	.747	−1.506	.018
	(.734)		(.691)		(.636)	
Candidate characteristics						
Stands up for beliefs	−.432	.462	−1.116	.215	2.507	.000
	(.587)		(.900)		(.699)	
Strong liberal	.140	.784	−.662	.446	−.273	.653
	(.510)		(.869)		(.606)	
Experience most						
important	—		—		−3.138	.005
					(1.124)	
Constant	−6.996	.000	−8.212	.001	−4.570	.008
	(1.604)		(2.400)		(1.715)	
Pseudo R^2	.42		.53		.48	
Log likelihood	−71.15		−42.46		−74.97	
N	183		138		210	

Note: Dependent variables: respondents who state they will participate in Democratic primary/caucus and vote for Obama coded 1, for all others coded 0. Unstandardized logistic regression coefficients; b is the unstandardized coefficient, and p is the p-value. Robust standard errors in parentheses. Probabilities based on two-tailed tests.

Multivariate Tables for Chapter 9

TABLE C.9.I. **Predictors of political participation and civic engagement in the 2008 Iowa caucuses**

Predictor variables	Online participation b (s.e.)	p	Offline participation b (s.e.)	p	Thought given to the election b (s.e.)	p	Following campaign news b (s.e.)	p
Political interest	.484 (.101)	.000	.312 (.093)	.001				
Internet use	1.394 (.095)	.000	.273 (.071)	.000	.216 (.083)	.010	.101 (.074)	.175
Education	.159 (.061)	.009	.287 (.057)	.000	.087 (.065)	.181	.166 (.060)	.005
Income	−.077 (.053)	.144	.081 (.050)	.106	−.116 (.058)	.047	−.012 (.052)	.834
Age	−.009 (.006)	.113	.034 (.006)	.000	.023 (.007)	.000	.023 (.006)	.000
Male	.199 (.164)	.227	.261 (.156)	.095	.061 (.183)	.741	.201 (.165)	.224
Married	.270 (.199)	.174	.184 (.185)	.319	−.296 (.219)	.177	−.158 (.192)	.411
Strong Democrat	.057 (.210)	.787	.446 (.195)	.022	1.221 (.257)	.000	1.086 (.207)	.000
Strong Republican	.055 (.196)	.780	.255 (.186)	.169	.430 (.208)	.039	.156 (.196)	.425
Religious attendance	−.034 (.068)	.622	.132 (.065)	.043	.099 (.075)	.185	−.003 (.067)	.970
Political efficacy	.440 (.119)	.000	.438 (.106)	.000	.282 (.121)	.020	.243 (.113)	.032

(*Continued*)

TABLE C. 9.I. *Continued*

Predictor variables	Online participation		Offline participation		Thought given to the election		Following campaign news	
	b (s.e.)	p	b (s.e.)	p	b (s.e.)	p	b (s.e.)	p
Pseudo R^2	.23		.09		.06		.07	
Log likelihood	−770.51		−830.59		−588.83		−500.71	
N	624		600		630		630	

Note: All models were estimated using ordered logistic regression, where b is the unstandardized coefficient, s.e. is the standard error, and p is the p-value. The p-values were calculated based on two-tailed tests. The model cut points are not presented to preserve space.

TABLE C. 9.2. Predictors of political participation and civic engagement, 2008 national sample (Super Tuesday and post–Super Tuesday voting states)

Predictor variables	Online participation		Offline participation		Thought given to the election		Following campaign news	
	b (s.e.)	p	b (s.e.)	p	b (s.e.)	p	b (s.e.)	p
Political interest	.296 (.079)	.000	.360 (.075)	.000				
Internet use	1.014 (.064)	.000	.218 (.052)	.000	.038 (.061)	.533	.117 (.054)	.029
Education	.095 (.045)	.036	.315 (.042)	.000	.085 (.050)	.087	.167 (.043)	.000
Income	−.021 (.036)	.569	.070 (.034)	.038	.088 (.039)	.026	−.007 (.035)	.837
Age	−.024 (.004)	.000	.023 (.004)	.000	.012 (.004)	.009	.020 (.004)	.000
Male	.519 (.121)	.000	.395 (.114)	.001	.151 (.137)	.271	.376 (.119)	.002
Married	.094 (.143)	.510	.115 (.131)	.379	.147 (.151)	.331	.057 (.135)	.674
Minority	−.498 (.326)	.126	−.331 (.325)	.309	−.761 (.319)	.017	−.530 (.309)	.086
Strong Democrat	.467 (.146)	.001	.359 (.134)	.007	.862 (.178)	.000	.659 (.139)	.000
Strong Republican	.521 (.153)	.001	.364 (.145)	.012	.207 (.171)	.226	.457 (.151)	.002
Religious attendance	−.070 (.039)	.073	.022 (.036)	.538	−.005 (.044)	.908	−.033 (.038)	.381
Political efficacy	.407 (.081)	.000	.441 (.077)	.000	.339 (.089)	.000	.441 (.079)	.000
Pseudo R^2	.20		.09		.04		.05	
Log likelihood	−1419.82		−1434.50		−871.66		−1143.54	
N	1,135		1,142		1,145		1,147	

Note: All models were estimated using ordered logistic regression, where b is the unstandardized coefficient, s.e. is the standard error, and p is the p-value. The p-values were calculated based on two-tailed tests. The model cut points are not presented to preserve space.

TABLE C.9.3. **Predictors of political participation and civic engagement in the 2008 presidential nominations (pooled samples—Iowa caucus and national sample)**

Predictor variables	Online participation b (s.e.)	p	Offline participation b (s.e.)	p	Thought given to the election b (s.e.)	p	Following campaign news b (s.e.)	p
Iowa registered voter	.571 (.103)	.000	2.204 (.110)	.000	−.370 (.114)	.001	−.471 (.101)	.000
Reference category— national registered voter	—	—	—	—	—	—	—	—
Political interest	.360 (.061)	.000	.359 (.059)	.000				
Internet use	1.136 (.053)	.000	(.245) (.042)	.000	.100 (.049)	.042	.116 (.043)	.007
Education	.109 (.036)	.002	.307 (.034)	.000	.089 (.039)	.023	.167 (.035)	.000
Income	−.043 (.030)	.145	.068 (.028)	.015	.018 (.032)	.572	−.006 (.029)	.829
Age	−.019 (.003)	.000	.028 (.003)	.000	.017 (.004)	.000	.021 (.003)	.000
Male	.404 (.097)	.000	.345 (.092)	.000	.139 (.109)	.204	.322 (.096)	.001
Married	.149 (.115)	.196	.145 (.106)	.172	−.020 (.123)	.873	.003 (.110)	.978
Minority	−.290 (.291)	.320	−.533 (.300)	.075	−.841 (.287)	.003	−.560 (.290)	.053
Strong Democrat	.341 (.119)	.004	.381 (.110)	.001	.962 (.145)	.000	.776 (.115)	.000
Strong Republican	.334 (.119)	.005	.315 (.114)	.006	.311 (.132)	.018	.337 (.118)	.004
Religious attendance	−.053 (.034)	.121	.053 (.031)	.090	.020 (.038)	.602	−.028 (.033)	.403
Political efficacy	.415 (.067)	.000	.445 (.063)	.000	.320 (.071)	.000	.380 (.064)	.000
Pseudo R^2	.21		.16		.05		.06	
Log likelihood	−2214.14		−2306.67		−1383.56		−1742.85	
N	1,759		1,742		1,775		1,777	

Note: All models were estimated using ordered logistic regression, where b is the unstandardized coefficient, s.e. is the standard error, and p is the p-value. The p-values were calculated based on two-tailed tests. The model cut points are not presented to preserve space.

TABLE C.9.4. **Predictors of political participation and civic engagement in the 2008 presidential nominations (pooled samples—Iowa caucus, national sample, and Pennsylvania primary)**

Predictor variables	Online participation		Offline participation		Thought given to election		Following campaign news	
	b (s.e.)	p	b (s.e.)	p	b (s.e.)	p	b (s.e.)	p
National sample (registered voters)	−1.064 (.111)	.000	−3.047 (.126)	.000	.268 (.110)	.015	.342 (.097)	.000
Pa. primary registered voter	−1.129 (.197)	.000	−3.450 (.237)	.000	.765 (.206)	.000	.408 (.165)	.013
Reference category— Iowa registered voter	—	—	—	—	—	—	—	—
Political interest	.466 (.069)	.000	.402 (.070)	.000				
Education	.163 (.037)	.000	.224 (.037)	.000	.129 (.035)	.000	.216 (.031)	.000
Income	.049 (.030)	.101	.086 (.031)	.006	.033 (.029)	.257	−.002 (.026)	.927
Age	−.038 (.003)	.000	.005 (.003)	.104	.013 (.003)	.000	.017 (.003)	.000
Male	.286 (.102)	.005	.410 (.105)	.000	.137 (.103)	.183	.355 (.090)	.000
Married	.228 (.119)	.056	−.136 (.121)	.264	.019 (.115)	.872	.044 (.102)	.669
Minority	−.008 (.304)	.978	−.304 (.360)	.398	−.630 (.267)	.019	−.434 (.264)	.101
Strong partisan	.349 (.103)	.001	.255 (.104)	.015	.711 (.102)	.000	.596 (.089)	.000
Religious attendance	−.018 (.035)	.603	.081 (.036)	.026	−.029 (.035)	.409	−.044 (.030)	.136
Pseudo R^2	.11		.25		.03		.04	
Log likelihood	−1363.74		−1399.17		−1561.19		−2000.96	
N	1,990		1,969		1,997		1,999	

Note: All models were estimated using ordered logistic regression, where b is the unstandardized coefficient, s.e. is the standard error, and p is the p-value. The p-values were calculated based on two-tailed tests. The model cut points are not presented to preserve space.

Multivariate Tables for Chapter 10

TABLE D.10.1. **Who supports a national primary? (2008 October Hawkeye Poll)**

Predictor variables	Baseline b (s.e.)	p	Interaction 1 b (s.e.)	p	Interaction 2 b (s.e.)	p
Population (log) of respondent's State	−.257 (.325)	.429	−.838 (.412)	.042	.123 (.464)	.791
State very or somewhat important in Pres. nomination ("state role")	.032 (.209)	.878	−5.691 (3.142)	.070	.022 (.213)	.916
Super Tuesday state	−.159 (.183)	.384	−.187 (.186)	.314	5.538 (3.305)	.094
Population X state role			.845 (.469)	.072		
Population X Super Tuesday state					−.827 (.481)	.086
Percentage of high school graduates in respondent's state	−.009 (.025)	.714	−.008 (.026)	.768	−.009 (.027)	.727
Political efficacy	−.206 (.085)	.016	−.204 (.087)	.019	−.205 (.085)	.017
Education	−.082 (.061)	.182	−.083 (.061)	.177	−.086 (.063)	.174
Male	−.448 (.125)	.000	−.458 (.126)	.000	−.436 (.125)	.001
Age	−.002 (.005)	.670	−.002 (.005)	.674	−.001 (.005)	.770
Income	.041 (.043)	.346	.040 (.044)	.361	.046 (.044)	.296
Republican	−.297 (.180)	.098	−.283 (.185)	.126	−.296 (.178)	.098

(*Continued*)

TABLE D.IO.I. *Continued*

Predictor variables	Baseline b (s.e.)	p	Interaction 1 b (s.e.)	p	Interaction 2 b (s.e.)	p
Democrat	−.314 (.171)	.066	−.319 (.175)	.068	−.284 (.174)	.103
African American	.404 (.339)	.233	.417 (.339)	.219	.402 (.340)	.238
Intercept	4.913 (3.538)	.165	8.685 (3.786)	.022	2.253 (4.021)	.575
N (respondents)	1,026		1,026		1,026	
N (states)	40		40		40	
Pseudo R^2	.02		.02		.02	
Log likelihood	−580.773		−579.419		−578.969	
Wald χ^2	77.183		100.400		90.195	

Source: National Registered Voter Survey surrounding February 5, 2008, primaries, University of Iowa Hawk-eye Poll.

Note: The dependent variable is coded 1 if the respondent favors a national primary and 0 if otherwise. Unstandardized logistic regression coefficients; b is the unstandardized coefficient, and p is the p-value. Robust standard errors in parentheses, and probabilities based on two-tailed tests. Standard errors clustered by state to account for spatial autocorrelation.

TABLE D.IO.2. **Who supports a national primary? (2008 October CCAP Survey)**

	Model 1		Model 2	
	b (s.e.)	p	b (s.e.)	p
State population (log)	.1807 (.102)	.078	.1213 (.102)	.235
Perceive state has influence	−.0583 (.081)	.470		
Resides in a state with nominating event before Feb. 5 (IA, NH, NV, SC)			−.6186 (.329)	.060
Democrat	.0543 (.189)	.774	.0090 (.193)	.963
Republican	−.1118 (.186)	.548	−.1244 (.185)	.502
Age	.0126 (.005)	.018	.0124 (.005)	.016
Education	−.0196 (.079)	.805	−.0130 (.080)	.871
Income	.0060 (.028)	.832	.0054 (.028)	.850
Female	.0207 (.170)	.903	.0042 (.168)	.980
White non-Hispanic	.7957 (.214)	.000	.7913 (.219)	.000
Constant	−3.678 (1.741)	.035	−2.883 (1.820)	.113
N	959		961	
Log likelihood	−638.5355		−639.0206	

Source: 2008 Cooperative Campaign Analysis Panel (CCAP), October wave.

Note: The dependent variable is coded 1 if the respondent favors a national primary and 0 if otherwise. Unstandardized logistic regression coefficients; b is the unstandardized coefficient, and p is the p-value. Robust standard errors in parentheses, and probabilities based on two-tailed tests. Since both individual- and state-level effects are considered, model coefficients are clustered by standard errors by state to account for spatial autocorrelation. Question wording: "Others have proposed a national primary, similar to Super Tuesday, where every state would hold their caucuses or primaries on the same day. Would you strongly favor, favor, oppose or strongly oppose such a plan?"

TABLE D.10.3. **Who supports rotating primaries? (2008 October Hawkeye Poll)**

Predictor variables	Baseline b (s.e.)	p	Interaction 1 b (s.e.)	p	Interaction 2 b (s.e.)	p
Population (log) of respondent's State	.302 (.222)	.173	−.423 (.455)	.353	.400 (.228)	.079
State very or somewhat important in pres. nomination ("state role")	−.480 (.172)	.005	−7.116 (3.595)	.048	−.482 (.172)	.005
Super Tuesday state	−.064 (.133)	.632	−.095 (.136)	.485	1.458 (2.503)	.560
Population X "state role"			.985 (.541)	.069		
Population X Super Tuesday state					−.221 (.368)	.547
Percentage of high school graduates in respondent's state	.001 (.016)	.943	.002 (.016)	.907	.001 (.016)	.946
Political efficacy	.001 (.142)	.995	.004 (.142)	.975	.002 (.141)	.991
Education	.133 (.056)	.018	.133 (.056)	.018	.132 (.056)	.018
Male	−.360 (.129)	.005	−.372 (.126)	.003	−.355 (.130)	.006
Age	−.018 (.005)	.000	−.019 (.005)	.000	−.018 (.005)	.000
Income	.062 (.044)	.160	.061 (.043)	.159	.063 (.044)	.153
Republican	−.173 (.211)	.412	−.164 (.213)	.442	−.175 (.213)	.410
Democrat	−.012 (.177)	.946	−.018 (.177)	.917	−.006 (.177)	.973
African American	.074 (.323)	.819	.091 (.327)	.780	.076 (.321)	.814
Intercept	−.556 (2.531)	.826	4.235 (3.808)	.266	−1.238 (2.535)	.625
N (respondents)	913		913		913	
N (states)	40		40		40	
Pseudo R^2	.05		.05		.05	
Log likelihood	−512.936		−511.3845		−512.819	
Wald χ^2	75.095		101.882		69.599	

Source: National Registered Voter Survey surrounding February 5, 2008, primaries, University of Iowa Hawkeye Poll.

Note: The dependent variable is coded 1 if the respondent favors rotating state primaries and 0 if otherwise. Unstandardized logistic regression coefficients; b is the unstandardized coefficient, and p is the p-value. Robust standard errors in parentheses, and probabilities based on two-tailed tests. Standard errors clustered by state to account for spatial autocorrelation.

Notes

Chapter Two

1. The amount of money raised by the presidential candidates for the nomination contests ($296 million for Obama, $238 million for Clinton, and $122 million for McCain through May 2008) shattered all previous records. Obama and Clinton opted out of public financing. See Thomas E. Mann, "Money in the 2008 Elections" (Brookings Institution, 2007). Available online: http://www.brookings.edu/opinions/2008/0701_publicfinance_mann.aspx (accessed April 3, 2010).

2. See Stone, Rapoport, and Atkeson (1995); Stone, Rapoport, and Abramowitz (1992, 1989); Hull (2007) for exceptions.

3. Many local elections are run on a nonpartisan basis, so voters do not have party cues in making their choices, and often must choose from more than two candidates on the ballot for one office. But such elections are rare at the state and national levels.

4. While Hull's work is the first systematic look at Iowa in quite a while, some problems with imputed data and retrospectively asked survey questions as well as issues of statistical analysis cast some doubt on the precision of the findings he reports. However, we are convinced of his general claim that Iowa has gained in importance in recent years.

5. CNN, 2006, online at http://transcripts.cnn.com/TRANSCRIPTS/0608/18/ltm.04.html (accessed April 3, 2010).

6. 1980 is not included due to a lack of data. In 1992, Iowa senator Tom Harkin ran for the Democratic nomination with a Republican incumbent, and thus this year is omitted as well, as the Iowa caucus was not contested.

7. Complete data and survey instruments are available on our Web site at http://www.whyiowa.org. The Hawkeye Polls were quite accurate in terms of the head-to-head candidate comparisons. The October survey was the first to show a Huckabee surge and also one of the first to show Obama rising as Edwards fell.

Details on the polls, including toplines, can be found online at http://www.uiowa
.edu/election/news-events/archives/hawkeyepoll.html.

8. For those who are familiar with multivariate methods, these include logistic regression (for binary outcome variables), ordinal logistic regression (for ordinal outcome variables), and calculations of the standard errors that correct for
potentially biased estimates by using robust standard errors. Depending on the
coding of the dependent variables, these methods are used in models in various
chapters.

Chapter Three

1. For those interested in more details of the history of the caucus process,
Winebrenner (1998) provides an excellent summary along with detailed descriptions of the caucuses from 1972 to 1996. Squire (1989, 1–3) also provides a quick
summary of how Iowa became first in the nation.

2. It is difficult to find much detailed history on the Iowa caucuses before
1972. Two articles by Horack (1910, 1923) discuss the development of the Iowa
primary, indicating that a law establishing it was passed in 1907, though it does
not appear to have been used for presidential nominations except in 1916. Horack's description suggests that during those years the county convention delegates from a political party were selected by voters through this primary, not the
party caucuses. At the same time, Horack also points out that in general, voters
simply pasted names provided by party leaders onto gummed sheets for county
committee and delegate positions on the ballot; thus, the parties retained control of both the county committees and the county conventions. We have been
unable to find a source indicating when this practice was abandoned, since it is
clear that in the 1960s and beyond, committee people and convention delegates
were selected at caucuses.

3. A vestige of this remains even today. The Iowa caucuses are held every
two years, not just during presidential election cycles. County committee people
hold their office for two years, and the county, district, and state conventions are
also held every two years. But in the off years when there is no presidential election, or when in presidential years there is no nomination contest, no one cares
and virtually no one comes. One of us, David Redlawsk, chaired the Democratic
caucus in his precinct every two years from 2000 to 2008. Attendance varied
drastically—118 people in 2000, 6 in 2002, 299 in 2004, 4 in 2006, and 570 in
2008. Yet no matter the turnout, those who attend the caucus elect members of
the county committee and delegates to the county convention. Obviously, these
positions are more competitive in competitive presidential nomination years.

4. In low-population counties there are generally very few precincts—as few
as 4—while the largest county, Polk, had 183 precincts during the 2008 caucuses.

5. Iowa has no-excuse absentee voting, which begins as early as forty days before a primary or general election. This is among the earliest of all states, and perhaps makes all the more ironic Iowa's requirement that a caucus participant show up in person at a designated time.

6. It is worth thinking of the process in Iowa as a pyramid. At the base are the precinct caucuses; in 2008 there were 1,784 of them throughout the state. The next stage is the county convention, generally held about six weeks after the caucus in each of the 99 counties in the state. The congressional district conventions—five, until redistricting after 2010 loses Iowa another congressional seat—are held a month later. Finally, the state convention is at the top, held in June of the election year.

7. Brady (1988) reports on attending a Republican caucus in 1988 at which the attendees chose delegates to the county convention essentially based on who wanted to go, without consideration of candidate preference. Thus, while Kansas senator Bob Dole won the precinct straw poll with 35 out of 81 votes, delegates elected to the county convention included eight supporters of Dole, one supporter of New York representative Jack Kemp, and one uncommitted. Dole's plurality allowed his supporters to elect nearly all the delegates, though supporters for four other candidates had listed their names.

8. This 15% threshold is not unique to Iowa, nor is it always 15%. Because the national Democratic Party since 1990 has required that states allocate delegates proportionally whether through a caucus or a primary process, every state has a threshold, below which a candidate receives no national convention delegates. This threshold is applied at both a congressional district and a statewide level, so candidates may win district delegates while falling below the statewide threshold, as happened with John Edwards in Florida in 2008. At the Iowa caucuses, while 15% is the usual threshold, there are no preference groups in precincts that elect only one county convention delegate, so whoever has 50% + 1 supporter gets the delegate. In precincts electing two delegates, the threshold is 25%; any candidate receiving less support than that will not win any delegates. Similarly, in precincts electing three delegates, the threshold is 16.67%. Finally, the 15% threshold comes into play where there are four or more delegates to be elected. The number of county convention delegates is determined by the county party, and apportioned to precincts based on prior Democratic vote performance. For a detailed look at the issue of threshholds and the history of the Democratic Party's use of proportional representation, see Kamarck (2009), 81–118.

9. This final vote includes twelve more unpledged "Party Leader and Elected Official" delegates (otherwise known as superdelegates) not elected at the district and state conventions. Data on the delegate numbers come from The Green Papers, online at http://www.thegreenpapers.com/P08/IA-D.phtml, and verified by one of the authors, David Redlawsk, who was elected as a pledged Edwards national convention delegate at the Iowa Second District Democratic con-

vention. Redlawsk was involved in the negotiations with the Obama campaign that moved him and the other three Edwards district delegates to Obama, announced June 3, 2008, and ensured that three additional Edwards supporters would be elected to the national convention as Obama delegates.

10. Some random examples include a Republican blogging at http://polipundit .com/?p=1769, and a Democrat at http://poljunk.gloriousnoise.com/2008/01/ caucus_report_a_poljunk_eyewitness.php, while an observer, not a participant, posted this: http://www.talkleft.com/story/2008/1/3/192445/8044.

11. The number of delegates to the county convention allocated to each precinct is determined before the caucuses are held, and is based on party performance in that precinct at the preceding two general elections. So no matter how many people show up at the precinct on caucus night, the number of delegates is preset. This leads to criticisms of the Democrats' process as violating the one-person one-vote principle, since it can take a different number of supporters to elect a single delegate in different precincts.

12. Technically, any caucus participant can change his or her candidate between the first and second alignment. Most, of course, do not. However, sometimes people move from one viable group to another for strategic reasons. As we will see, groups may have "excess" support that does not translate into an additional delegate but may be deployed to deny some other candidate a delegate.

13. Kamarck (2009) describes how the number of delegates in individual districts affects candidate strategies because of this rounding process. While she is writing generally about primaries and congressional-level delegates, the same considerations apply for Iowa precinct delegates. Typically, precincts with an odd number of delegates are potentially more valuable to the winner than those with an even number of delegates. Consider that in a precinct with 4 delegates, winning 60% of the vote will earn only 2 delegates (.6 × 4 = 2.4, rounds to 2.0). But in a precinct with 5 delegates, 60% will win 3 delegates. The difference is stark—between having the result reported as a "tie" versus a clear win.

14. Other categories include "straightforward" voting, where the voter chooses the candidate he or she feels is both the most viable and the most highly rated. This is presumably an easy vote, since subjective rating and assessment of viability correspond. Abramson et al. (1992) also include an "irrational" category, where the voter chooses a candidate who is both less viable and lower rated.

15. Our categorization of respondents into voter types was based on feeling thermometer questions for voters' predispositions toward a candidate (favorability ratings) and the candidate's chance of winning the party's nomination (viability). Such questions ask voters to rate candidates from zero (very cold) to one hundred (very warm). We use the late October Iowa caucus survey and national Super Tuesday primary survey in this analysis, along with our survey of Pennsylvania Democrats before their April 2008 primary; each was a preelection sur-

vey. Voter types were built replicating Abramson et al. (1992) and comparing our findings with theirs based on the 1988 presidential nomination.

16. In fact, among a number of "reforms" that former *Des Moines Register* political columnist David Yepsen (2008a, 2008b) urged on the Democrats was that they report the actual results of the caucus and that the process be managed by Iowa county auditors just as other elections are. We have more to say about this in our final chapter.

17. On July 28, 2009, the Iowa Republican and Democratic parties announced that for the first time, their off-year caucuses would be held on a Saturday afternoon, January 23, beginning at 1:00 p.m. The joint announcement read in part: "Our decision to hold these important organizational meetings on a Saturday was made to encourage greater participation in an off-year caucus and get more Iowans actively involved with the work of our Parties." An informal canvass of several precincts by one of the authors suggested that actual turnout was a dismal as ever in the 2010 off-year caucus.

Chapter Four

1. Data on candidate visits to Iowa was viewed at George Washington University's Democracy in Action Web site at http://www.gwu.edu/~action/2008/chrniowa08.html (accessed April 18, 2010). Days spent by the candidates in Iowa are also from the same source, as are the number of field offices each candidate established in 2008.

2. Some work has been done in the past to get a sense of how much mail voters in Iowa receive during a caucus campaign. See, for example, Redlawsk and Sanders (2000).

3. We limit our focus to simplify things. As it turns out, there are relatively few differences in reported contacts among those in the middle age groups. Voters thirty to forty-four years old reported far fewer in-person contacts from the Edwards campaign than from either of the two others, but among those in the 45–59 age group, in-person contacts by Edwards were ahead of Clinton and not far behind Obama. Telephone and mail contacts did not vary much within these age groups by candidate.

Chapter Five

1. We have no intention of denigrating the contributions of this work or of other papers published by Abramowitz, Stone, and Rapoport. In fact, they have compiled a comprehensive multiyear data set of caucus voters in a number of states across many years (Abramowitz et al. 2001). From these data they pub-

lished a number of papers developing many different arguments about the role of activists in the nominating process, including valuable studies of how their respondents perceived and responded to candidates (Stone and Rapoport 1994), the effects of the gender gap in nomination politics (Rapoport, Stone, and Abramowitz 1994), and mobilization in presidential nomination campaigns (Stone, Atkeson, and Rapoport 1992), among others.

2. The media entrance poll reported that about 22% of all Democratic attendees and 11% of all Republicans were between the ages of 17 and 29 years (http://www.cnn.com/ELECTION/2008/primaries/results/state/#IA [accessed April 7, 2010]).

3. We should note that one major advantage we have is that our in-caucus survey was collected on caucus night immediately before the caucuses began, while Stone and colleagues relied on mail surveys completed and returned sometime after the caucuses were over.

4. With President Bush running for reelection in 2004, the Republican caucus did not include a presidential preference poll and the turnout for Republicans was very small.

5. Figure 5.3 reports only the telephone survey results. Party differences in the in-caucus survey are essentially the same with one exception. In the in-caucus survey, Democrats are much less likely to say they attended to be involved in their party organization, while in the telephone survey there is no difference between the parties.

6. As we described in chapter 2, we have a series of telephone surveys taken during the Iowa caucus campaigns (March, July/August, October), followed by the January surveys (telephone and in-caucus). The results we report in this chapter are from the January surveys. In chapter 9 we will also examine participation, but we will do so using the October precaucus survey in order to compare more directly with our national and Pennsylvania samples, which were also collected before any voting took place in those states. However, since this chapter focuses specifically on voters who actually did caucus (as opposed to those who said they were likely to do so), we use only the January surveys here.

7. We should note that in our October telephone sample, a larger percentage of respondents reported making online contributions than did in our January postcaucus sample. This is most likely due to sampling error, given the very small percentage reporting this activity in the first place.

8. But one important similarity must be noted first—activists were neither older nor younger than nonactivists. The average age of activists in our telephone survey was 55.1 years, compared with 56.3 years for nonactivists. So the results we report here are not confounded by age.

9. It is worth noting that on rare occasions, other states have jumped ahead of Iowa. For example, in 1996 Louisiana and Alaska held Republican nomination

contests ahead of Iowa, and it may be that Texas senator Phil Gramm's loss to conservative political commentator Patrick Buchanan in Louisiana contributed to his fourth-place showing in Iowa. But of course the media paid no attention to these contests, nor did most candidates. We are indebted to Chris Hull for pointing this out to us.

Chapter Six

An earlier version of this chapter was published as David P. Redlawsk, Daniel Bowen, and Caroline J. Tolbert, "Comparing Caucus and Registered Voter Support for the 2008 Presidential Candidates in Iowa," *PS: Political Science and Politics* 41, no. 1 (2007): 129–38.

1. McDonald and Popkin (2001) argue that the correct base for calculation of voter turnout is not the typical "voting age population" or even registered voters. Instead, it is an estimate of those who are potentially eligible voters, whether registered or not. This voting eligible population essentially takes the census estimates of the voting age population and adjusts for resident aliens and others who are barred from voting (such as convicted felons, in a number of states).

2. Officially, superdelegates are known as "unpledged and pledged party leaders and elected official delegates" (Democratic National Committee, www.democrats.org). Their presence, while theoretically allowing them to tip a convention, has not really been tested, since no nomination battle has gone to convention since they were created. At this writing, the Democrats may be making a significant change to these delegates for 2012, requiring them to run as pledged to candidates rather than unpledged (Romm 2009).

3. Though Wang (2007) does not provide a baseline to compare this number to, approximately 42% of Iowa adults aged 18 or over are over 50 years old, suggesting that this skew is not quite as dramatic as it seems at first. Entrance poll reports of the 2008 caucuses suggest that about 60% of Democratic caucusgoers were 45 and over, which indicates that younger voters showed up in 2008 at a greater rate than in 2004.

4. The Northern Iowa study's mean includes both presidential-year and off-year caucuses and voters from both parties. While not generally recognized by those who comment on the caucuses, the parties hold their precinct caucuses every two years in order to conduct a range of party business.

5. Iowa Commission of Latino Affairs, drawing on data from the U.S. census; online at http://www.iowalatinoaffairs.iowa.gov/Pages/Data.htm (accessed April 10, 2010).

6. Contrast this to the New Hampshire primary, where nonparty voters may

choose to vote in either party's primary and then may immediately fill out a form to return to nonparty status while still at the polls. Iowa independents who wish to caucus automatically become party members unless they submit a new registration form reregistering as "no party" to the county election office. They cannot do this until the next working day at the earliest.

7. Turnout was reported at 124,000 people for the 2004 Democratic caucus, out of a base of about 540,000 registered Democrats.

8. Democrats: approximately 239,000 caucus attendees out of 649,000 party members (including 43,000 registrations on caucus night). Republicans: approximately 118,000 attendees out of 585,000 Republicans (including 9,500 registrations on caucus night). Registration data source: Iowa Secretary of State, http://www.sos.state.ia.us/press/2008/2008_01_18.html (accessed September 24, 2009).

9. More information regarding the University of Iowa's Hawkeye Polls can be found online at http://www.uiowa.edu/election/news-events/index.html#hawkeyepoll or at http://www.whyiowa.org.

10. Registered voter results using the March and August samples were weighted by gender. Neither sample in the October survey was weighted because of more even gender representation in the unweighted sample.

11. We identified likely caucusgoers from a series of questions. Respondents were asked to self-identify their likelihood of caucusing on a four-point scale. Those who said they were "very likely" or "somewhat likely" to caucus were also asked for the party they planned to caucus for. Those who could not identify a party were removed from the sample of likely caucusgoers. We also asked if respondents had caucused in previous years.

12. Estimates from media entrance polls suggest that about 20% of Democratic caucusgoers were independents.

13. Due to space constraints, only the March and October precaucus survey results are presented in table 6.2, along with the January postcaucus. August results available from the authors.

14. In the surveys, the question was posed as "Which one policy is the most important for your vote for president in 2008?" Respondents were given the following choices: terrorism, Iraq war, economy, gay marriage, abortion, immigration, health care, energy policy, environment, education, agriculture policy, or other. Respondents who chose abortion, gay marriage, or immigration as the most important issue were given an additional question: "How important is [abortion] to your vote for president in 2008? Is it very important, somewhat important, or not that important?"

15. We recognize that there are generally some systematic biases in telephone surveys such as ours. The most obvious is that it is much more diffiuclt to reach young people. Comparing our results to the U.S. Census Bureau's 2006 Current Population Survey of Iowa points this out. Our estimates for the composition

of the electorate in terms of education, income, and age track fairly well with the demographic profile of Iowa registered voters in the CPS; our survey data slightly overrepresent the better educated (postgraduate degree) and underrepresents the least educated (high school graduates or less) but are otherwise quite close. However, we see significant differences based on age. Among Iowa registered voters, the CPS estimates that 16% are between 18 and 29 years of age, while in our October sample of registered voters only 5.3% fall within this range. Of Iowa's registered voter population, only 29% are over 60 years of age, yet of the October survey respondents 44% were in this age cohort. Even so, the difficulty of reaching young people with telephone surveys is not biased more in the registered voters samples than in the likely caucusgoer samples. Thus, there is no systematic bias in comparing the two samples based on age. Additionally, comparison to the U.S. Census Bureau's demographic profile of Iowans gives us more confidence that our estimates of education, income, and gender are accurate. This provides additional confidence that the small differences we find between Iowa registered voters and caucus attenders based on income, age, and gender are in fact accurate.

16. For the Republicans, the official results were Huckabee, 35%; Romney, 25%; and McCain and former Tennessee senator Fred Thompson, both at 13%, followed by Texas representative Ron Paul at 10% and former New York City mayor Rudy Giuliani at 4%. The Democrats reported that Obama won about 38% of the state delegates, Edwards 30%, and Clinton 29%, followed by New Mexico governor Bill Richardson at 2%. No other candidate got more than 1% of the delegates.

Chapter Seven

An earlier version of this chapter was published as Todd Donovan and Rob Hunsaker, "Beyond Expectations: Effects of Early Elections in U.S. Presidential Nominating Contests," *PS: Political Science and Politics* 42, no. 1 (January 2009): 45–51.

1. Bartels (1985) demonstrates that candidate preferences are strongly projected onto expectations, so the relationship is reciprocal, and that the effects of expectations depend on whether a contest is close.

2. These phrases are taken from *New York Times* headlines. Dean's 26% "Overwhelming Defeat" was a second-place showing in New Hampshire, 12% behind Kerry in 2004. Bill Clinton's 25% "comfortable second" was 8% behind Massachusetts senator Paul Tsongas in 1992.

3. Morton and Williams (2001) employ laboratory experiments to test their hypotheses about simultaneous versus sequential elections. Many previous fore-

casting models estimate aggregate primary vote share or nomination outcome as a simultaneous election, either with (Adkins and Dowdle 2001) or without (Mayer 1996, 2003) accounting New Hampshire as part of an additive model, and most omit Iowa.

4. Substantive results are unaffected when sitting presidents are omitted.

5. Double counting of stories was avoided by coding post-Iowa stories with Iowa bylines and/or headlines as Iowa content, and pre–New Hampshire stories with New Hampshire bylines and/or headlines as New Hampshire content.

6. The value for Bill Clinton is inflated by limited initial attention to Iowa that largely focused on Iowa senator Tom Harkin. Harkin had the largest decline in share of press attention (–47 points), followed by President Gerald Ford (1976, –36 points), Edwards (2008, –28 points), Forbes (1996, –27 points), and former New Jersey senator Bill Bradley (2000, –17 points).

7. There is clearly a causal morass in arguing that initial press attention simply reflects expectations that are unique from pure reporting of results. The two are highly correlated. However, change in media attention from pre-Iowa to post-Iowa coverage is not well correlated with Iowa vote ($r = -.22$), and change in attention is inversely correlated with initial Iowa attention (–.41).

8. Ford in 1976; Carter in 1980.

9. This is limited to Tom Harkin of Iowa, who ran in 1992.

10. The correlation between proportion of mentions and poll strength is .68; mentions and money, .43; money and poll strength, .50. Days spent in Iowa is uncorrelated with money and poll standing.

11. Values here converted to year 2000 dollars.

12. Recall that these variables are not well correlated with each other.

13. http://www.usatoday.com/news/polls/tables/live/2004-01-25-poll-results.htm (accessed September 29, 2009).

14. A related phenomenon occurred in the 2008 Nevada precinct caucuses, where Clinton beat Obama 50% to 45% in a tally of the 10,740 delegates elected by 117,600 voters to 17 county conventions. The geographic distribution of support across counties led the state party to acknowledge that Obama would receive more national convention delegates than Clinton. As in Iowa, actual preferences of the 117,000 voters were not reported by the party. Most outlets reported the state as a Clinton victory.

Chapter Eight

1. Respondents were asked, "Now I'll read a name and ask you to rate the candidate on another scale from 0 to 100. Ratings between 51 and 100 mean you feel favorable toward that person, with 100 being most favorable. Ratings be-

tween 0 and 49 degrees mean you feel unfavorable. Use 50 if you feel neither. You may use any number from 0 to 100."

2. Simulations were run using the Clarify software.

Chapter Nine

1. In Iowa, at least, independents can participate, but only if they are willing to officially register with a party, at which point they are no longer independents (on the books, at least). While it is possible to change one's registration back to "no party" as soon as the day after the caucus, this requires the extra step of re-registering to vote. Thus, most independents who caucus find themselves party members since they do not bother to change back.

2. http://www.civicyouth.org/PopUps/PR_08_Iowa_turnout_Jan4.pdf (accessed April 14, 2010).

3. The only difference among the registered voter samples was that for the last 200 Iowa respondents, those who said they "absolutely would not caucus" were screened out. Those who said they were "very likely" to caucus, "somewhat likely" to caucus, or "not very likely" to caucus were retained. When the analysis is reestimated on only the 500+ Iowa registered voters who did not receive this screen, the results remain unchanged.

4. One small caveat, however. The October survey took place about nine weeks before the Iowa caucuses, while the other surveys mostly occurred immediately before the contests they covered. This means that the participation measures for Iowa almost certainly *underestimate* the final levels of participation for those who actually attended the caucus. At the same time, the Iowa caucus campaign had been under way for a year or more by the time of our survey, longer than the campaigns in any other state in our surveys.

5. When including the Pennsylvania primary sample in the pooled analyses, both the online and offline participation variables range from 0 to 2 activities. This is because some questions were not asked in the Pennsylvania survey. When using all three samples, the common online activities include visiting a candidate's Web site or contributing money online. The common offline activities include attending a campaign event or meeting a candidate.

6. "How much thought have you given to the coming 2008 presidential election?" coded 1 for "none," 2 for "a little," 3 for "some," and 4 for "quite a lot."

7. "How closely have you followed news about the candidates for president?" with responses ranging from "not at all closely" (coded 1), "not too closely" (coded 2), "fairly closely" (coded 3), and "very closely" (coded 4).

8. Poisson and negative binomial regressions were estimated for the count dependent variables (online and offline participation) without significant changes

in the substantive effects. To aid in comparison of the factors predicting participation and civic engagement, ordered logistic regression was used for all model
estimations.

9. Substituting the *following campaign news* variable as an approximation of
political interest produced results similar to those found by using *thought given
to election*.

10. Responses to how often the respondent uses the Internet include "never,"
"occasionally," "weekly," "daily," and "hourly," which are respectively coded
from 1 to 5.

11. *Political efficacy* is operationalized as a binary variable that is coded 1 for
those who agreed with the statement "People like me can influence government."

12. Given that the coefficient is not statistically significant ($p = .11$) by conventional threshold, the model technically finds that in Iowa, it is Internet use, political interest, education, and political efficacy that explain online participation—
and that, controlling for those factors, we cannot say with certainty that age
plays any role. However, the young are more likely to be frequent Internet users
(Mossberger, Tolbert, and McNeal 2008).

13. This variable was not used in the Iowa caucus models, because the low
number of minority participants interviewed would not have produced reliable
results.

14. Two variables were omitted (Internet use and political efficacy) because
the Pennsylvania primary survey did not ask the corresponding questions. Also,
the binary variables for strong Democrats and Republicans were replaced by a
single binary variable indicating a *strong partisan*, since only registered Democrats were surveyed for the Pennsylvania primary.

Chapter Ten

An earlier version of this chapter was published as Caroline J. Tolbert, David P.
Redlawsk, and Daniel C. Bowen, "Reforming Presidential Nominations: Rotating State Primaries or a National Primary?" *PS: Political Science and Politics*
42, no. 1 (2009): 71–79.

1. The Republicans did not sanction any state nominating events before this
date, though several, including Iowa and New Hampshire, were held. States that
run GOP caucuses and primaries before the official date were to be sanctioned
by losing half their delegates, which is in fact what happened to Michigan and
Florida. The others—including Iowa and New Hampshire—avoid sanction by officially separating the election of delegates from the caucus or primary voting, so
that delegates are technically not selected until after the window opens.

2. "Democrats Set Primary Calendar and Penalties," *New York Times*, August 20, 2006.

3. Near the end of primary season, the Democrats reversed their earlier decision and agreed to seat delegations from both Michigan and Florida, but gave each state only half its votes.

4. The Democrats generally do not report voter turnout in their caucuses, and what numbers they do produce cannot be independently verified. This occurs because the results the Democrats report from caucuses are not votes, but shares of delegates. The Republicans, on the other hand, do report actual votes in caucus, and therefore turnout numbers as well; but as party-run events, again there is no independent verification of the results.

5. The Cooperative Campaign Analysis Panel (CCAP) is a collaborative effort that brought together over 60 political scientists from 25 institutions to produce a six-wave panel study conducted on the Internet. This sample was constructed using a technique called sample matching. The researchers created a list of all U.S. consumers to generate a set of demographic characteristics that should be mirrored in the survey sample. Then, using a matching algorithm, the researchers selected respondents who most closely resembled the consumer data from a pool of opt-in participants. The sample was stratified to ensure large samples within states. More information regarding sample matching is available at http://web.mit.edu/polisci/portl/cces/material/sample_matching.pdf. The models are estimated using Polimetrix survey weights. Using this same technique, the 2006 Cooperative Congressional Election Survey (CCES) produced more precise estimates than more conventional probability designs such as random-digit-dialed (RDD) phone surveys (Vavreck and Rivers 2008).

6. This question was worded slightly differently in the Iowa postcaucus survey, but is substantively the same. Iowa respondents were asked: "Some people have proposed a plan that would rotate the states going first in the presidential nomination process. Would you strongly favor, favor, oppose or strongly oppose such a plan?"

7. The threshold between small- and large-population states is a population of 6 million, approximately the mean population of the forty states included in the survey; 55% of survey respondents reside in states thus categorized as small.

8. Logistic regression is an appropriate method to use when dealing with models that have dichotomous dependent variables, and is utilized in the models presented here.

9. Population size is logged for theoretical and practical reasons. Theoretically, population size will likely have a diminishing effect on support for reform, with the effect of a unit change in population on the probability of supporting reform decreasing as size gets larger. This is borne out in the data: descriptive analysis shows the strongest relationship between aggregate levels of support for reform and state population when logged population is used.

10. In the Hawkeye Polls, education is measured with a 7-point ordinal variable from the question, "What is the last grade or class that you completed in

school?" The variable ranges from 1 ("None, or grade 1–8") to 7 ("Post-graduate training or professional schooling after college [e.g., toward a master's degree or Ph.D.; law or medical school]"). The variable income comes from answers to the question, "Last year, that is, in 2006, what was your total family income from all sources, before taxes? Just stop me when I get to the right category." Respondents were given nine categories, ranging from "less than $10,000" to "$150,000 or more." Age of the respondent is measured in years. For these three variables only, all missing cases were coded at the variable's mean value to save cases from pairise deletion. Gender is measured with a dummy variable, where males are coded 1 and females 0. Race is measured by a binary variable coded 1 if the respondent is African American and 0 otherwise. African Americans are the only racial minority with enough respondents in the survey to be included. Similar variable codes were used for the CCAP survey, except that all missing cases were coded as missing.

11. In both the CCAP and the Hawkeye Poll, respondents were asked, "In politics today, do you consider yourself a Republican, Democrat, or Independent?" Two variables were created from this question. The first is a dichotomous variable for Republicans, where all those who reported being Republican coded 1 and all other respondents coded 0. A similar variable was created for Democrats.

12. Respondents were asked if they strongly agree, agree, disagree, or strongly disagree with the statement "People like me can influence government." A four-point ordinal variable was created from this question, with those strongly agreeing with the statement coded 4 and those strongly disagreeing with the statement coded 1.

13. Such autocorrelation, if not accounted for, tends to artificially deflate the standard errors of the aggregate variables and to upwardly bias the standard errors of individual-level variables (Primo, Jacobsmeier, and Milyo 2007). Preliminary versions of the models presented here were run using multilevel models with a logit link function. The multilevel models produced results nearly identical to those achieved by clustering standard errors.

14. Using a the three-point scale for partisanship, 77% of independents favor a national primary, compared with 73% of Democrats and 72% of Republicans. Roughly equal percentages of Republicans, Democrats, and independents favor rotating state primaries (71%–72%).

Chapter Eleven

1. In conversation with one of the authors, John Edwards's national campaign manager, David Bonior, gave the Edwards campaign credit for much of the even-

tual Democratic platform, arguing that many of the key planks were ones Edwards had originally championed.

2. Data from the Wisconsin Advertising Project show that McCain and the Republican National Committee spent $429,000 on television advertisements in Iowa between October 21 and October 28, 2008, while $298,000 was spent on TV ads on behalf of Obama.

References

Abramowitz, Alan I. 1989. "Viability, Electability, and Candidate Choice in a Presidential Primary Election: A Test of Competing Models." *Journal of Politics* 51 (4): 977–92.

Abramowitz, Alan I., John McGlennon, and Ronald B. Rapoport. 1981. "A Note on Strategic Voting in a Primary Election." *Journal of Politics* 43 (3): 899–904.

Abramowitz, Alan I., John McGlennon, Ronald B. Rapoport, and Walter J. Stone. 2001. "Activists in the United States Presidential Nomination Process, 1980–1996." Inter-university Consortium for Political and Social Research 6143, Second ICPS Version.

Abramson, Paul R., John H. Aldrich, Phil Paolino, and David Rohde. 1992. "'Sophisticated' Voting in the 1988 Presidential Primaries." *American Political Science Review* 86 (1): 55–69.

Adkins, Randall E., and Andrew J. Dowdle. 2001. "How Important Are Iowa and New Hampshire to Winning Post-Reform Presidential Nominations?" *Political Research Quarterly* 54 (2): 431–44.

Aldrich, John H. 1980. "A Dynamic Model of Presidential Nomination Campaigns." American Political Science Review 74 (3): 651–69.

———. 2009. "The Invisible Primary and Its Effects on Democratic Choice." *PS: Political Science and Politics* 42 (1): 33–38.

Altschuler, Bruce E. 2008. "Selecting Presidential Nominees by National Primary: An Idea Whose Time Has Come?" *The Forum* 5 (4): Article 5. Online at http://www.bepress.com/forum/vol5/iss4/art5 (accessed April 19, 2010).

Alvarez, R. Michael, and Jonathan Nagler. 2000. "A New Approach for Modeling Strategic Voting in Multiparty Elections." *British Journal of Political Science* 30 (1): 57–75.

Anderson, Christopher J., Andre Blais, Shaun Bowler, Todd Donovan, and Ola Listhaug. 2005. *Loser's Consent: Elections and Democratic Legitimacy.* Oxford: Oxford University Press.

Anderson, Christopher J., and Christine A. Guillory. 1997. "Political Institutions and Satisfaction with Democracy: A Cross-National Analysis of Consensus and Majoritarian Systems." *American Political Science Review* 91 (1): 66–81.

Anderson, Christopher J., and Andrew J. LoTempio. 2002. "Winning, Losing and Political Trust in America." *British Journal of Political Science* 32 (2): 335–51.

Anderson, Christopher J., and Yuliya V. Tverdova. 2001. "Winners, Losers, and Attitudes toward Government in Contemporary Democracies." *International Political Science Review* 22 (4): 321–38.

Andrews, Josephine, and Robert Jackman. 2005. "Strategic Fools: Electoral Rule Choice under Extreme Uncertainty." *Electoral Studies* 24 (1): 65–84.

Associated Press. 2003. "Young Political Staff Flock to Iowa for Grass-Roots Experience." December 26, 2003. Online at http://www.usatoday.com/news/politicselections/2003-12-26-iowa-staff_x.htm (accessed April 19, 2010).

Atkeson, Lonna, and Cherie Maestas. 2009. "Meaningful Participation and the Evolution of the Reformed Presidential Nominating System." *PS: Political Science and Politics* 42 (1): 59–64.

Baldwin, Tom. 2008. "Swept Away by a Tide of Young Idealists, Hillary Clinton Knows She Must Bounce Back." *Times* (London), January 5.

Balz, Dan. 2008. "Obama Team Seeks Changes in Primaries." *Washington Post,* August 21.

Banducci, Susan A., Todd Donovan, and Jeffrey A. Karp. 1999. "Proportional Representation and Attitudes about Politics: Results from New Zealand." *Electoral Studies* 18 (4): 533–55.

Banducci, Susan A. and Jeffrey A. Karp. 1999. "Perceptions of Fairness and Support for Proportional Representation." *Political Behavior* 21 (3): 217–38.

———. 2003. "How Elections Change the Way Citizens View the Political System: Campaigns, Media Effects and Electoral Outcomes in Comparative Perspective." *British Journal of Political Science* 33 (1): 175–99.

Barber, Benjamin R. 1984. *Strong Democracy: Participatory Politics for a New Age.* Berkeley and Los Angeles: University of California Press.

Bartels, Larry M. 1985. "Expectations and Preferences in Presidential Nominating Campaigns." *American Political Science Review* 79:804–15.

———. 1987. "Candidate Choice and the Dynamics of the Presidential Nominating Process." *American Journal of Political Science* 31 (1): 1–30.

———. 1988. *Presidential Primaries and the Dynamics of Public Choice.* Princeton, NJ: Princeton University Press.

———. 1989. "After Iowa: Momentum in Presidential Primaries." In *The Iowa Caucuses and the Presidential Nominating Process,* edited by Peverill Squire, 121–48. Boulder, CO: Westview Press.

——. 2008. *Unequal Democracy: The Political Economy of the New Gilded Age.* Princeton, NJ: Princeton University Press.

Battaglini, Marco, Rebecca Morton, and Thomas Palfrey. 2007. "Efficiency, Equity, and Timing of Voting Mechanisms." *American Political Science Review* 101 (3): 404–29.

Best, Samuel J., and Brian S. Krueger. 2005. "Analyzing the Representativeness of Internet Political Participation." *Political Behavior* 27 (2): 183–216.

Bimber, Bruce. 2001. "Information and Political Engagement in America: The Search for Effects of Information Technology at the Individual Level." *Political Research Quarterly* 54 (1): 53–67.

——. 2003. *Information and American Democracy: Technology in the Evolution of Political Power.* Cambridge: Cambridge University Press.

Blais, André, and Agnieszka Dobrzynska. 1998. "Turnout in Electoral Democracies." *European Journal of Political Research* 33 (2): 239–61.

Blais, André, and Richard Nadeau. 1996. "Measuring Strategic Voting: a Two-Step Procedure." *Electoral Studies* 15:39–52.

Blais, André, Richard Nadeau, Elisabeth Gidengil, and Neil Nevitte. 2001. "Measuring Strategic Voting in Multiparty Plurality Elections." *Electoral Studies* 20 (3): 343–52.

Blumenthal, Sidney. 1982. *The Permanent Campaign.* New York: Simon and Schuster.

Boots, Ralph S. 1920. *The Presidential Primary: A Comprehensive Examination of the Presidential Primary at Work with Proposals of Reform.* Concord, NH: National Municipal League.

Bowler, Shaun, David Brockington, and Todd Donovan. 2001. "Election Systems and Voter Turnout: Experiments in the United States." *Journal of Politics* 63 (3): 902–15.

Bowler, Shaun, and Todd Donovan. 2007. "Reasoning about Institutional Change: Winners, Losers, and Support for Electoral Reforms." *British Journal of Political Science* 37:455–76.

Bowler, Shaun, Todd Donovan, and David Brockington. 2003. *Electoral Reform and Minority Representation: Local Experiments with Alternative Elections.* Columbus: Ohio State University Press.

Bowler, Shaun, Todd Donovan, and Jeffrey A. Karp. 2002. "When Might Institutions Change? Elite Support for Direct Democracy in Three Nations." *Political Research Quarterly* 55 (4): 731–54.

——. 2006. "Why Politicians Like Electoral Institutions: Self-Interest, Values, or Ideology?" *Journal of Politics* 68 (2): 434–46.

Bowler, Shaun, and David J. Lanoue. 1992. "Strategic and Protest Voting for Third Parties: The Case of the Canadian NDP." *Political Research Quarterly* 45:485–99.

Brady, Henry E. 1988. "Strategy on the Campaign Trail in Iowa." *PS: Political Science and Politics* 21 (2): 269–73.

———. 1989. "Is Iowa News?" In *The Iowa Caucuses and the Presidential Nominating Process*, ed. Peverill Squire, 89–119. Boulder, CO: Westview Press.

Brady, Henry E., and Richard Johnston. 1987. "What's the Primary Message: Horse Race or Issue Journalism?" In *Media and Momentum: The New Hampshire Primary and Nomination Politics*, ed. Gary R. Orren and Nelson W. Polsby, 60–103. Chatham, NJ: Chatham House.

Burnham, Walter Dean. 1970. *Critical Elections and the Mainsprings of American Politics*. New York: W. W. Norton.

Burns, Nancy, Kay Lehman Schlozman, and Sidney Verba. 2001. *The Private Roots of Public Action: Gender, Equality, and Political Participation*. Cambridge, MA: Harvard University Press.

Busch, Andrew E., and William G. Mayer. 2004. "The Front-Loading Problem." In *The Making of the Presidential Candidates 2004*, ed. William G. Mayer, 1–44. Lanham, MD: Rowman & Littlefield Publishers.

Cain, Bruce E. 1978. "Strategic Voting in Britain." *American Journal of Political Science* 22 (3): 639–55.

Cain, Bruce, Todd Donovan, and Caroline J. Tolbert, eds. 2008. *Democracy in the States: Experiments in Election Reform*. Washington, DC: Brookings Institution Press.

Campbell, Angus, Phillip E. Converse, Warren E. Miller, and Donald E. Stokes. 1960. *The American Voter*. New York: John Wiley & Sons.

Cohen, Marty, David Karol, Hans Noel, and John Zaller. 2008. *The Party Decides: Presidential Nominations Before and After Reform*. Chicago: University of Chicago Press.

Cook, Rhodes. 2003. *The Presidential Nominating Process: A Place for Us?* Lanham, MD: Rowman & Littlefield Publishers.

———. 2007. *Race for the Presidency 2008: Winning the 2008 Nomination*. Washington, DC: CQ Press.

Copeland, Gary. 1983. "Activating Voters in Congressional Elections." *Political Behavior* 5:391–401.

Cox, Gary. 1997. *Making Votes Count: Strategic Coordination in the World's Electoral Systems*. Cambridge: Cambridge University Press.

Cox, Gary W., and Michael C. Munger. 1989. "Closeness, Expenditures and Turnout in the 1982 U.S. House Elections." *American Political Science Review* 83 (1): 217–31.

CQ Press. 2005. *Guide to U.S. Elections*. Washington, DC: CQ Press.

Dahl, Robert. 1961. *Who Governs?* New Haven, CT: Yale University Press.

Dalton, Russell. 2004. *Democratic Challenges, Democratic Choices: The Erosion of Political Support*. Oxford: Oxford University Press.

Deeth, John. 2008. "GOP Calendar Plan Passes Quietly." *Iowa Independent*.

Online at http://iowaindependent.com/4967/gop-calendar-plan-quietly-passes (accessed September 3, 2008).

di Gennaro, Corinna, and William Dutton. 2006. "The Internet and the Public: Online and Offline Political Participation in the United Kingdom." *Parliamentary Affairs* 59 (2): 299–313.

Donovan, Todd. 2007. "The Goal for Reform—make Elections Worth Stealing." *PS: Political Science and Politics* 40 (4): 681–86.

Donovan, Todd, and Shaun Bowler. 2004. *Reforming the Republic: Democratic Institutions for the New America*. Englewood Cliffs, NJ: Prentice Hall.

Donovan, Todd, and Rob Hunsaker. 2009. "Beyond Expectations: Effects of Early Elections in US Presidential Nomination Contests." *PS: Political Science and Politics* 42 (1): 45–52.

Donovan, Todd, Caroline J. Tolbert, and Daniel Smith. 2008. "Priming Presidential Votes by Direct Democracy." *Journal of Politics* 70 (4): 1217–31.

———. 2009. "Political Engagement, Mobilization and Direct Democracy." *Public Opinion Quarterly* 73 (1): 98–118.

Dowdle, Andrew J., Randall E. Adkins, and Wayne P. Steger. 2009. "The Viability Primary: Modeling Candidate Support before the Primaries." *Political Research Quarterly* 62 (1): 77–91.

Eby, Charlotte. 2007. "Iowa 1, Michigan 0." *Iowa Insider*. Online at http://www.wcfcourier.com/app/blogs/eby/?p=156 (accessed April 18, 2010).

Fiorina, Morris P., Samuel J. Abrams, and Jeremy C. Pope. 2004. *Culture War? The Myth of a Polarized America*. New York: Pearson Longman.

Fowler, Mayhill. 2008. "Clinton Betrays the Elder Vote; Edwards and Obama Grassroots Broker a Deal. What an Evening in Iowa!" *Huffington Post*, January 4. Online at http://www.huffingtonpost.com/mayhill-fowler/clinton-betrays-the-elder_b_79881.html (accessed March 15, 2010).

Franklin, Mark N. 2004. *Voter Turnout and the Dynamics of Electoral Competition in Established Democracies since 1945*. Cambridge: Harvard University Press.

Fund, John. 2007. "What's the Matter with Iowa? The Caucuses Are Anything but a Norman Rockwell Exercise in Small-Town Democracy." *Wall Street Journal*, December 31. Online at http://www.opinionjournal.com/diary/?id=110011061 (accessed April 18, 2010).

Gavrilovic, Maria. 2008. "Obama Makes Up for Skipped Iowa Stop." CBD News Online. http://www.cbsnews.com/8301-502443_162-4561374-502443.html (accessed April 7, 2010).

Geer, John G. 1988. "Assessing the Representativeness of Electorates in Presidential Primaries." *American Journal of Political Science* 32 (4): 929–45.

Gerber, Alan S., Donald P. Green, and Christopher W. Larimer. 2008. "Social Pressure and Voter Turnout: Evidence from a Large-Scale Field Experiment." *American Political Science Review* 102 (1): 33–48.

Gibson, Rachel K., Wainer Lusoli, and Stephen Ward. 2005. "Online Participation in the UK: Testing a 'Contextualised' Model of Internet Effects." *British Journal of Politics and International Relations* 7 (4): 561–83.

Gimpel, John, Karen M. Kaufmann, and Shanna Pearson-Merkowitz. 2007. "The Battleground vs. the Blackout States: Behavioral Implications of Modern Presidential Campaigns." *Journal of Politics* 69 (3): 786.

Greenfield, Jeff. 2007. "The Brigadoon Complex: Where the Iowa Caucuses Went Wrong." Slate.com, December 31. Online at http://www.slate.com/id/2181096/ (accessed April 18, 2010).

Griffin, John, and Brian Newman. 2005. "Are Voters Better Represented?" *Journal of Politics* 67 (4): 1206–27.

Grose, Christian R., and Carrie A. Russell. 2008. "Avoiding the Vote: A Theory and Field Experiment of the Social Costs of Public Political Participation." SSRN. Online at http://ssrn.com/abstract=1310868 (accessed April 10, 2010).

Hagen, Michael G., and William G. Mayer. 2000. "The Modern Politics of Presidential Selection: How Changing the Rules Really Did Change the Game." In *In Pursuit of the White House 2000: How We Choose Our Presidential Nominees*, ed. William G. Mayer, 1–56. Chatham, NJ: Chatham House Publishers.

Hansen, Susan B. 1997. "Talking about Politics: Gender and Contextual Effects on Political Proselytizing." *Journal of Politics* 59 (1): 73–103.

Haynes, Audrey, and Brian Pitts. 2009. "Making an Impression in the 21st Century: New Media in 2008 Presidential Nomination Campaigns." *PS: Political Science and Politics* 42 (1): 53–58.

Hero, Rodney E. 1998. *Faces of Inequality: Social Diversity in American Politics*. New York: Oxford University Press.

Hill, David, and Seth C. McKee. 2005. "The Electoral College, Mobilization, and Turnout in the 2000 Presidential Election." *American Politics Research* 33 (5): 700–725.

Hitchens, Christopher. 2007. "The Iowa Scam: The Undemocratic Caucuses Are a Terrible Way to Choose a Presidential Candidate." Slate.com, December 31. Online at http://www.slate.com/id/2181008/ (accessed April 2, 2010).

Hofstadter, Richard 1955. *The Age of Reform: From Bryant to F. D. R.* New York: Vintage Books, Random House.

Holbrook, Thomas M., and Scott D. McClurg. 2005. "The Mobilization of Core Supporters: Campaigns, Turnout, and Electoral Composition in United States Presidential Elections." *American Journal of Political Science* 49 (4): 689–703.

Horack, Frank E. 1910. "Primary Elections in Iowa." *Proceedings of the American Political Science Association* 7:175–86.

———. 1923. "The Workings of the Direct Primary in Iowa, 1908–1922." *Annals of the American Academy of Political and Social Science* 106 (1): 148–57.

Huckfeldt, Robert, and John Sprague. 1995. *Citizens, Politics and Social Communication*. New York: Cambridge University Press.

Hull, Christopher C. 2007. *Grassroots Rules: How the Iowa Caucus Helps Elect American Presidents*. Stanford, CA: Stanford University Press.

Jackson, Robert A. 1996. "A Reassessment of Voter Mobilization." *Political Research Quarterly* 49:331–49.

———. 1997. "The Mobilization of U.S. State Electorates in the 1988 and 1990 Elections." *Journal of Politics* 59 (2): 520–37.

———. 2002. "Gubernatorial and Senatorial Campaign Mobilization of Voters." *Political Research Quarterly* 55 (4): 825–44.

Johnston, Richard. 1992. *Letting the People Decide: Dynamics of a Canadian Election*. Stanford, CA: Stanford University Press.

Kahn, Kim Fridkin, and Patrick J. Kenney. 1999. "Do Negative Campaigns Mobilize or Suppress Turnout? Clarifying the Relationship between Negativity and Participation." *American Political Science Review* 93 (4): 877–89.

Kamarck, Elaine C. 2009. *Primary Politics: How Presidential Candidates Have Shaped the Modern Nominating System*. Washington, DC: Brookings Institution Press.

Karp, Jeffrey A. 2007. "Reforming the Electoral College and Support for Proportional Outcomes." *Representation* 43 (4): 239–50.

Karp, Jeffrey, Jack Vowles, Susan Banducci, and Todd Donovan. 2002. "Strategic Voting, Party Activity, and Candidate Effects: Testing Explanations for Split Voting in New Zealand's New Mixed System." *Electoral Studies* 21:1–22.

Kathlene, Lyn. 1994. "Power and Influence in State Legislatures: The Interaction of Gender and Position in Committee Hearing Debates." *American Political Science Review* 88 (3): 560–76.

Kenney, Patrick J., and Tom W. Rice. 1994. "The Psychology of Political Momentum." *Political Research Quarterly* 47 (4): 923–38.

Kenski, Kate, and Natalie Jomini Stroud. 2006. "Connections between Internet Use and Political Efficacy, Knowledge, and Participation." *Journal of Broadcasting and Electronic Media* 50 (2): 173–92.

Kiely, Kathy. 2008a. "Politicians Love, Loathe Iowa Caucus System." *USA Today*, January 1.

———. 2008b. "Edwards Squeezes Out Second-Place Finish; Record Democratic Turnout Favors Obama, Hands Clinton Disappointing Third." *USA Today*, January 4.

Kipling, Rudyard. 1899. "The White Man's Burden." *McClure's Magazine* (February): 12.

Knight, Brian, and Nathan Schiff. 2007. "Momentum and Social Learning in Presidential Primaries." NBER Working Paper no. W13637. Cambridge, MA: National Bureau of Economic Research.

Krueger, Brian S. 2002. "Assessing the Potential of Internet Political Participation in the United States: A Resource Approach." *American Politics Research* 30 (5): 476–98.

———. 2006. "A Comparison of Conventional and Internet Political Mobilization." *American Politics Research* 34 (6): 759–76.

Kurtz, Howard. 2007. "The Press's Post-Iowa Tailwinds: As Nature Intended It?" *Washington Post*, November 26.

Lacey, Robert J. 2005. "The Electoral Allure of Direct Democracy: The Effect of Initiative Salience on Voting, 1990–96." *State Politics and Policy Quarterly* 5 (2): 168–81.

Lane, Joseph. 2008. "The Iowa Caucus: Chicanery or Democracy?" *Encyclopaedia Britannica* Blog, January 7. Online at http://www.britannica.com/blogs/2008/01/the-iowa-caucus-chicanery-or-democracy/ (accessed January 8, 2008).

Lau, Richard R., and David P. Redlawsk. 2001. "Advantages and Disadvantages of Cognitive Heuristics." *American Journal of Political Science* 45, no. 4 (October): 951–71.

———. 2006. *How Voters Decide: Information Processing during Election Campaigns.* New York: Cambridge University Press.

Lewis-Beck, Michael S. 1988. "Economics and the American Voter: Past, Present, Future." *Political Behavior* 10 (1): 5–21.

Lewis-Beck, Michael S., Helmut Norpoth, William G. Jacoby, and Herbert F. Weisberg. 2008. *The American Voter Revisited.* Ann Arbor: University of Michigan Press.

Lewis-Beck, Michael S., and Martin Paldam. 2000. "Economic Voting: An Introduction." *Electoral Studies* 19:113–21.

Lewis-Beck, Michael, and Peverill Squire. 2009. "Iowa: The Most Representative State?" *PS: Political Science and Politics* 42 (1): 39–44.

Lijphart, Arend. 1997. "Unequal Participation: Democracy's Unresolved Dilemma." *American Political Science Review* 91 (1): 1–14.

Lupia, Arthur. 1994. "Shortcuts versus Encyclopedias." *American Political Science Review* 88:63–76.

Madonna, Terry. 2004. "A Crazy System." In *Politically Uncorrected.* Online at http://www.fandm.edu/x4092 (accessed July 25, 2009).

Mann, Thomas E. 2009. "Is This Any Way to Pick a President?" In *Reforming the Presidential Nominating Process*, ed. Stephen S. Smith and Melanie J. Springer, 115–72. Washington, DC: Brookings Institution Press.

Mansbridge, Jane. 1986. *Why We Lost the ERA.* Chicago: University of Chicago Press.

Mayer, William G. 1987. "The New Hampshire Primary: A Historical Overview." In *Media and Momentum: The New Hampshire Primary and Nomination Politics*, ed. Gary R. Orren and Nelson W. Polsby, 9–41. Chatham, NJ: Chatham House Publishers.

———. 1996. "Forecasting Presidential Nominations." In *In Pursuit of the White House 2000: How We Choose Our Presidential Nominees*, ed. William G. Mayer, 44–71. Chatham, NJ: Chatham House.

———, ed. 2000. *In Pursuit of the White House 2000: How We Choose Our Presidential Nominees*. Chatham, NJ: Chatham House Publishers.

———. 2003. "Forecasting Presidential Nominations, or My Model Worked Just Fine, Thank You." *PS: Political Science and Politics* 36 (2): 153–57.

———. 2004. *The Making of the Presidential Candidates 2004*. Lanham, MD: Rowman & Littlefield Publishers.

———. 2009. "An Incremental Approach to Presidential Nomination Reform." *PS: Political Science and Politics* 42 (1): 65–69.

Mayer, William G., and Andrew E. Busch. 2004. *The Front-Loading Problem in Presidential Nominations*. Washington, DC: Brookings Institution Press.

McAllister, Ian, and Donley T. Studlar. 1991. "Bandwagon, Underdog, or Projection? Opinion Polls and Electoral Choice in Britain, 1979–1987." *Journal of Politics* 53 (3): 720–41.

McDermott, Monika L. 1997. "Voting Cues in Low-Information Elections: Candidate Gender as a Social Information Variable in Contemporary United States Elections." *American Journal of Political Science* 41 (1): 270–83.

———. 1998. "Race and Gender Cues in Low-Information Elections." *Political Research Quarterly* 51:895–918.

McDonald, Michael P. 2008a. United States Election Project: 2004 Presidential Primary Turnout Rates. Online at http://elections.gmu.edu/Voter_Turnout_2004_Primaries.htm (accessed February 3, 2008).

———. 2008b. United States Election Project: 2008 Presidential Primary Turnout Rates. Online at http://elections.gmu.edu/Voter_Turnout_2008_Primaries.htm (accessed February 3, 2008).

McDonald, Michael P., and Samuel Popkin. 2001. "The Myth of the Vanishing Voter." *American Political Science Review* 95 (4): 963–74.

McDonald, Michael P., and John Samples, eds. 2006. *The Marketplace of Democracy: Electoral Competition and American Politics*. Washington, DC: Brookings Institution Press.

McSweeney, Dean. 2007. "The Front-Runner Fails." *Party Politics* 13 (1): 109–26.

Moran, Jack, and Mark Fenster. 1982. "Voter Turnout in Presidential Primaries: A Diachronic Analysis." *American Politics Research* 10:453–76.

Morton, Rebecca B., and K. C. Williams. 2001. *Learning by Voting: Sequential Choices in Presidential Primaries and Other Elections*. Ann Arbor: University of Michigan Press.

Mossberger, Karen, and Caroline J. Tolbert. 2010. "Digital Democracy." In *Oxford Encyclopedia of American Elections and Political Behavior*, ed. Jan Leighley. New York: Oxford University Press.

Mossberger, Karen, Caroline J. Tolbert, and Ramona S. McNeal. 2008. *Digital Citizenship: the Internet, Society, and Participation.* Cambridge, MA: MIT Press.

Mossberger, Karen, Caroline J. Tolbert, and Mary Stansbury. 2003. *Virtual Inequality: Beyond the Digital Divide.* Washington, DC: Georgetown University Press.

Muhlberger, Peter. 2003. "Political Values, Political Attitudes, and Attitude Polarization in Internet Political Discussion: Political Transformation or Politics as Usual?" *Communications* 28 (2): 107–34.

Mutz, Diana. 1995. "Effects of Horse-Race Coverage on Campaign Coffers: Strategic Contributing in Presidential Primaries." *Journal of Politics* 57 (4): 1015–42.

——. 1997. "Mechanisms of Momentum: Does Thinking Make It So?" *Journal of Politics* 59 (1): 104–25.

Nadeau, Richard, and Andre Blais. 1993. "Accepting the Election Outcome: The Effect of Participation on Losers' Consent." *British Journal of Political Science* 23 (4): 553–63.

New York Times. 2003. "The Iowa Bypass." Editorial, October 21. Online at http://www.nytimes.com/2003/10/21/opinion/the-iowa-bypass.html (accessed April 18, 2010).

Norrander, Barbara. 1986a. "Correlates of Vote Choice in the 1980 Presidential Primaries." *Journal of Politics* 48 (1): 156–66.

——. 1986b. "Selective Participation: Presidential Primary Voters as a Subset of General Election Voters." *American Politics Quarterly* 14:35–53.

——. 1989. "Ideological Representativeness of Presidential Primary Voters." *American Journal of Political Science* 33 (3): 570–87.

——. 1991. "Patterns of Voting in the Super Tuesday Primaries: Momentum and Ideology." Paper presented at the annual meeting of the Western Political Science Association, Seattle.

——. 1992. *Super Tuesday: Regional Politics and Presidential Primaries.* Lexington: University Press of Kentucky.

——. 1993. "Nomination Choices: Caucus and Primary Outcomes, 1976–1988." *American Journal of Political Science* 37 (2): 343–64.

——. 1996. "Presidential Nomination Politics in the Post-Reform Era." *Political Research Quarterly* 49 (4): 875–915.

——. 2000. "The End Game in Post-Reform Presidential Nominations." *Journal of Politics* 62 (4): 999–1013.

Norris, Pippa. 1999. *Critical Citizens: Global Support for Democratic Government.* Oxford: Oxford University Press.

Pacheco, Julianna Sandell. 2008. "Political Socialization in Context: The Effect of Political Competition on Youth Voter Turnout." *Political Behavior* 30:415–36.

Patterson, Samuel C., and Gregory A. Caldeira. 1983. "Getting Out the Vote: Participation in Gubernatorial Elections." *American Political Science Review* 77 (3): 675–89.

Pinckney, Darryl, Gary Wills, Joan Didion, David Bromwich, and Paul Krugman. 2008. "A Fateful Election." *New York Review of Books.* Online at http://www.nybooks.com/articles/archives/2008/nov/06/1-fateful-election/?page=2 (accessed April 19, 2010).

Polsby, Nelson W. 1983. *The Consequences of Party Reform.* New York: Oxford University Press.

Primo, David M., Matthew L. Jacobsmeier, and Jeffrey Milyo. 2007. "Estimating the Impact of State Policies and Institutions with Mixed-Level Data." *State Politics and Policy Quarterly* 7 (4): 446–59.

Putnam, Robert D. 2000. *Bowling Alone: The Collapse and Revival of American Community.* New York: Simon and Schuster.

Rainey, James, and Seema Mehta. 2008. "Not Caucusing? Most of Iowa Won't Either." *Los Angeles Times,* January 2.

Ranney, Austin. 1977. *Participation in American Presidential Nominations, 1976.* Washington, DC: AEI Press.

———. 1978. "Changing the Rules of the Presidential Nominating Game: Party Reform in America." In *Parties and Elections,* ed. Jeff Fishel. Bloomington: Indiana University Press.

Rapoport, Ronald B., Walter J. Stone, and Alan I. Abramowitz. 1994. "Sex and the Caucus Participant: The Gender Gap and Presidential Nominations." *American Journal of Political Science* 34 (3): 725–40.

Redlawsk, David P., Daniel C. Bowen, and Caroline J. Tolbert. 2008. "Comparing Caucus and Registered Voter Support for the 2008 Presidential Candidates in Iowa." *PS: Political Science and Politics* 41 (1): 129–38.

Redlawsk, David P., and Arthur Sanders. 2000. "Groups and Grassroots in the Iowa Caucuses." *PS: Political Science and Politics* 34 (2): 206.

Riker, William H. 1962. *The Theory of Political Coalitions.* New Haven, CT: Yale University Press.

Romm, Tony. 2009. "DNC Commission Recommends End to Superdelegate System." *The Hill,* December 30.

Rothenberg, Lawrence S., and Richard A. Brody. 1988. "Participation in Presidential Primaries." *Political Research Quarterly* 41 (2): 253–71.

Savage, Luis Ch. 2008. "Democracy in One Hand, a Brownie in the Other." *MacLean's,* January 4. Online at http://www.macleans.ca/canada/features/article.jsp?content=20080104_174325_2448 (accessed April 15, 2010).

Schattschneider, E. E. 1960. *The Semi-Sovereign People.* New York: Harcourt Brace.

Seelye, Katharine Q. 2004. "A Presidential Fraternity Helps Clinton Open Library in Arkansas." *New York Times,* November 19.

Shafer, Byron E. 1983. *Quiet Revolution: The Struggle for the Democratic Party and the Shaping of Post-Reform Politics.* New York: Russell Sage Foundation.

Shah, Dhavan V., Jaeho Cho, William P. Eveland, and Nojin Kwak. 2005. "Information and Expression in a Digital Age: Modeling Internet Effects on Civic Participation." *Communication Research* 32 (5): 531–65.

Shear, Michael D. 2008. "GOP to Consider Major Changes in Primary Calendar." *Washington Post*, August 22.

Sigelman, Lee. 1989. "The 1988 Presidential Nominations: Whatever Happened to Momentum?" *PS: Political Science and Politics* 22 (1): 35–39.

Smith, Daniel A., and Caroline J. Tolbert. 2004. *Educated by Initiative: The Effects of Direct Democracy on Citizens and Political Organizations in the American States.* Ann Arbor: University of Michigan Press.

Smith, Mark. 2001. "The Contingent Effects of Ballot Initiatives and Candidate Races on Turnout." *American Journal of Political Science* 45: 700–706.

Smith, Steven S., and Melanie J. Springer, eds. 2009. *Reforming the Presidential Nomination Process.* Washington, DC: Brookings Institution Press.

Squire, Peverill, ed. 1989. *The Iowa Caucuses and the Presidential Nominating Process.* Boulder, CO: Westview Press.

———. 2008. "The Iowa Caucuses, 1972–2008: A Eulogy." *Forum* 5 (4): Article 1. Online at http://www.bepress.com/forum/vol5/iss4/art1 (accessed April 18, 2010).

Stone, Walter J., Alan I. Abramowitz, and Ronald B. Rapoport. 1989. "How Representative Are the Iowa Caucuses?" In *The Iowa Caucuses and the Presidential Nominating Process*, ed. Peverill Squire, 19–50. Boulder, CO: Westview Press.

Stone, Walter J., Lonna Rae Atkeson, and Ronald Rapoport. 1992. "Turning On or Turning Off? Mobilization and Demobilization Effects of Participation in Presidential Nomination Campaigns." *American Journal of Political Science* 36 (3): 665–91.

Stone, Walter J., and Ronald B. Rapoport. 1994. "Candidate Perception among Nomination Activists: A New Look at the Moderation Hypothesis." *Journal of Politics* 56 (4): 1036–52.

Stone, Walter J., Ronald B. Rapoport, and Alan I. Abramowitz. 1992. "Candidate Support in Presidential Nomination Campaigns: The Case of Iowa in 1984." *Journal of Politics* 54 (4): 1074–97.

Stone, Walter J., Ronald B. Rapoport, and Lonna Rae Atkeson. 1995. "A Simulation Model of Presidential Nomination Choice." *American Journal of Political Science* 39 (1): 135–61.

Tolbert, Caroline J. 2003. "Direct Democracy and Institutional Realignment in the American States." *Political Science Quarterly* 118 (3): 467–89.

Tolbert, Caroline J., Daniel C. Bowen, and Todd Donovan. 2009. "Initiative Campaigns: Direct Democracy and Voter Mobilization." *American Politics Research* 37 (1): 155–92.

Tolbert, Caroline J., John A. Grummel, and Daniel A. Smith. 2001. "The Effects of Ballot Initiatives on Voter Turnout in the American States." *American Politics Research* 29 (6): 625–48.

Tolbert, Caroline J., and Ramona S. McNeal. 2003. "Unraveling the Effects of the Internet on Political Participation?" *Political Research Quarterly* 56 (2): 175–85.

Tolbert, Caroline J., David P. Redlawsk, and Daniel C. Bowen. 2009. "Reforming the Presidential Nomination Process: Rotating State Primaries or a National Primary?" *PS: Political Science and Politics* 42 (1): 71–79.

Tolbert, Caroline J., Daniel A. Smith, and John Green. 2009. "Strategic Voting and Legislative Redistricting Reform: District and Statewide Representational Winners and Losers." *Political Research Quarterly* 62 (1): 92–109.

Tolbert, Caroline J., and Peverill Squire. 2009. "Editors' Introduction. Reforming the Presidential Nomination Process (Back to the Drawing Board: The Broken Presidential Nomination Process)." *PS: Political Science and Politics* 42:27–32.

Trish, Barbara. 1999. "Does Organization Matter? A Critical-Case Analysis from Recent Presidential Nomination Politics." *Presidential Studies Quarterly* 29 (4): 873–96.

University of Iowa Hawkeye Polls. Online at http://www.uiowa.edu/election/news-events/index.html#hawkeyepoll (accessed November 5, 2009).

University of Northern Iowa. Iowa Caucus Survey. Online at http://www.uni.edu/iowacaucus/main.htm (accessed January 31, 2008).

Vavreck, Lynn, and Douglas Rivers. 2008. "The 2006 Cooperative Congressional Election Study." *Journal of Elections, Public Opinion and Parties* 18:355–66.

Vavreck, Lynn, Constantine J. Spiliotes, and Linda L. Fowler. 2002. "The Effects of Retail Politics in the New Hampshire Primary." *American Journal of Political Science* 46 (3): 595–610.

Verba, Sidney, Nancy Burns, and Kay Lehman Schlozman. 1997. "Knowing and Caring about Politics: Gender and Political Engagement." *Journal of Politics* 59 (4): 1051–72.

Verba, Sidney, Kay Lehman Schlozman, and Henry Brady. 1995. *Voice and Equality: Civic Voluntarism in American Politics.* Cambridge, MA: Harvard University Press.

Wang, Tova Andrea. 2007. "Has America Outgrown the Caucus? Some Thoughts on Reshaping the Nomination Contest." New York: Century Foundation.

Ware, Alan. 2009. *The American Direct Primary: Party Institutionalization and the Transformation in the North.* Cambridge: Cambridge University Press.

Webb, Justin. 2008. "The Trouble with Caucuses." BBCNews.com. Online at http://www.bbc.co.uk/blogs/thereporters/justinwebb/2008/01/the_trouble _with_caucuses.html (accessed April 18, 2010).

Wenzel, James P., Shaun Bowler, and David J. Lanoue. 2000. "Citizen Opinion and Constitutional Choices: The Case of the UK." *Political Behavior* 22 (3): 241–65.

Wilgoren, Jodi, and Rachel L. Swarns. 2004. "2000 Tape Shows Dean Maligning Iowa Caucuses." *New York Times*, January 9.

Winebrenner, Hugh. 1998. *The Iowa Precinct Caucuses: The Making of a Media Event.* 2nd ed. Ames: Iowa State University Press.

Wolfinger, Raymond E., and Steven J. Rosenstone. 1980. *Who Votes?* New Haven, CT: Yale University Press.

Yepsen, David. 2008a. "Parties Must Probe Caucus Complaints, Make Fixes." *Des Moines Register*, January 10.

———. 2008b. "Do It Yourself, Iowa: Improve the Caucuses." *Des Moines Register*, September 7.

Youngman, Sam, and Andy Barr. 2008. "Obama's Movement Campaign Moves to the Top." *The Hill*, January 3.

Index